PRO/CON VOLUME 13

U.S. HISTORY

Published 2004 by Grolier,
an imprint of Scholastic Library Publishing
Old Sherman Turnpike
Danbury, Connecticut 06816

Library of Congress Cataloging-in-Publication Data

Pro/con
   p. cm
   Includes bibliographical references and index.
   Contents: v. 13. U.S. History – v. 14. International Development – v. 15. Human
Rights – v.16. Education – v. 17. New Science – v. 18. Commerce and Trade.
   ISBN 0-7172-5927-7 (set : alk. paper) – ISBN 0-7172-5930-7 (vol. 13 : alk. paper) –
ISBN 0-7172-5929-3 (vol. 14 : alk. paper) – ISBN 0-7172-5931-5 (vol. 15 : alk. paper)
– ISBN 0-7172-5928-5 (vol. 16 : alk. paper) – ISBN 0-7172-5932-3 (vol. 17 : alk.
paper) – ISBN 0-7172-5933-1 (vol. 18 : alk. paper)
   1. Social problems. I. Scholastic Publishing Ltd Grolier (Firm)

HN17.5 P756 2002
361.1–dc21

                                                                      2001053234

Printed and bound in Singapore

SET ISBN 0-7172-5927-7
VOLUME ISBN 0-7172-5930-7

For The Brown Reference Group plc
Project Editor: Aruna Vasudevan
Editors: Rachel Bean, Mark Fletcher, Chris Marshall,
Lesley Henderson, Jonathan Dore, Fiona Plowman
Consultant Editor: Ronald Lee, Chairman of the Social Studies Department
at Keith Country Day School in Rockford, Illinois
Designer: Sarah Williams
Picture Researchers: Clare Newman, Susy Forbes
Set Index: Kay Ollerenshaw

Managing Editor: Tim Cooke
Art Director: Dave Goodman
Production Director: Alastair Gourlay

GENERAL PREFACE

"All that is necessary for evil to triumph is for good men to do nothing."
—Edmund Burke, 18th-century English political philosopher

Decisions

Life is full of choices and decisions. Some are more important than others. Some affect only your daily life—the route you take to school, for example, or what you prefer to eat for supper—while others are more abstract and concern questions of right and wrong rather than practicality. That does not mean that your choice of presidential candidate or your views on abortion are necessarily more important than your answers to purely personal questions. But it is likely that those wider questions are more complex and subtle and that you therefore will need to know more information about the subject before you can try to answer them. They are also likely to be questions where you might have to justify your views to other people. In order to do that you need to be able to make informed decisions, be able to analyze every fact at your disposal, and evaluate them in an unbiased manner.

What is *Pro/Con*?

Pro/Con is a collection of debates that presents conflicting views on some of the more complex and general issues facing Americans today. By bringing together extracts from a wide range of sources—mainstream newspapers and magazines, books, famous speeches, legal judgments, religious tracts, government surveys—the set reflects current informed attitudes toward dilemmas that range from the best

way to feed the world's growing population to gay rights, from the connection between political freedom and capitalism to the fate of Napster.

The people whose arguments make up the set are for the most part acknowledged experts in their fields, making the vast difference in their points of view even more remarkable. The arguments are presented in the form of debates for and against various propositions, such as "Should Americans Celebrate Columbus Day?" or "Are human rights women's rights?" This question format reflects the way in which ideas often occur in daily life: in the classroom, on TV shows, in business meetings, or even in state or federal politics.

The contents

The subjects of the six volumes of *Pro/Con 3—U.S. History, International Development, Human Rights, Education, New Science,* and *Commerce and Trade*—are issues on which it is preferable that people's opinions are based on information rather than personal bias.

Special boxes throughout *Pro/Con* comment on the debates as you are reading them, pointing out facts, explaining terms, or analyzing arguments to help you think about what is being said.

Introductions and summaries also provide background information that might help you reach your own conclusions. There are also tips about how to structure an argument that you can apply on an everyday basis to any debate or conversation, learning how to present your point of view as effectively and persuasively as possible.

VOLUME PREFACE
U.S. HISTORY

The study of history has been a major component of school curricula for centuries. Scholars have long regarded the subject as essential in creating and promoting a sense of national identity, and for understanding how past political, economic, and social changes have shaped today's institutions. They stress that history is relevant not only for what it tells us about significant events and people in the past, but for how it can inform our knowledge of the present and help us to make decisions for the future.

Relevance today

Knowledge of our national history enhances our understanding of our country as well as its relationship with other nations. Countering the arguments of critics who claim that history teaching has no demonstrable practical benefit or advantage, many historians and educators argue that it is crucial to citizenship and the creation of a cohesive and informed population. It enhances people's sense of their shared heritage and pride in their country. It also, they argue, puts people on their guard against activities and attitudes that threaten to undermine American values.

Educators also stress that history is more than a list of facts—of dates, revolutions, battles, and treaties. It can also encourage awareness and understanding of contemporary local, national, and international issues. It can inform by example and precedent, showing us how people acted in the past and what resulted from their actions. With the benefit of hindsight, we can evaluate people's actions in the light of their outcomes. We can learn from this knowledge and apply it to the modern world. History can help us to avoid past inequities and bloodshed; in the words of philosopher George Santayana (1863-1952): "Those who do not remember the past are condemned to relive it."

In addition to knowledge of specific past events and their relevance to today's world, the study of history can also stimulate modes of thinking that help us to make sense of our own times. It can encourage us to think analytically and objectively: to evaluate data in order to identify the facts, separating them out from partisan viewpoints, both those of historical figures and of later historians, who might interpret events in light of their own agendas. We can use these skills to evaluate critically the speeches and policies of politicians today, and the way that they are reported on the television, radio, and Internet, and in newspapers and magazines.

Pro/Con

This volume of *Pro/Con* invites you to consider the complexities inherent in some key topics in U.S. history. Using texts from a variety of sources, ranging from historical documents to articles by authors working today, it presents different viewpoints on some of the most important events, institutions, and ideas that have shaped the nation. By stimulating an analytical approach to history, the book encourages a questioning attitude to the nation's past and its relevance to life today.

HOW TO USE THIS BOOK

Each volume of *Pro/Con* is divided into sections, each of which has an introduction that examines its theme. Within each section are a series of debates that present arguments for and against a proposition, such as whether or not the death penalty should be abolished. An introduction to each debate puts it into its wider context, and a summary and key map (see below) highlight the main points of the debate clearly and concisely. Each debate has marginal boxes that focus on particular points, give tips on how to present an argument, or help question the writer's case. The summary page to the debates contains supplementary material to help you do further research.

Boxes and other materials provide additional background information. There are also special spreads on how to improve your debating and writing skills. At the end of each book is a glossary and an index. The glossary provides explanations of key words in the volume. The index covers all 18 books, so it will help you trace topics in this set and the previous ones.

marginal boxes
Marginal boxes highlight key points of the argument, give extra information, or help you question the author's meaning.

summary boxes
Summary boxes are useful reminders of both sides of the argument.

background information
Frequent text boxes provide background information on important concepts and key individuals or events.

further information
Further Reading lists for each debate direct you to related books, articles, and websites so you can do your own research.

other articles in the *Pro/Con* series
This box lists related debates throughout the *Pro/Con* series.

key map
Key maps provide a graphic representation of the central points of the debate.

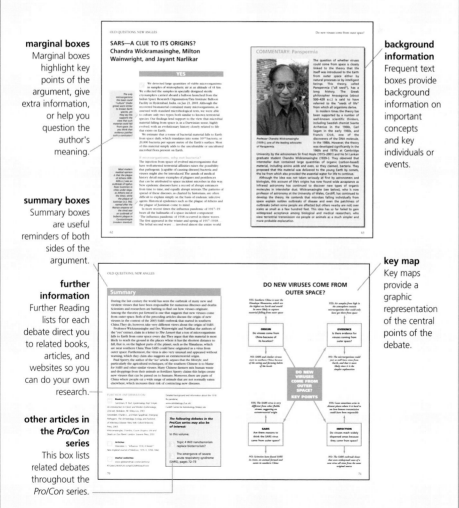

CONTENTS

PART 1
EARLY AMERICAN HISTORY

The early American history covered in this section of the book encompasses a long period—some 400 years from the arrival of Christopher Columbus in 1492 to the reorganization of the states during Reconstruction (1865-1877). It includes 300 years of colonization by European powers and such momentous events in the creation of the United States as the American Revolution (1775-1783) and the Civil War (1861-1865). Historians traditionally regard the years from the 16th century to the 19th century as the formative period in which the modern nation was shaped and defined.

A shared history?

While the arrival of European settlers signaled the beginning of a new era— radically changing the ethnic, racial, social, political, and economic makeup of the American continent— it also signaled the destruction of the lives and cultures of indigenous peoples who had lived on the land for thousands of years. By the 1530s Native Americans had been ravaged by diseases, wars, and slavery introduced by the new settlers. The colonists forged agreements with some peoples while displacing others in order to obtain land. This pattern of exploitation and subjugation continued for centuries as European settlers moved westward. Acts such as the 1830 Indian Removal Act allowed the government to negotiate removal treaties with peoples living east of the Mississippi River in exchange for land further west. Although some tribes signed treaties voluntarily, the Cherokee were forcibly removed in 1838, an event known as the Trail of Tears, during which 4,000 Cherokee died.

Reassessing traditional views

National and international institutions began to recognize and address the subjugation of and discrimination against Native Americans only in the 20th century, particularly in the 1970s following the Civil Rights Movement. Society's values in the 21st century enable us to reassess traditional interpretations of early American history. Equally, knowledge of this history enables us to understand issues in contemporary life: Why, for example, the relationship between Native American communities and the government is often problematic, and why Native Americans often try to retain traditional cultures and lifestyles, even, critics argue, at the cost of development.

Independence for all?

The perspective of the 21st century also enables us to evaluate other inequities that were enshrined in the institutions and economy of the emerging nation. The best known of these is slavery. The trade in African slaves and the enforced labor they provided, particularly in the cotton plantations of the South, was of fundamental importance to the wealth of North America. Unlike Native American rights, however, slavery became a major political issue during the period of early American history. Although the Framers of the Constitution did nothing to abolish slavery in the Bill of Rights (1791)—recognizing the essential part it played in the new nation's economy—it

exploitative relationships pursued for economic gain are acceptable today, for example, the use of illegal labor from poor regions, and the commercial interaction between developed and developing countries.

Questioning history

Slavery and the treatment of Native Americans are just two issues in a long and immensely rich period of the nation's past—other key themes include territorial expansion (to the

"A moment comes, which comes but rarely in history, when we step out from the old to the new, when an age ends, and when the sound of a nation, long suppressed, finds utterance."

— JAWAHARLAL NEHRU, POLITICIAN AND STATESMAN (1947)

became a growing cause of friction between North and South in the 19th century. In the North, the states had voluntarily outlawed slavery by 1804—they drew instead on cheap labor from Europe for their rapidly growing industrial workforce—but in the South reliance on slave labor grew. Cotton plantations came increasingly to underpin the region's economy. Some commentators believe that slavery was one of the main factors that led to the Civil War. It was not abolished until 1865, when the Thirteenth Amendment outlawed slavery.

Understanding the role played by slavery in the formation of the nation can help address related issues in contemporary society, such as racial prejudice and discrimination. It can also stimulate us to question whether

west and south), relationships with former colonial powers, immigration, and industrialization. However, these two subjects illustrate that history is rarely a straightforward progression; the nation's independence, democracy, and wealth were not achieved without cost.

The four topics that follow deal with various aspects of questions about slavery, race, and the experience of Native Americans. In Topic 1 the issue of whether Americans should celebrate Columbus Day is debated or whether it is an offensive outdated holiday. Topic 2 looks at the controversial issue of whether the Framers were racist. Topic 3 examines if slavery was the main cause of the Civil War, and finally, Topic 4 questions whether Reconstruction was a success.

Topic 1
SHOULD AMERICANS CELEBRATE COLUMBUS DAY?

YES
FROM "REMARKS BY THE PRESIDENT ON SIGNING OF COLUMBUS DAY PROCLAMATION"
THE EAST ROOM, OCTOBER 8, 2001
GEORGE W. BUSH

NO
"NATION SHOULD NOT CELEBRATE COLUMBUS DAY, TERRORISM OF NATIVE PEOPLE"
THE STATE NEWS, OCTOBER 8, 2001
DARREN KROENKE

INTRODUCTION

On August 3, 1492, the Italian navigator Christopher Columbus (1451–1506) set sail on his ship *Santa Maria* from Palos de la Frontera, Spain. Columbus's aim was to find a route to the East Indies by sailing west. In the early hours of October 12, 1492, he and his crew landed on the Bahamian island of Guanahani, off the coast of the United States. Although millions of Native Americans lived on the islands and on the mainland of the New World, Columbus has for more than 500 years been heralded as "discovering" America.

For most of this time Americans have celebrated Columbus's achievement. During the 19th century Italian Americans in particular organized events to honor Columbus, and in 1905 Colorado became the first state to officially observe Columbus Day. Thirty-two years later Franklin D. Roosevelt announced that October 12 would be celebrated as Columbus Day, and in 1971 Richard Nixon proclaimed it a federal public holiday to be celebrated on the second Monday in October.

Many Americans object to Columbus Day, however. They argue that Native Americans had been living on the land for centuries before Columbus came to the New World, and that celebrating the explorer's landing is offensive to that community.

Supporters of Columbus Day, President George W. Bush included, counter that Columbus Day is important since he did discover America in the sense that he brought it to the attention of the "civilized" world, and that ultimately led to the formation of the modern United States. They argue that critics of the holiday are just taking political correctness too far. But which argument is right?

Columbus's voyage was sponsored by the Spanish monarchy. King Ferdinand and Queen Isabella had financed many voyages of discovery, partly to extend the influence of the Catholic church, partly to increase Spain's wealth and empire. Even so, it took Columbus many years to convince them to support his journey to find a route to the East Indies by traveling West. In fact, when Columbus first spotted land in October 1492, he believed he was in the East Indies, and he named the native Arawaks he came across "Indians" in his mistaken belief.

"We can build him up to be a great man, or on the other side we can see that he is the symbol of white man's oppression."
—WILLIAM WALKSALONG, SOCIOLOGIST

Some critics claim that Columbus's landing, far from heralding an "age of discovery," began an "age of conquest" that saw the end of Native American culture and freedom. Academics estimate that when Columbus landed in the islands, the Caribbean was populated by hundreds of tribes, with as many as nine million Arawaks living there. By 1532 the natives had virtually been wiped out as a result of war, slavery, and disease brought to the New World by European settlers. Some critics argue that Columbus's intentions toward the native population were from the beginning exploitative. He wrote in his journal in 1492 that the natives he encountered, "… would make good servants. With 50 men we could subjugate them all and make them do whatever we want." This has led many

people to believe that Columbus's landing should not be celebrated since it began an age in which the native peoples were victims of genocide, racism, and enslavement. They claim that Columbus Day should be abolished because it is insulting to Native Americans. Some cities, including Berkeley, Pasadena, and Santa Cruz (CA), do not celebrate Columbus Day, and South Dakota has changed Columbus Day to Native American Day.

However, Michael S. Berliner, senior adviser to the Ayn Rand Institute, states in "Did Christopher Columbus 'Discover' America?" (2002) that Columbus "is the carrier of Western civilization and the very values attacked by terrorists on September 11, [2001]" and that he should be honored, "for in doing so we honor Western civilization." Others see Columbus Day as a way of honoring a courageous man who achieved a remarkable feat of navigation and was not to blame for what happened after him. They argue that Columbus's achievements were great and that celebrating his landing in the Bahamian islands also honors the contribution that the Italian American community has made to U.S. culture and society. Some supporters also point out that Columbus's contribution to America is no less significant than that of, say, Martin Luther King, Jr., whose life and achievements are also celebrated by a national holiday.

The following pieces examine the issue further. The first is a speech by President George W. Bush celebrating Columbus Day and the achievements of the Italian American community. The second article argues that Columbus Day should not be celebrated because Christopher Columbus's landing brought terror to the native people.

REMARKS BY THE PRESIDENT ON SIGNING OF COLUMBUS DAY PROCLAMATION
George W. Bush

YES

 THE PRESIDENT: Thank you very much. I'm glad I invited you.

Thank you all for coming. Laura and I are delighted to have you here to celebrate Columbus Day. Since 1934, when Franklin Roosevelt first proclaimed the national holiday, our entire nation has observed Columbus Day to mark that moment when the Old World met the New. We honor the man from Genoa and the vision that carried him throughout his ten-week voyage. And we recognize—as well we recognize the unique contributions that people of Italian descent have made here in our country for more than five centuries.

Italian Americans and September 11, 2001

Italian Americans were among the many public servants last month who gave extraordinary service in an hour of dire emergency. Some are with us today. The Fire Department of Arlington, Virginia was first on the scene after the attack on the Pentagon. And we're so honored to have Battalion Chief, Jim Bonzano with us today.

We have representatives of the New York Police and Fire Departments with us, representatives of people who showed incredible bravery and sacrifice and determination. Please welcome Joe Esposito and Chief Dan Nigro.

Chief Nigro is the successor of Peter Ganci, Jr., whom I had the privilege of meeting two years ago. Chief Ganci gave his life at the World Trade Center and was laid to rest on September the 15th. We're so delighted today to have heroes here representing the Ganci family: his wife, his two sons and his daughters. Welcome, and thank you for being here.

I can't remember if it was Chris or Peter III who looked out at the South Lawn and said, God, I wish Dad were here. He could hit a three wood right over the fence. I said, it might make him nervous; he might shank it into the water. He said, no, you don't know my Dad.

Christopher Columbus planting the Spanish flag to mark the discovery of the New World on October 12, 1492.

Order Sons of Italy in America (OSIA) is an organization of Italian Americans. It was founded in 1905 in New York City as a mutual aid society for early Italian immigrants. It aims to preserve Italian American traditions. UNICO National is an organization that "strives to promote and disseminate the culture and ethnic heritage of our Italian immigrant ancestors." The name (translated from the Italian) means "only one of its kind," and the letters also stand for unity, neighborliness, integrity, charity, and opportunity.

President Bush calls the people who carried out the terrorist attacks on September 11, 2001, the "evil ones." Does using such emotional language strengthen his argument, or does it work against it?

I want to thank the Sons of Italy who have joined us today, as well as the leadership of the National Italian American Foundation and UNICO National who are here as well. Thank you all for coming.

Ambassador Salleo from Italy; we're so glad you're here, and thank you for bringing your wife with you as well. I just got off the phone call with your Prime Minister, Prime Minister Berlusconi, who is a good friend of mine and a good friend of America's. He sends his best, by the way. Welcome.

I want to thank the members of Congress who are here. Thank you all for coming. And I also am so pleased that the first Italian American to serve on our Supreme Court, has agreed to join us as well. Justice Scalia, thank you for being here, sir.

I'm proud to have a number of Italian Americans in my administration. A member of my Cabinet unfortunately is not here, but I can assure you he's doing a great job, and that's Tony Principi. [I'm] so proud of Tony's service to the veterans of our country. He's doing a really outstanding job....

I was in New York last week. Like all Americans, I am amazed at what a great job the New York City folks are doing. The spirit of New York. The willingness for people to pull together and to help a neighbor in need. And I'm most impressed by the character of the leadership there. Two people of Italian heritage, I might add: The Governor—and Mayor Rudy Giuliani.

The evil ones thought they were going to hurt us, and they did, to a certain extent. But what they really did was, they enabled the world to see the true character and compassion and spirit of our country. And no finer example of that than New York City.

Columbus Day and national pride

This Columbus Day should be one of deep pride for all Americans—all Americans—especially those of Italian descent. From the very beginning of our country, the sons and daughters of Italy have brought honor to themselves and have enriched our national life. In the beauty of this capital city we see the hand of Italian immigrants who spent more than 10 years carving the great seated figure in the Lincoln Memorial, who adorned the National Cathedral with statues, and who graced the dome and corridors of the Capitol building with magnificent art.

Our freedom itself was gained with the help of three Italian regiments that crossed the Atlantic to fight in the Revolutionary War. Our Declaration of Independence bears the signatures of two Italian Americans. In later struggle, dozens of Italian Americans would receive the Medal of Honor. And today, when Americans pay tribute to the Greatest Generation, we have in mind people like Captain Don Gentile, the fighting ace whom General Eisenhower described as a "one-man air force."

Take any field of endeavor—any achievement of this country—and Italian Americans are part of it. For generation after generation, the success of our country has drawn heavily from the industry and resourcefulness of Italian immigrants and their families. The same can be said for the values that make us [a] great nation. The millions who came here brought with them a distinct strength of character, faith in God, devotion to family, and love of life.

An immigrant nation

This summer I visited Genoa, where, 550 years ago, Christopher Columbus was born. All around that vibrant, modern city are glimpses of the ancient civilization that still inspires the world's admiration, and always will. In so many ways, that culture has added to our own—first on three small ships, then on many more. It is our good fortune to be an immigrant nation—to be the keepers of traditions and gifts that have come to us from great nations like Italy.

More than 15 million Americans claim Italian heritage. And all Americans have reason to be grateful, because we would be poorer without it. I now have the singular honor of signing the official document proclaiming October 8th, 2001 as Columbus Day in the United States of America.

Captain Don Gentile (1920–1950) was born in Ohio and became a celebrated fighter pilot in the Army Air Force. During World War II (1939–1945) he shot down more than 30 Nazi planes. General Eisenhower presented him with the Distinguished Service Cross. Gentile died at the age of 30 during a training incident.

What are the benefits of a country being based on immigration? Do you think the Native American community views immigration since Columbus as "good fortune"?

NATION SHOULD NOT CELEBRATE COLUMBUS DAY, TERRORISM OF NATIVE PEOPLE
Darren Kroenke

NO

A direct opening can be a very good way of immediately capturing the reader's attention. Is the author successful?

America was attacked

The innocent lives of countless Americans were lost as the result of acts of violence incomprehensible to most people. Children were left without parents. Husbands were left without wives. Sisters were left without brothers. The promising futures of so many people were taken from them, their hopes and dreams cut short by the hands of individuals who did not know the names or the families of their victims. We, the survivors, are left to mourn our losses, but we will continue to honor the memory of the fallen.

Is comparing Columbus's arrival to a "campaign of terrorism" fair? Do Columbus's own motives make any difference?

Not September 11, 2001

I'm not talking about the events of Sept. 11. What I am talking about is a campaign of terrorism that started in 1492 with the arrival of an Italian mariner named Christopher Columbus. This man's voyage initiated the first invasion of America. The terrorists came from foreign lands to the east.

Highly organized and with a mission supposedly given to them by their God, they subjugated, intimidated and killed our people through acts of terror and violence not much different from the terrorists of modern times. They used germ warfare, in the form of small pox infested blankets, and every other technology known to them. They killed men, women and children indiscriminately. These acts of violence were both horrific and unprovoked. The lives of the original Americans were thus changed forever.

Do a search on www.google.com, and research the coverage of September 11, 2001, at the time of the event. Can you find evidence to support the author's statement that some people looked at the terrorist action with "joy"?

Justification of terrorism

In other parts of the world, and even in our own country, there are people who look upon the events of Sept. 11 with joy and would even go so far as to celebrate such a catastrophe. As a nation, we look upon these individuals with bitter hatred and we ask ourselves how anyone could celebrate such an event or find some sort of justification for these acts of terrorism.

COMMENTARY: Native American holiday

Although some people support Christopher Columbus's achievements and claim that he deserves to be remembered by a public holiday, many Americans, including Native American groups and civil rights groups, disagree. They believe that Columbus Day, which falls on the second Monday of October, is insulting to the Native American population because it celebrates a colonial view of the "discovery" of America. They argue that far from discovering America, Columbus landed in an already populated country where Native American tribes had lived for around 10,000 years, and that his arrival brought misery and death to the native communities. These critics assert that there should be a Native American Day instead. In fact, several states, including South Dakota and Louisiana, refuse to celebrate Columbus Day and have already established a Native American Day. Other states choose to celebrate both Columbus Day and a day for Native Americans. Those groups in favor of celebrating Columbus Day include the Knights of Columbus, an international Roman Catholic society that was instrumental in the establishment of the official holiday, and the Order Sons of Italy in America (OSIA), who campaign to preserve Italian American traditions. These groups and others who approve of Columbus Day claim that Columbus's discovery led to the influx of ideas and people on which the United States was founded and that refusing to celebrate is a case of political correctness gone too far.

First Americans Day

An organization called United Native America started campaigning on the National Native American holiday issue in 1993. On August 1, 2000, they set up an online petition calling for Congress to rename Columbus Day as First Americans Day. They contended that the petition was an attempt to introduce a holiday that would appeal to all Americans and was not an attack on Christopher Columbus. United Native America claim that the polls they conducted showed that the "vast majority of Americans prefer changing Columbus Day to creating a whole new holiday" for Native Americans. By May 2003 they had gathered 28,919 signatures.

Resolution before Congress

On March 31, 2003, the National Native American Day resolution was submitted to the 108th Congress. The main point of the proposed bill was to honor "the achievements and contributions of Native Americans to the United States." It urged "the establishment and observation of a paid legal public holiday in honor of Native Americans." Critics of the resolution argue that Columbus Day celebrates the achievement of an individual; it does not attack an ethnic group, and therefore it does not need to change.

A protester holds up a Columbus Wanted poster in Denver, Colorado, October 7, 1992.

Indigenous peoples ask themselves the same thing every year Columbus Day is celebrated. So why is it that this country celebrates Columbus Day? What does this day mean to "Americans?" Do those who celebrate it do so to recognize the "discovery" of America?

Why celebrate?

America was not discovered by anyone. To discover something you need to be the first person to find something, to see something or know about that which you claim to have discovered. So, if there were already people living in the Americas since Creation, how did Columbus discover this land?

Few textbooks today would call Columbus a discoverer. Do you think Kroenke is writing about the past?

Oh, but wait, as of a little over 20 years ago, U.S. history books were still being used in high school education that claimed while people were enjoying the fruits of their collective intellect elsewhere in the world (read "Europe"), the continents we know as the Americas stood empty of mankind and its works. I suppose if you want to believe in such fictions, why don't the same history books teach us the United States discovered the moon? Neil Armstrong, an American, was the first person to walk on it, wasn't he?

Let's assume for a moment that everyone reading this is a relatively well-informed person and you have already rid yourselves of the absurdity of Columbus's discovery of America. So, why do Americans continue to celebrate Columbus Day? Do people in this country recognize it as the beginning of civilization in the Americas? Maybe Hernán Cortés had the same thoughts the Sept. 11 terrorists did when he and his troops leveled Tenochtitlán, the Aztec version of New York, in 1521. Such acts can only be fueled by an extreme hatred for a whole nation and its "morally corrupt" culture.

Neither Cortés and his conquistadors nor the terrorist attackers of several weeks ago knew the people they were killing as individuals, and therefore they had no personal reason to take these lives. They targeted a very visible symbol of a nation to subjugate the people as a whole.

So maybe in some sick and twisted way, all terrorists, be they European explorers or some other group, feel their acts of violence are in some way "civilizing."

Hernán Cortés (1485–1547) was a Spanish conquistador in Mexico and Central America. He is probably most remembered for his famous march to Tenochtitlán (Mexico City), capital of the Aztec Empire, in August 1519. He entered the city on November 8, took Montezuma, the Aztec emperor, hostage, and claimed Mexico in the name of Spain.

Acts against civilization

But these acts are against civilization. The Sept. 11 attacks on the World Trade Center and the Pentagon are nothing for U.S. citizens to celebrate, and the European invasion of the Americas that begin in 1492 is nothing for indigenous people to celebrate. The 500 years of violence, racism and genocide perpetrated through acts of terrorism against the first Americans since that fateful landing of Christopher Columbus is hardly a joyous occasion.

Will future U.S. history texts describe Sept. 11 the same way European terrorism of the Americas has been described?

People are talking about how this day has changed our lives as Americans forever. The same can certainly be said for every descendant of the original peoples of this country.

We carry in our hearts and in our minds the same sorrow, fear and anger almost every American now knows. Let us seriously ask ourselves then, why does this nation celebrate Columbus Day?

Kroenke compares Columbus's arrival to September 11, 2001. Does the fact that it happened so long ago make the comparison less effective?

Summary

For centuries Christopher Columbus's landing in the New World has been celebrated, first unofficially and then in the 20th century by an official holiday. Many people, however, believe that it is wrong to honor a man who started the process that helped to kill and enslave millions of Native Americans. Others argue that Columbus's achievements were great and very much in the American tradition. He followed his dreams and by doing so changed the history of a nation.

President George W. Bush states in his speech on the signing of the Columbus Day Proclamation that Columbus Day marks the time when the "Old World met the New" and also recognizes the great contribution that Italian Americans have made to the United States, including their efforts to deal with the September 11, 2001, terrorist attacks.

Darren Kroenke, the author of the second article, published in *The State News*, however, disagrees. He argues that Columbus's voyage was the first invasion of America. He says, "there are people who look upon the events of September 11 with joy.... As a nation ... we ask ourselves how anyone could celebrate such an event or find some sort of justification for these acts of terrorism. Indigenous peoples ask themselves the same thing every year Columbus Day is celebrated." He asks why the nation needs to celebrate Columbus Day when it is offensive to Native Americans.

FURTHER INFORMATION:

 Books:

Altman, Ida, *Emigrants and Society: Extremadura and America in the Sixteenth Century.* Berkeley, CA: University of California Press, 1989.

Bedini, Silvio A. (ed.), *The Christopher Columbus Encyclopedia.* 2 vols. New York: Simon and Schuster, 1992.

Bitterli, Urs, *Cultures in Conflict: Encounters between European and Non-European Cultures, 1492–1800,* translated by Ritchie Robertson. Stanford, CA: Stanford University Press, 1989.

Hebert, John R. (ed.), *1492: An Ongoing Voyage.* Washington, D.C.: Library of Congress, 1992.

Kehow, Alice Beck, *America before the European Invasions.* London and New York: Longman, 2002.

Russell, Jeffrey Burton, *Inventing the Flat Earth: Columbus and Modern Historians.* New York: Praeger, 1991.

Sinovcic, Vincent, *Columbus: Debunking of a Legend.* New York: Rivercross Publishing, 1990.

Stannard, David E., *American Holocaust: Columbus and the Conquest of the New World.* New York: Oxford University Press, 1992.

 Useful websites:

www1.minn.net/~keithp/
Examines various aspects of Christopher Columbus and his achievements.

www.ibiblio.org/expo/1492.exhibit/Intro.html
Site for 1492: An Ongoing Voyage, an online exhibit by the Library of Congress, Washington, D.C.

The following debates in the Pro/Con series may also be of interest:

In this volume:
 Part 1: Early American history, pages 8–9

SHOULD AMERICANS CELEBRATE COLUMBUS DAY?

YES: Although the New World was populated by tribes, Columbus discovered it in the sense that he brought it to the attention of the civilized world

YES: It is important to celebrate the achievements of significant people, and without doubt Columbus is one of them. To let political correctness prevent that is wrong.

DISCOVERY
Did Christopher Columbus "discover" America?

POLITICAL CORRECTNESS
Are critics of Columbus Day just giving in to political correctness?

NO: It is not possible to discover somewhere already populated by millions of people

NO: Columbus Day is insulting to Native Americans because it celebrates their misery. It is more than just political correctness to object to this day.

SHOULD AMERICANS CELEBRATE COLUMBUS DAY?

KEY POINTS

YES: Renaming the day would give Native Americans the message that Americans realize that they were treated wrongly and cruelly by European settlers

YES: Columbus's arrival marked the start of the process of the killing and enslaving of millions of Native Americans

RENAMING
Should Columbus Day be renamed as Native American day?

AGE OF CONQUEST
Can Columbus be blamed for what happened after his voyage?

NO: Christopher Columbus was a courageous individual who fought for his dreams. He is the essence of modern America.

NO: Columbus was simply a sailor who was interested in navigating to new lands

Topic 2
WERE THE FRAMERS RACIST?

YES
"THE BICENTENNIAL SPEECH"
THE ANNUAL SEMINAR, MAUI, HAWAII, MAY 6, 1987
SAN FRANCISCO PATENT AND TRADEMARK LAW ASSOCIATION
THURGOOD MARSHALL

NO
"SPIKE LEE AND *THE PATRIOT*"
WWW.ENTERSTAGERIGHT.COM, JULY 17, 2000
STUART BUCK

INTRODUCTION

There is a well-known contradiction between the Constitution's declaration of the rights to freedom and its failure to grant such rights to slaves. It is equally well known that some of the Framers were themselves slave owners, notably George Washington (1732-1799) and Thomas Jefferson (1743-1826). But does the Framers' treatment of slaves reflect their own views or simply the spirit of the times? Is it fair to judge 18th-century views by 21st-century standards, such as "racism," which was not seen the same way then?

From May to September 1787, 55 delegates—including Benjamin Franklin (1706-1790) and James Madison (1751-1836)—representing 12 states met at the Constitutional Convention in Philadelphia to establish a governmental framework. The Constitution, which is still the basis of government, arose from discussions between the delegates, or Framers, as they came to be known.

The Constitution, as originally written, preserved the institution of slavery by failing to abolish it. The Bill of Rights (1791), which was passed to protect the rights of the individual, also failed to mention slavery. In fact, the word "slavery" did not appear in the Constitution until 1865, when the Thirteenth Amendment abolished it.

In the late 18th century the economy relied on slave labor: In the South slaves were an integral part of the cotton industry, while the New England shipowners made great profits from the slave trade. Few of the delegates even considered the possibility of abolishing slavery in those states where it was still legal, such as Georgia. There was no suggestion that slaves should be given a vote: Slaves were counted only in order to determine the number of representatives each state should have in government (they were counted as three-fifths of a person each) and the amount of direct taxation the states should bear.

A more sensitive issue involved the effort to prevent the new central government from ending the slave trade. Some states had already outlawed the practice, including New Hampshire, Massachusetts, and Connecticut, and they demanded that the federal government do the same. But delegates from Southern states, in particular South Carolina and Georgia, protested, and a compromise was reached whereby Congress would not prohibit the trade until 1808, but would meanwhile levy a tax on all slaves imported.

> *"When the architects of our republic wrote ... the Constitution and the Declaration ... they were signing a promissory note to which every American was to fall heir."*
>
> —DR. MARTIN LUTHER KING, JR.,
> "I HAVE A DREAM," AUGUST 28, 1963

Some critics argue that the Framers must have been racist because they did not give slaves the vote. If they had been liberals in the modern sense, how could they have committed such an injustice, advocates of this view ask.

But critics claim that in the late 18th century, modern notions of racial equality were literally unthinkable. Slavery had existed in America for over 200 years and had for thousands of years been accepted as normal in societies around the world.

However, this argument has been countered by other critics who point out that there was a moral case against slavery in the early republic. Some of the speakers at the Constitutional Convention, such as George Mason, argued against the ownership of slaves on humanitarian grounds. Many Christian churches—the Quakers, the Presbyterian Church, and the Methodist Church—also actively opposed slavery.

Other apologists for the Framers have suggested that although their own conduct may not have been what we would now regard as enlightened, they were trying to achieve consensus: It was necessary to accept slavery so as to bring the South into the Union. The Constitution was thus founded on compromise. That, too, can be countered by those who say that political compromise would not have prevented powerful citizens such as George Washington from freeing their own slaves.

The following two articles examine the issue further. The first is a speech made by the late Supreme Court Justice Thurgood Marshall (1908-1993), a leader of the civil rights movement, on the 200th anniversary of the Constitution. Marshall argues that the Framers were racist because they failed to abolish slavery and put economics before personal freedom.

Journalist Stuart Buck focuses on comments made by the black filmmaker and activist Spike Lee (1963-) about the film *The Patriot*. Lee argues that the Framers, because they owned slaves themselves, were racist. Buck asserts that although many of the Framers opposed slavery, they had no choice but to reach a compromise in order to create a strong United States that could fight for the greater good.

THE BICENTENNIAL SPEECH
Thurgood Marshall

YES

Justice Thurgood Marshall (1908–1993), the author of this speech, had a leading role in the civil rights movement. The grandson of a slave, Marshall became the first African American to be appointed to the Supreme Court (1967–1991).

See Volume 7, The Constitution, for various debates about the Constitution in the modern world.

Under the Three-Fifths Clause the three southern-most states were allowed to count three-fifths of their slave population in apportioning representation. This was to give the South extra representation in government and extra votes in the Electoral College.

 1987 marks the 200th anniversary of the United States Constitution....

Patriotic feelings will surely swell, prompting proud proclamations of the wisdom, foresight, and sense of justice shared by the Framers and reflected in a written document now yellowed with age. This is unfortunate, not the patriotism itself, but the tendency for the celebration to oversimplify, and overlook the many other events that have been instrumental to our achievements as a nation. The focus of this celebration invites a complacent belief that the vision of those who debated and compromised in Philadelphia yielded the "more perfect Union" it is said we now enjoy.

I cannot accept this invitation, for I do not believe that the meaning of the Constitution was forever "fixed" at the Philadelphia Convention. Nor do I find the wisdom, foresight, and sense of justice exhibited by the Framers particularly profound. To the contrary, the government they devised was defective from the start, requiring several amendments, a civil war, and momentous social transformation to attain the system of constitutional government, and its respect for the individual freedoms and human rights, we hold as fundamental today. When contemporary Americans cite "The Constitution," they invoke a concept that is vastly different from what the Framers barely began to construct two centuries ago.

For a sense of the evolving nature of the Constitution we need look no further than the first three words of the document's preamble: "We the People." When the Founding Fathers used this phrase in 1787, they did not have in mind the majority of America's citizens. "We the People" included, in the words of the Framers, "the whole Number of free Persons." On a matter so basic as the right to vote, for example, Negro slaves were excluded, although they were counted for representational purposes at threefifths each. Women did not gain the right to vote for over a hundred and thirty years.

These omissions were intentional. The record of the Framers' debates on the slave question is especially clear: The Southern States acceded to the demands of the New England

States for giving Congress broad power to regulate commerce, in exchange for the right to continue the slave trade. The economic interests of the regions coalesced: New Englanders engaged in the "carrying trade" would profit from transporting slaves from Africa as well as goods produced in America by slave labor. The perpetuation of slavery ensured the primary source of wealth in the Southern States.

Slavery and morality

Despite this clear understanding of the role slavery would play in the new republic, use of the words "slaves" and "slavery" was carefully avoided in the original document. Political representation in the lower House of Congress was to be based on the population of "free Persons" in each State, plus threefifths of all "other Persons." Moral principles against slavery, for those who had them, were compromised, with no explanation of the conflicting principles for which the American Revolutionary War had ostensibly been fought: the selfevident truths "that all men are created equal, that they are endowed by their Creator with certain unalienable Rights, that among these are Life, Liberty and the pursuit of Happiness."…

And so again at the Constitutional Convention eloquent objections to the institution of slavery went unheeded, and its opponents eventually consented to a document which laid a foundation for the tragic events that were to follow.

Pennsylvania's Governor [Gouverneur] Morris provides an example. He opposed slavery and the counting of slaves in determining the basis for representation in Congress. At the Convention he objected that:

> *The inhabitant of Georgia [or] South Carolina who goes to the coast of Africa, and in defiance of the most sacred laws of humanity tears away his fellow creatures from their dearest connections and damns them to the most cruel bondages, shall have more votes in a Government instituted for protection of the rights of mankind, than the Citizen of Pennsylvania or New Jersey who views with a laudable horror, so nefarious a Practice.*

And yet Governor Morris eventually accepted the threefifths accommodation.…

As a result of compromise, the right of the southern States to continue importing slaves was extended, officially, at least until 1808. We know that it actually lasted a good deal longer,

From 1700 to 1850 over 10 million Africans were forcibly removed from their homelands in West and Central Africa to work on the plantations in America and the Caribbean. The treatment of slaves was notoriously bad even before they arrived in the South. On the trip across the Atlantic Ocean, known as the Middle Passage, the slaves were bound in shackles and crowded into quarters below deck. Thousands died from disease on the journey.

Gouverneur Morris (1752–1816) was one of the original Framers. One of the leading figures at the Constitutional Convention, he is believed to have written the final draft of the Constitution.

as the Framers possessed no monopoly on the ability to trade moral principles for selfinterest. But they nevertheless set an unfortunate example. Slaves could be imported, if the commercial interests of the North were protected. To make the compromise even more palatable, customs duties would be imposed at up to ten dollars per slave as a means of raising public revenues.

No doubt it will be said, when the unpleasant truth of the history of slavery in America is mentioned during this bicentennial year, that the Constitution was a product of its times, and embodied a compromise which, under other circumstances, would not have been made. But the effects of the Framers' compromise have remained for generations. They arose from the contradiction between guaranteeing liberty and justice to all, and denying both to Negroes.

The original intent of the phrase, "We the People," was far too clear for any ameliorating construction. Writing for the Supreme Court in 1857, Chief Justice Taney penned the following passage in the Dred Scott case, on the issue whether, in the eyes of the Framers, slaves were "constituent members of the sovereignty," and were to be included among "We the People":

In 1846 slaves Dred Scott (about 1799–1858) and his wife Harriet filed suit for their freedom in the St. Louis Circuit Court. Eleven years later the case reached the Supreme Court, which issued a landmark decision declaring that Scott and his wife should remain slaves. The issue of continued slavery was one of the main factors that led to the Civil War (1861–1865).

> *We think they are not, and that they are not included, and were not intended to be included.... They had for more than a century before been regarded as beings of an inferior order, and altogether unfit to associate with the white race...; and so far inferior, that they had no rights which the white man was bound to respect; and that the Negro might justly and lawfully be reduced to slavery for his benefit.... [A]ccordingly, a Negro of the African race was regarded ... as an article of property, and held, and bought and sold as such.... [N]o one seems to have doubted the correctness of the prevailing opinion of the time.*

The Thirteenth Amendment was introduced in 1865. It states, "Neither slavery nor involuntary servitude, except as a punishment for crime whereof the party shall have been duly convicted, shall exist within the United States, or any place subject to their jurisdiction."

… It took a bloody civil war before the 13th Amendment could be adopted to abolish slavery, though not the consequences slavery would have for future Americans.

A new basis for justice

While the Union survived the civil war, the Constitution did not. In its place arose a new, more promising basis for justice and equality, the 14th Amendment, ensuring protection of the life, liberty, and property of all persons against deprivations without due process, and guaranteeing equal protection of the laws. And yet almost another century would pass before any significant recognition was obtained of the rights of black Americans to share equally even in such basic opportunities as education, housing, and employment, and to have their votes counted, and counted equally. In the meantime, blacks joined America's military to fight its wars and invested untold hours working in its factories and on its farms, contributing to the development of this country's magnificent wealth and waiting to share in its prosperity.

What is striking is the role legal principles have played throughout America's history in determining the condition of Negroes. They were enslaved by law, emancipated by law, disenfranchised and segregated by law; and, finally, they have begun to win equality by law. Along the way, new constitutional principles have emerged to meet the challenges of a changing society. The progress has been dramatic, and it will continue.

The men who gathered in Philadelphia in 1787 could not have envisioned these changes. They could not have imagined, nor would they have accepted, that the document they were drafting would one day be construed by a Supreme Court to which had been appointed a woman and the descendent of an African slave. "We the People" no longer enslave, but the credit does not belong to the Framers. It belongs to those who refused to acquiesce in outdated notions of "liberty," "justice," and "equality," and who strived to better them.

And so we must be careful, when focusing on the events which took place in Philadelphia two centuries ago, that we not overlook the momentous events which followed, and thereby lose our proper sense of perspective. ... If we seek, instead, a sensitive understanding of the Constitution's inherent defects, and its promising evolution through 200 years of history, the celebration of the "Miracle at Philadelphia" will, in my view, be a far more meaningful and humbling experience. We will see that the true miracle was not the birth of the Constitution, but its life, a life nurtured through two turbulent centuries of our own making, and a life embodying much good fortune that was not....

Some may more quietly commemorate the suffering, struggle, and sacrifice that has triumphed over much of what was wrong with the original document, and observe the anniversary with hopes not realized and promises not fulfilled.

I plan to celebrate the bicentennial of the Constitution as a living document, including the Bill of Rights and the other amendments protecting individual freedoms and human rights.

Do you think slaves could have won their freedom through any other method rather than by changes in the law? See Volume 1, Individual and Society, Topic 10 Is violent protest ever justified?

If the Framers cannot take credit for what has happened since they drafted the Constitution, why should they take the blame for its defects?

The first 10 Amendments to the Constitution were ratified in 1791. They became known as the Bill of Rights. See Volume 7, The Constitution, The Bill of Rights, pages 24–25.

SPIKE LEE AND *THE PATRIOT*
Stuart Buck

Spike Lee (1963–) is America's foremost African American filmmaker. His films include Do the Right Thing (1989), Malcolm X (1992), Get on the Bus (1996), and Summer of Sam (1999).

NO

Spike Lee, never known for concealing his feelings, published a letter Friday in which he charged that Mel Gibson's latest movie, *The Patriot*, is a "complete whitewashing of history." "For three hours, *The Patriot* dodged around, skirted about or completely ignored slavery…. Let's not forget that two of 'The Framers,' founding fathers George Washington and Thomas Jefferson, owned numerous slaves. *The Patriot* is pure, blatant American Hollywood propaganda."

Lee has a point. In *The Patriot*, Gibson's character, Benjamin Martin, employs only freed blacks on his large plantation. The film's main black character fights in the South Carolina militia alongside Martin because he was promised his freedom after 12 months of service—but in fact South Carolina was one of only two states (Georgia being the other) in which blacks were NOT allowed to gain their freedom in that way. Only one white soldier shows any sign of racism towards the black soldier, and later apologizes before the final battle scene, saying that he is "honored" to serve with the black. When Martin's family is being hunted by the British, they take refuge in a seaside town of happy-go-lucky free blacks. So, Lee is correct that *The Patriot* is hardly an accurate picture of race relations in 1776.

But Lee's own version of history leaves much to be desired as well. Lee makes clear that he would have preferred a movie which portrayed our country 's Founders [Framers] as thoroughly racist. Lee might well have quoted Supreme Court Justice Thurgood Marshall, who once charged the Framers with thinking that blacks were "so far inferior, that they had no rights which the white man was bound to respect."

This view of our Founders is false. Though Jefferson certainly owned slaves, he made efforts throughout his life to end slavery. In the original version of the Declaration of Independence, Jefferson accused King George of waging "cruel war against human nature itself, violating its most sacred rights of life and liberty in the persons of a distant people who never offended him, captivating and carrying them into slavery in another hemisphere." As a state legislator, Jefferson proposed a law that would have led to

Go to www.common-place.org/vol-01/no-04/garrett/ for more discussion of Thomas Jefferson's attitude toward slavery.

COMMENTARY: *The Patriot*

The film *The Patriot* was released to mixed reception in 2000. Set in South Carolina in 1776 during the American Revolutionary War (1775–1783), it tells the story of widower Benjamin Martin (Mel Gibson) and his son Gabriel (Heath Ledger), who find themselves thrust into the fighting against the British Army. Reluctantly Martin takes up arms against the British Redcoats and recruits a band of volunteers to help him in his struggle to protect his family. The American Revolutionary War was caused by such factors as unpopular taxation and a lack of representation in the British Parliament. The Colonial Army was mainly made up of farmers, supplemented by state militias. In contrast, the British had a much larger professional army. Despite the clear advantage of the British troops, the Americans proved to be an effective fighting force, winning major victories at Saratoga and Yorktown. At the end of war Britain's North American colonies won independence, later joining together to become the United States.

The film is based on true events and people. Martin's character was inspired by several people, including Francis Marion, an American general who was known as "The Ghost." The climactic battle is based on the Battle of Cowpens (1781) and the Battle of Guilford Courthouse (1781).

Gabriel Martin (front left, played by Heath Ledger) and his father Benjamin (Mel Gibson) fight side by side against the British in the film The Patriot.

The filmmaker Spike Lee. A successful actor, writer, and director, Lee has brought the story of African Americans to a wide audience.

emancipation in Virginia, and he later proposed a law that would have banned slavery from the entire US West. Jefferson wrote some of the most haunting words on the subject of slavery: "I tremble for my country when I reflect that God is just: that his justice cannot sleep forever."

Among other Founders, George Washington said, "There is not a man living who wishes more sincerely than I do, to see a plan adopted for the abolition of [slavery]." Madison ... wrote that he had seen "the mere distinction of color made in the most enlightened period of time, a ground of the most oppressive dominion ever exercised by man over man." Benjamin Franklin wrote that slavery was "an atrocious debasement of human nature." And as for South Carolina, the setting of *The Patriot*, Alexander Hamilton proposed to give slaves their freedom in exchange for joining the revolutionary army, writing that "an essential part of the plan is to give them their freedom with their muskets."

Alexander Hamilton (1757–1804) was one of the delegates from New York at the Constitutional Convention. He later became secretary of the treasury under George Washington.

So why did not the Founders abolish slavery outright? Weren't they hypocritical? Isn't that Spike Lee's point?

The motives of the Framers

In an ideal world, the Founders [Framers] would have been able to abolish slavery in 1776, along with hunger, poverty, sexism, and the common cold. But political actors have to bend to social reality. And the reality in 1776 was that many people in our country, especially in the South, were not yet willing to abolish slavery. In order to form the Union, our Founders had to make certain compromises, including the toleration of slavery for a while. Had they not been willing to make that compromise, the South might never have joined the Union in the first place, and there would never have been the occasion for a Civil War to free the slaves.

Buck makes a startling comparison to try to suggest the impossibility of abolishing slavery.

If the South had never joined the Union and been subject to Northern pressure, might slavery still exist today?

What distinguishes the American Founding is that while it made a compromise on the slavery issue, the Founders nevertheless laid out in bold terms the principle of human equality. As the Declaration of Independence states, all men are created equal and are endowed by their Creator with inalienable rights. By putting forward this noble principle, even though they were unable to live up to it in every respect, the Founders gave later generations an ideal towards which to strive. As Professor Thomas West says… , "Lincoln and the Republican party of the 1850s were able to mobilize a national majority against …slavery only because of the commitment the Founders had made to the proposition that all men are created equal."

Do you believe it is possible for filmmakers to accurately reproduce history? Should films simply be considered entertainment?

So, both the filmmakers of *The Patriot* and Spike Lee have it wrong. *The Patriot* whitewashes history by portraying South Carolina as a picture of racial harmony. But Spike Lee's answer—to call the Founders racist—is equally wrongheaded. Both *The Patriot* and Lee ignore the complicated nature of humanity's struggle for justice. In that struggle, the Founders may have made concessions to evils like slavery, but at the same time they overcame their lower natures and established the principle of human equality. For that, we should be grateful.

Summary

In the first article Thurgood Marshall suggests that the Framers were indeed racist. He claims the patriotic fervor that accompanied the 1987 celebrations to mark the bicentenary of the Constitution obscured some unpalatable truths about the men who drafted it. He states that although the opening phrase of the historic document—"We the people"—may now be taken as inclusive of all Americans, at the time it was anything but: The Framers had no intention of giving votes to African Americans or to women. Negroes, he says, were disenfranchised because slavery was essential to the economies of the Southern states. He points out that some of the delegates at the Constitutional Convention opposed slavery on moral grounds—so it was not as if no one thought of abolition—but that they were eventually persuaded to accept an iniquitous compromise.

The second article was written by Stuart Buck in response to criticisms by the radical black film director Spike Lee of the film *The Patriot*. Lee objected that the film "whitewashed" the issue of slavery in the late 18th century and ignored the fact that some of the Framers themselves owned slaves. But Buck points out that at least one of them, George Washington, wanted to abolish slavery, while another, Thomas Jefferson, tried to legislate against it. His central point is that they abhorred the practice, but there was only so much they could do. Without the agreement of the Southern states the Constitution would never have been ratified. So the most enlightened of the Framers had to compromise in order to achieve the greater good of creating the United States. The matter of slavery would be dealt with later.

FURTHER INFORMATION:

Books:

Bradford, M.E., *Founding Fathers: Brief Lives of the Framers of the United States Constitution* Lawrence, KS: University Press of Kansas, 1994.

Greene, Thurston, *Language of the Constitution: A Sourcebook and Guide to the Ideas, Terms and Vocabulary Used by the Framers of the United States Constitution*. Westport, CT: Greenwood Press, 1991.

Kampinski, John P., and Richard Leffler (eds.), *A Necessary Evil? Slavery and the Debate over the Constitution (Constitutional Heritage, Vol. 2)*. Lanham, MD: Madison House Publishing, 1995.

Levy, Leonard W., *Original Intent and the Framers' Constitution*. New York: Macmillan, 1988.

Useful websites:

www.usconstitution.net/constframe.html
Site dedicated to the Constitution and the Framers.
www.law.ou.edu/hist/constitution/
Transcripts of the Amendments.

The following debates in the Pro/Con series may also be of interest:

In this volume:

Topic 3 Was slavery the cause of the Civil War?

Topic 12 Did the civil rights movement improve the position of blacks in society?

WERE THE FRAMERS RACIST?

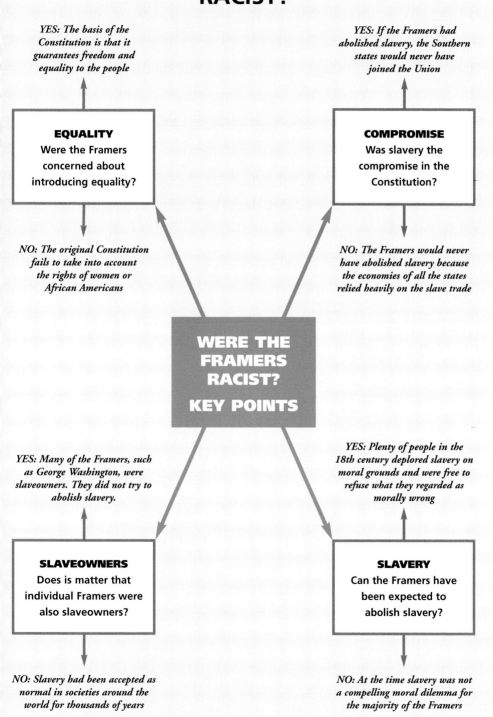

YES: The basis of the Constitution is that it guarantees freedom and equality to the people

YES: If the Framers had abolished slavery, the Southern states would never have joined the Union

EQUALITY
Were the Framers concerned about introducing equality?

COMPROMISE
Was slavery the compromise in the Constitution?

NO: The original Constitution fails to take into account the rights of women or African Americans

NO: The Framers would never have abolished slavery because the economies of all the states relied heavily on the slave trade

WERE THE FRAMERS RACIST?
KEY POINTS

YES: Many of the Framers, such as George Washington, were slaveowners. They did not try to abolish slavery.

YES: Plenty of people in the 18th century deplored slavery on moral grounds and were free to refuse what they regarded as morally wrong

SLAVEOWNERS
Does is matter that individual Framers were also slaveowners?

SLAVERY
Can the Framers have been expected to abolish slavery?

NO: Slavery had been accepted as normal in societies around the world for thousands of years

NO: At the time slavery was not a compelling moral dilemma for the majority of the Framers

Topic 3
WAS SLAVERY THE CAUSE OF THE CIVIL WAR?

YES
FROM "CORNERSTONE SPEECH"
SAVANNAH, GEORGIA, MARCH 21, 1861
ALEXANDER H. STEPHENS

NO
FROM "CAUSES OF THE CIVIL WAR"
WWW.NGEORGIA.COM/HISTORY/WHY.HTML
RANDY GOLDEN

INTRODUCTION

The Civil War was fought between the U.S. federal government and the secessionists of the Confederate States of America. Between April 12, 1861, when the first shots were fired at Fort Sumter, South Carolina, and May 1865, when the last Confederate forces surrendered, at least 620,000 soldiers died out of a total American population of around 32 million. The conflict is often portrayed as a battle between the antislave President Abraham Lincoln (1809-1865) and the proslavery leader of the Confederacy, Jefferson Davis (1808-1889). But was slavery really the main cause of the Civil War?

Slavery was a central pillar of Southern culture, whereas it had disappeared in the North. Even Northerners who were not avowedly antislavery tended to disapprove of the practice, while others, including Lincoln himself, opposed slavery on humanitarian grounds and sought to stop its spread into the western territories. Meanwhile, abolitionist groups fought (sometimes literally) for the emancipation of slaves in the South, and actions such as John Brown's 1859 attempt to steal arms from the arsenal at Harpers Ferry (then in Virginia, now West Virginia) to use against slaveholders alarmed Southerners. Nevertheless, the Northern states were not havens of liberalism. Racism was common, and Jefferson Davis accused the North of using the moral issue of slavery as a smokescreen to cover its efforts to dominate the South.

However, slavery was clearly vital to the South's economy. Although the majority of whites did not own slaves—according to the 1860 census only 384,000 whites out of a total white population of 8,099,00 in the South owned slaves—slaves kept the whole of society wealthy. If slavery was abolished, poor whites feared that there would be heightened competition for jobs, while small farmers might never have the opportunity of being slaveowners themselves one day. White Southerners, even though they did not benefit directly from slavery, overwhelmingly supported the Confederacy in the war.

Another interpretation, however, is that slavery was not the only important issue dividing the North and the South at this time. For example, some commentators claim that Abraham Lincoln only first stated that the war was about slavery in the Emancipation Proclamation (1863), two years after the start of the war. They argue that Lincoln at first stressed that the conflict was about preserving the union.

"It is not humanity that influences you ... you want ... to promote the industry of the United States, at the expense of the people of the South."

—JEFFERSON DAVIS, PRESIDENT OF THE CONFEDERATE STATES OF AMERICA (1861–1865)

Historians point to the differences in the regions' economies. At the end of the 1850s the North was industrializing, while the Southern economy remained based on plantation crops like cotton. The plantations depended on slave labor and the state of the world cotton market. When the price of cotton was high, the plantation owners made huge profits, but they did not invest them to diversify the South's economic base.

The South's lack of economic diversity led to friction with the North. Only 8 percent of U.S. manufactures came from the Southern states, so most manufactured goods for sale in the South were imported from overseas or elsewhere in the country. Goods imported from overseas, however, were subject to a federal tax that made them expensive. This tariff was viewed by Southerners as a means of protecting Northern manufacturing interests (which competed with overseas imports) at the expense of the South.

Divisions also arose in the political field. A mistrust of the aims and sympathies of the federal government plus traditional local loyalties caused Southerners to lean toward the doctrine of states' rights. This notion asserts that the states retain all powers not specifically granted to the federal government under the Constitution. Attitudes tended to be different in the North, where more extensive central government meant more effective economic development.

The following articles debate the causes of the Civil War. The first piece is a transcript of a speech given by Alexander H. Stephens (1812-1883), vice president of the then recently formed Confederacy, at Savannah, Georgia, on March 21, 1861. Stephens argues that slavery is "the proper status of the negro in our form of civilization." He is in no doubt that slavery was the immediate cause of the war.

In the second article Randy Golden argues that slavery was just one of a number of tensions between the North and the South. He cites slavery in conjunction with states' rights and economic issues as factors that contributed to secession and the war.

CORNERSTONE SPEECH
Alexander H. Stephens

The "new constitution" to which the author/speaker refers is that of the Confederacy, which was adopted on March 11, 1861.

To soften his criticism of respected persons, Stephens carefully exonerates them (in this case the Framers) from blame as he prepares to reject their views.

YES

✓ …The new constitution has put at rest, forever, all the agitating questions relating to our peculiar institution— African slavery as it exists amongst us—the proper status of the negro in our form of civilization. This was the immediate cause of the late rupture and present revolution. Jefferson in his forecast, had anticipated this, as the "rock upon which the old Union would split." He was right. What was conjecture with him, is now a realized fact. But whether he fully comprehended the great truth upon which that rock stood and stands, may be doubted. The prevailing ideas entertained by him and most of the leading statesmen at the time of the formation of the old constitution, were that the enslavement of the African was in violation of the laws of nature; that it was wrong in principle, socially, morally, and politically. It was an evil they knew not well how to deal with, but the general opinion of the men of that day was that, somehow or other in the order of Providence, the institution would be evanescent and pass away. This idea, though not incorporated in the constitution, was the prevailing idea at that time. The constitution, it is true, secured every essential guarantee to the institution while it should last, and hence no argument can be justly urged against the constitutional guarantees thus secured, because of the common sentiment of the day. Those ideas, however, were fundamentally wrong. They rested upon the assumption of the equality of races. This was an error. It was a sandy foundation, and the government built upon it fell when the "storm came and the wind blew."

Stephens links the institution of slavery to a "greater truth" of racial inequality. Could a politician make similar claims today?

Subordination to the superior race
Our new government is founded upon exactly the opposite idea; its foundations are laid, its corner-stone rests upon the great truth, that the negro is not equal to the white man; that slavery—subordination to the superior race—is his natural and normal condition. This, our new government, is the first, in the history of the world, based upon this great physical, philosophical, and moral truth. This truth has been slow in the process of its development, like all other truths in the various departments of science. It has been so even amongst us. Many who hear me, perhaps, can recollect well, that this

Alexander H. Stephens of Georgia, vice president of the Confederacy (1861–1865).

truth was not generally admitted, even within their day. The errors of the past generation still clung to many as late as twenty years ago. Those at the North, who still cling to these errors, with a zeal above knowledge, we justly denominate fanatics. All fanaticism springs from an aberration of the mind—from a defect in reasoning. It is a species of insanity. One of the most striking characteristics of insanity, in many instances, is forming correct conclusions from fancied or erroneous premises; so with the anti-slavery fanatics; their conclusions are right if their premises were. They assume that the negro is equal, and hence conclude that he is entitled to equal privileges and rights with the white man. If their premises were correct, their conclusions would be logical and just—but their premise being wrong, their whole argument fails.

Stephens' conclusion applies equally to his own argument.

Warring against principle?

I recollect once of having heard a gentleman from one of the northern States, of great power and ability, announce in the House of Representatives, with imposing effect, that we of the South would be compelled, ultimately, to yield upon this subject of slavery, that it was as impossible to war successfully against a principle in politics, as it was in physics or mechanics. That the principle would ultimately prevail. That we, in maintaining slavery as it exists with us, were warring against a principle, a principle founded in nature, the principle of the equality of men. The reply I made to him was, that upon his own grounds, we should, ultimately, succeed, and that he and his associates, in this crusade against our institutions, would ultimately fail. The truth announced, that it was as impossible to war successfully against a principle in politics as it was in physics and mechanics, I admitted; but told him that it was he, and those acting with him, who were warring against a principle. They were attempting to make things equal which the Creator had made unequal.

In the conflict thus far, success has been on our side, complete throughout the length and breadth of the Confederate States. It is upon this, as I have stated, our social fabric is firmly planted; and I cannot permit myself to doubt the ultimate success of a full recognition of this principle throughout the civilized and enlightened world.

As I have stated, the truth of this principle may be slow in development, as all truths are and ever have been, in the various branches of science. It was so with the principles announced by Galileo—it was so with Adam Smith and his

Galileo Galilei (1564–1642) was an Italian scientist. Among his discoveries was that objects fall at the same velocity no matter how heavy they are.

principles of political economy. It was so with Harvey, and his theory of the circulation of the blood. It is stated that not a single one of the medical profession, living at the time of the announcement of the truths made by him, admitted them. Now, they are universally acknowledged. May we not, therefore, look with confidence to the ultimate universal acknowledgment of the truths upon which our system rests? It is the first government ever instituted upon the principles in strict conformity to nature, and the ordination of Providence, in furnishing the materials of human society. Many governments have been founded upon the principle of the subordination and serfdom of certain classes of the same race; such were and are in violation of the laws of nature. Our system commits no such violation of nature's laws. With us, all of the white race, however high or low, rich or poor, are equal in the eye of the law. Not so with the negro. Subordination is his place. He, by nature, or by the curse against Canaan, is fitted for that condition which he occupies in our system.

> Scientific method does not accept a theory until it has been proven: Is that what Stephens is proposing here?

> The "curse against Canaan" refers to Genesis 9:24–27, in which Biblical passage Noah places a curse on Canaan, dooming him to be a servant to his brothers.

The architect, in the construction of buildings, lays the foundation with the proper material—the granite; then comes the brick or the marble. The substratum of our society is made of the material fitted by nature for it, and by experience we know that it is best, not only for the superior, but for the inferior race, that it should be so. It is, indeed, in conformity with the ordinance of the Creator. It is not for us to inquire into the wisdom of his ordinances, or to question them. For his own purposes, he has made one race to differ from another, as he has made "one star to differ from another star in glory."

The cornerstone of the Confederacy

The great objects of humanity are best attained when there is conformity to his laws and decrees, in the formation of governments as well as in all things else. Our confederacy is founded upon principles in strict conformity with these laws. This stone which was rejected by the first builders "is become the chief of the corner"—the real "cornerstone"—in our new edifice.

I have been asked, what of the future? It has been apprehended by some that we would have arrayed against us the civilized world. I care not who or how many they may be against us, when we stand upon the eternal principles of truth, if we are true to ourselves and the principles for which we contend, we are obliged to, and must triumph....

CAUSES OF THE CIVIL WAR
Randy Golden

NO

X Some say simplistically that the Civil War was fought over slavery. Unfortunately, there is no "simple" reason. The causes of the war were a complex series of events, including slavery, that began long before the first shot was fired. Competing nationalisms, political turmoil, the definition of freedom, the preservation of the Union, the fate of slavery and the structure of our society and economy could all be listed as significant contributing factors in America's bloodiest conflict.

The author is deliberately tailoring his argument to appeal to his readership.

Complaints of Georgians

Many of the problems Georgians saw more than one hundred fifty years ago are being reiterated today. The "oppressive" federal government. High taxes (tariffs before the war). A growing government unwilling to listen to law abiding citizens. Sound familiar? They were complaints levied from 1816 on in Georgia.

John C. Calhoun (1782–1850) was vice president of the United States under both John Quincy Adams and Andrew Jackson. He was also the architect of South Carolina's 1832 nullification of the tariff. Go to http://gi.grolier.com /presidents/ea/vp/ vpcal.html for a detailed biography.

Constitutional questions

People argued about the meaning of the Constitution since its infancy. From a legal standpoint, the document defines the relationship between the people of the United States and the federal government, detailing the powers and responsibilities of each. In 1828 Vice-president John C. Calhoun said if a state felt a federal law extended beyond the Constitutional rights of the government that state had the right to ignore (or "nullify") the law. This concept dated back [to] the Articles of Confederation. President Andrew Jackson felt the federal government was the highest authority (Article VI, Section 2) and the states had to abide by its law.

Tariffs and the Nullification Crisis

As industry in the North expanded it looked towards southern markets, rich with cash from the lucrative agricultural business, to buy the North's manufactured goods. However, it was often cheaper for the South to purchase the goods abroad. In order to "protect" the northern industries Jackson slapped a tariff on many of the imported goods that could be manufactured in the North. When South Carolina passed the Ordinance of Nullification in November 1832, refusing to collect the tariff and threatening to withdraw from the Union, Jackson ordered federal troops to Charleston. A secession crisis was averted when Congress revised the Tariff of Abominations in February 1833.

The "Tariff of Abominations" was the disparaging nickname that Southerners gave to the unpopular Tariff Act of 1828.

The rhetoric changes

However, the political climate changed during this "Nullification Crisis." Designations of States Rightist, pro-Union, loose or strict constructionalist became more important than Whig or Democrat. In North Georgia when John Thomas, a local politician, was asked what to name a new county he said, "Name it Union, for none but Union-like men live here." Most of the northern tier of Georgia counties remained pro-Union until the outbreak of war almost 30 years later. From this point on factional politics would play an increasing part in the division of a country.

Economic changes affect society

The Panic of 1837 and the ensuing depression began to gnaw like a hungry animal on the flesh of the American system. The disparity between northern and southern economies was exacerbated. Before and after the depression the economy of the South prospered. Southern cotton sold abroad totaled 57% of all American exports before the war. The Panic of 1857 devastated the North and left the South virtually untouched. The clash of a wealthy, agricultural South and a poorer, industrial North was intensified by abolitionists who were not above using class struggle to further their cause.

The panics of 1837 and 1857 were major U.S. financial crises. Visit www. u-s-history.com/ pages/h967.html and ...h159.html to find out about their causes and effects.

The breakdown of the political system

The ugliness of the political process quickly began to show as parties turned upon themselves and politics on a national level were more like local Georgia politics. Feuds and fights in political arenas were common. From 1837 until 1861 eight men became president, but no man served more than a single term in office. One sitting president was not renominated by his own party and another withdrew his name after being nominated. New political parties were created with names like Constitutional Union, American, Free-Soilers and Republican. In Georgia, Democrats were strong, but factional fighting broke the party along pro-Union and States Rights lines.

With the disintegration of the Whig party in the early 1850's the political turmoil increased. Howell Cobb, former Speaker of the House, molded pro-Union Democrats, mostly from North Georgia, with former Whigs to grab the governorship in 1851. His attempts to help slaves fell on the deaf ears of our state legislature. Although Georgia began to prosper during his first year the coalition fell apart as the Democrats reunited. The increasing power of the West and self-serving politicians like Stephen A. Douglas churned the political environment as the North and South battled for philosophic control.

By the time [James] Buchanan was elected [president] (1856) the country was divided on many issues, including slavery. Former Governor Cobb spoke in the North as a moderate Southerner for Buchanan and served on his cabinet. Over the next 4 years Cobb changed from pro-Union to secessionist. A similar process occurred across much of Georgia. In 1860 the state was equally divided between secessionist and pro-Union.

A concise history of slavery

At Jamestown, Va. in 1611 a group of Scottish women and children were sold as slaves. 7 years later in Jamestown the first Africans were sold in[to] slavery. From 1611 until 1865 people from virtually every society on earth were sold into slavery in North America. Citizens in each of the thirteen colonies enslaved people, but slavery was viewed as a southern institution after the early 1800's. Along the coastal areas of the South a majority of the slaves were black. In some inland areas whites and Native Americans outnumbered black slaves. Slavery is still legal in the United States as a criminal punishment, but is not practiced.

The gin is a device that separates cotton fibers from cotton seeds. The mechanization of separation reduced the price of Southern cotton, leading to increased demand for the product and thus to a need for more slaves to work on the plantations.

In 1789 Georgians, as did much of the rest of the country, saw slavery as a dying institution. Eli Whitney's stolen modification of the cotton gin (1793) created a greater demand for slaves, so rather than "wither on the vine" the institution prospered. The Northwest Ordinance, adopted in 1787 banned the practice in the Northwest Territories. In 1798 Georgia forbade further importation of slaves and the Constitution allowed Congress to outlaw importation of slaves in 1808, which they did. Over the next 40 years lesser skirmishes were fought over slavery including the Compromise of 1820. In North Georgia slavery was not widespread and a majority of the slaves were of Native American, Scottish or Irish descent.

Slaves often spoke of "our cotton" or "our cattle". The only item they would concede was the master's carriage. Trusted slaves were permitted to go to town unescorted. Others suffered horribly. Conditions in northern factories were as bad or worse than those for a majority of the slaves, but it would be 40 years after the war when they were properly addressed.

Beginning in the late 1840's the conflict over slavery began to boil over. The Compromise of 1850 contributed heavily to the split in Georgia's Democratic Party. On a national scale David Wilmot, Lloyd Garrison, and Harriet Beecher Stowe enflamed the abolitionists. James G. Birney and Theodore Weld were more effective against slavery. The Dred Scot[t] decision, Kansas-Nebraska Act, and harsher Fugitive Slave Laws gave the South some redress.

The measures mentioned in this paragraph represent landmark legislation in the history of slavery. Go to www.pbs.org/wgbh/aia/home.html for an in-depth treatment of slavery in the United States.

The new Republican Party became a home to the alienated abolitionists. Although they totaled less than 3% of the population at large, they formulated the Republican platform to include the abolition of slavery as a plank. The party then nominated Abraham Lincoln for president. Few gave him any chance of success, but 3 other candidates split the popular vote and Lincoln won. Convinced that Lincoln would ruin the South economically, possibly by freeing the slaves, the heartland of the South withdrew from the Union. Shortly thereafter the upper south joined them. The attack on Fort Sumter launched America's bloodiest conflict.

So what caused the war?

The United States had been moving towards a fractured, divisive society for a number of years. Cultural and economic differences served to widen the rift. Battles among North, South, and West grew more heated, especially after 1850. Politicians and the judiciary sent conflicting signals trying to appease each of the groups involved, yet all remained dissatisfied. Georgians saw a federal government controlled by northern industrialists who were unresponsive to the problems of their state. Tariffs paid by Georgians bought improvements in northern and western states. Now the federal government, they thought, was going to take away personal property without compensation, a clear violation of their Fourth Amendment rights.

Would cultural and economic differences in the United States inevitably have caused war even without slavery?

The South was wrong to assume Lincoln intended to free the slaves. He had never advocated action to abolish slavery nor did he speak out against the Illinois rules prohibiting blacks from testifying against whites. The true abolition candidate, Gerrit Smith of New York, drew few votes. In his inaugural address Lincoln made it clear he would not interfere with slavery where it existed. Even though he made this speech after the South seceded he left the door open for their return....

Summary

The speech given in March 1861 by Alexander H. Stephens, vice president of the secessionist Confederate States of America, declares the Confederacy's clear belief in the correctness of "African slavery." Stephens states that the Confederacy was founded on the basis that "the negro is not equal to the white man" and that "slavery … is his [the negro's] natural and normal condition." Stephens boasts that the government of the South was "the first, in the history of the world, based upon this great physical, philosophical, and moral truth." Faced with the South having "arrayed against us the civilized world," Stephens responds that "when we stand upon the eternal principles of truth … we are obliged to, and must triumph." Stephens cites slavery as the immediate cause of the breach between North and South, recalling the prophecy of Thomas Jefferson (1743–1826) that slavery would be the "rock upon which the old Union would split."

Randy Golden asserts that to explain the Civil War as a struggle between slavers and antislavers is too simplistic. He maintains that slavery was one of several longstanding sources of friction between North and South. Among the other ingredients in a simmering cocktail, according to Golden, were federal versus state responsibilities and powers, the relative economic development of the North and South, and the linked issue of tariffs, which seemed to penalize the agricultural South to the advantage of the manufacturing North. As to the war having been fought over slavery, Golden argues that for his part, Abraham Lincoln did not intend to abolish slavery, having "made it clear he would not interfere with slavery where it existed."

FURTHER INFORMATION:

Books:

Fehrenbacher, Don E., *The Dred Scott Case: Its Significance in American Law and Politics*. New York: Oxford University Press, 2001.

Holt, Michael F., *The Political Crisis of the 1850s*. New York: W.W. Norton and Co., 1983.

Potter, David Morris, *The Impending Crisis: 1848–1861*. New York: Harper & Row, 1977.

Stamp, Kenneth Milton (ed.), *The Causes of the Civil War*. New York: Simon & Schuster, 1991.

Useful websites:

www.members.aol.com/TeacherNet/civilwar.html
Extensive Civil War resources site, including several links to pages on the conflict's causes.
www.suite101.com/links.cfm/civil_war
Extensive Civil War resources site.

The following debates in the Pro/Con series may also be of interest:

In this volume:
 Civil War timeline, pages 46–47

 Topic 4 Was Reconstruction a success?

In *The Constitution*:
Topic 1 Does it matter what the original intentions of the Framers were?

WAS SLAVERY THE CAUSE OF THE CIVIL WAR?

YES: The federal government set tariffs to protect Northern manufacturing at the expense of the agricultural South

YES: A stronger central government meant more effective economic development

ECONOMICS
Did tariffs aim to discriminate between the regions?

CENTRALIZATION
Did a stronger federal government benefit the country?

NO: Tariffs were the federal government's main source of income, and anyway, the South rejected industrialization, seeing it as a threat to its way of life

NO: A stronger central government infringed on freedom, and anyway, it cared little for the South

WAS SLAVERY THE CAUSE OF THE CIVIL WAR?

KEY POINTS

YES: Northern attitudes to slavery ranged from disapproval, through opposition to its spread, to militant abolitionism

MORALITY
Did the North oppose slavery on purely moral grounds?

NO: Opposition to slavery was simply a blind to mask political ambition. The North wanted to increase the number of free states over slave states so they could control the legislature.

CIVIL WAR TIMELINE

"In the present civil war it is quite possible that God's purpose is something different from the purpose of either party."

—ABRAHAM LINCOLN (1809–1865)

The Civil War was fought between the Northern states (the Union) and the Southern states (the Confederacy). The causes of the war included conflict about slavery—which by then existed only in the South—and disagreement over how much control the federal government should have over states. In 1860 the election of Abraham Lincoln, who was opposed to slavery, brought the conflict to a head.

1860 November 6: Republican Abraham Lincoln, an opponent of slavery, is elected president. **December 20:** South Carolina is the first state to withdraw from the United States of America.

1861 January: Following South Carolina, Mississippi, Florida, Alabama, Georgia, Louisiana, and Texas secede from the Union. **February:** Delegates from the seven seceding states meet in Montgomery, Alabama, and form a government. Jefferson Davis is elected president of the Confederate States of America. **March 4:** Abraham Lincoln is inaugurated as the 16th president of the United States. **April 12–13:** The Civil War begins when Confederate troops attack Fort Sumter in Charleston, South Carolina. **18:** Virginia, Arkansas, Tennessee, and North Carolina join the Confederacy. Richmond, Virginia, becomes the capital of the Confederacy. **20:** Colonel Robert E. Lee resigns his commission in the U.S. Army and later accepts command of Confederate forces in Virginia. **July 21:** On their march to take Richmond the Union Army is defeated by Confederate troops at the Battle of Bull Run, also known as the First Battle of Manassas. Union troops are driven back to Washington, D.C. Confederate General Thomas J. Jackson earns the nickname "Stonewall" for his

tenacity during the battle. **November:** George B. McClellan is appointed by Lincoln as general-in-chief of all Union forces.

1862 February 6–16: In the first major campaign of the war Union General Ulysses S. Grant captures Fort Henry and Fort Donelson in Tennessee, earning him the nickname "Unconditional Surrender Grant." **April 6–7:** Both sides suffer huge losses in the Battle of Shiloh in Tennessee; Union forces eventually prevail. **25:** Union fleet commander David G. Farragut captures New Orleans. **May 8:** "Stonewall" Jackson defeats Union forces at the Battle of McDowell in Virginia. **June 1:** Robert E. Lee takes command of the Confederate Army from the wounded Joseph E. Johnston at the Battle of the Seven Pines in Virginia. **June 25–July 1:** The Seven Days Battles reverse a tide of Union military successes as Lee's army drives McClellan's troops away from Richmond. **August 28–30:** Confederate forces are victorious at the Second Battle of Bull Run, or the Second Battle of Manassas. **September 17:** Confederate forces under General Lee are stopped at Antietam in Maryland by McClellan and his Union Army. Around 26,000 men are killed, wounded, or missing in the bloodiest battle of the war. General Lee withdraws to Virginia.

22: President Lincoln issues the preliminary Emancipation Proclamation freeing slaves. **November 7:** Lincoln replaces General McClellan with General Ambrose E. Burnside as the new commander of the Army of the Potomac. **December 13:** General Lee wins a decisive victory for Confederate forces at the Battle of Fredericksburg in Virginia.

1863 January 1: Lincoln issues the Emancipation Proclamation declaring that all slaves in areas held by the Confederates are, in the eyes of the federal government, free. The war to preserve the union becomes a struggle for the abolition of slavery. **March 3:** The Union Congress introduces a draft act making all male citizens between the ages of 20 and 45 liable to be called for military service, but exempts those who pay $300 or provide a substitute. **May 1–4:** Lee defeats Union forces at the Battle of Chancellorsville, Virginia. **10:** "Stonewall" Jackson dies from wounds suffered in fighting at Chancellorsville. **July 1–3:** Lee undertakes a second invasion of the north, but is defeated at the Battle of Gettysburg in Pennsylvania. Union General George G. Meade allows Lee to retreat south. **4:** In the west Confederates surrender Vicksburg, Mississippi, to Ulysses S. Grant, who secures the Mississippi River for the Union, effectively cutting the Confederacy in two. **13–15:** Violent antidraft riots breakout in New York. **September 19–20:** Confederate troops win a decisive victory at Chikamauga, Georgia. **November 19:** Lincoln delivers the Gettysburg Address at a ceremony dedicating the battlefield as a national cemetery. **23–25:** Union forces under General Grant defeat General Braxton Bragg's Army at Chattanooga, Tennessee.

1864 March 10: Lincoln appoints Ulysses S. Grant commander of all Union armies. **May 1864:** General Grant commands a coordinated campaign involving all the Union armies and begins a war of attrition that includes major battles at the Wilderness (May 5–6), Spotsylvania (May 8–12), and Cold Harbor (June 1–3). **September:** Union General William T. Sherman captures Atlanta, Georgia. **November 8:** Lincoln is reelected president. **16:** Sherman leaves Atlanta and begins his "march to the sea." **December:** Sherman's army takes Savannah, Georgia, without resistance. Sherman offers the city to Lincoln as a Christmas present.

1865 January 31: Congress passes the Thirteenth Amendment to the Constitution to abolish slavery. **February:** Sherman starts his Carolinas campaign. His army moves from Georgia through South Carolina. **March 4:** Lincoln is inaugurated as president for a second term. **March 24:** Sherman occupies Goldboro, North Carolina, ending his Carolinas campaign. **March 29:** The Appomattox campaign begins with Grant's move against Lee's defenses at Petersburg, Virginia. **April 2:** Petersburg falls to Union forces. Lieutenant General Ambrose P. Hill, a leading Confederate officer, is killed. The Confederate capital, Richmond, is evacuated. **3:** Union troops occupy Richmond. **9:** Robert E. Lee surrenders his Confederate Army to Ulysses S. Grant at Appomattox. **14:** Abraham Lincoln is shot by John Wilkes Booth at Ford's Theater in Washington, D.C. Secretary of State William H. Seward is stabbed and seriously wounded in an assassination attempt in his home. **15:** Lincoln dies at 7:22 A.M. Andrew Johnson is inaugurated as president. **18:** General Joseph E. Johnston surrenders to William T. Sherman in North Carolina. **26:** John Wilkes Booth is shot and killed in a barn in Virginia. **May 10:** Jefferson Davis is captured and taken prisoner near Irwinville, Georgia. Remaining Confederate forces surrender, and the nation is reunited.

Topic 4
WAS RECONSTRUCTION A SUCCESS?

YES
"THE FREEDMEN'S BUREAU"
HARPER'S WEEKLY, JULY 25, 1868
EDITORIAL

NO
FROM "RECONSTRUCTION AND ITS FAILURE"
BLACK EXPERIENCE, CHAPTER 6, 1976
PROFESSOR NORM COOMBS

INTRODUCTION

"Reconstruction" is the term commonly given to the period from the end of the Civil War in 1865 to 1877. Slavery was finally abolished in the United States under the Thirteenth Amendment, passed by Congress in 1865. During Reconstruction the federal government introduced measures to enable the defeated Southern states to be readmitted to the Union with governments based on racial equality. How successful Reconstruction was in ensuring equal political, civil, and economic rights for the newly freed slaves, though, is a controversial issue.

Andrew Johnson (1808–1875) succeeded President Abraham Lincoln (1809–1865) after the latter's assassination in April 1865. Like Lincoln, Johnson favored a lenient approach to the defeated South. He offered a generous amnesty to most Southern whites and a return to civil government for states that ratified the Thirteenth Amendment. Most of the Southern states complied, but Congress was far from satisfied with the situation.

Pointing to the presence in office of former Confederates and to the introduction in the South of Black Codes limiting the rights of ex-slaves, Congress rejected the new Southern state governments. Johnson was furious. But Congress now took over Reconstruction, and it was far less lenient toward the South.

In February 1866 Congress passed the Freedmen's Bureau Act, extending the life of the agency set up at the end of the war to help ex-slaves adjust to freedom. Two months later Congress enacted the Civil Rights Act, which established blacks as American citizens. Johnson rejected both measures, but Congress overrode his veto. That June Congress passed the Fourteenth Amendment, which was to place the citizenship clause of the Civil Rights Act in the Constitution. In the spring of 1867 Congress, which since the fall 1866 elections had a large Republican majority opposed to the "old South," began passing the Reconstruction acts, also over President Johnson's veto.

The Reconstruction acts barred the Southern states from Congress until their state constitutions included the Fourteenth Amendment. States still outside the Union after 1868 also had to accept the Fifteenth Amendment, which guaranteed black men the vote. By 1870 all the former Confederate states had been readmitted. Under mixed black and white Republican governments these states implemented policies that promoted civil and political equality for the races.

"Somebody must take them [freedmen] by the hand; not to support them but simply to help them to that work which will support them."

—CHARLES SUMNER (1811–1874), REPUBLICAN SENATOR

Southern whites resented these governments and the advancement of ex-slaves. Terror groups such as the Ku Klux Klan were formed. They intimidated white Republicans and blacks to keep them from voting. In 1869 a Democrat, white-only government was elected in Tennessee. More administrations of the same type came to power in other states of the old Confederacy. By the mid-1870s the tide was also running against the Republicans in the North. Many people believed their policies were extreme, and they were accused of corruption. In 1877 the last federal troops left the South, and the white population was once again firmly in control.

Historians still debate the successes and failures of Reconstruction. On the positive side three constitutional amendments were passed that transformed the position of ex-slaves, guaranteeing them their freedom and citizens' rights, and black males the vote. Blacks could at last take part in the political process, and they did. Another positive result was the introduction by the Freedmen's Bureau of public education for blacks.

Critics of Reconstruction, on the other hand, point out that it failed to help the ex-slaves economically. They had no wealth with which to back up their political rights. Redistribution of land among ex-slaves might have helped but did not take place. This lack of economic strength meant that once Reconstruction ended, the blacks could not prevent the white conservatives from regaining power. The old ways returned with heightened racial unease.

The following articles give two perspectives on Reconstruction. First, an 1868 editorial from *Harper's Weekly* outlines why the Freedmen's Bureau was vital in the years immediately after emancipation. It sums up the bureau's achievements to date and looks forward, in the words of General Howard, to a future "full of promise for the entire race redeemed from bondage and ignorance." In contrast, the second piece asserts that "most liberals assumed that the termination of slavery meant the end of their problems" and criticizes the Freedmen's Bureau for doing little outside the field of education "except to provide temporary help." The support given to ex-slaves under Reconstruction, it suggests, was far from enough to ensure meaningful freedom in the face of the advocates of white supremacy.

THE FREEDMEN'S BUREAU
Editorial, *Harper's Weekly*

YES

The writer grabs the reader's attention by beginning this editorial (an article that conveys the editors' or publishers' opinions) with a series of provocative statements.

✓ The Freedmen's Bureau has always been an object of Democratic hatred; but no institution was ever more imperatively necessary, and none has been more useful. Naturally a party which was steadily hostile to the abolition of slavery loudly clamored for the abolition of any system of defense for the emancipated class. But there is no doubt whatever that the war of races which that party has prophesied and encouraged, and which it would gladly have seen begun in the hope of the extermination of a race guilty of a colored skin, has been prevented by no means so powerful as that of the Freedmen's Bureau.

The war

The war left the late slaves free among a population that had always despised them as a servile race, and that now hated them as men who had loved and trusted the Government. The freedmen had the habit of dependence which a severe system of slavery develops. They had no resource, no hope whatever, but their labor, in a region where all the land belonged to the employers, and all the employers were their enemies. The circumstances of their emancipation were a constant exasperation to the late master class that waited only for the moment to reduce them again to some kind of peonage or to actual slavery.

"Peonage" was a system under which people who got into debt were forced to work on their creditors' property until their debt was paid off. Peonage provided cheap labor, and in some cases employers deliberately got workers into debt so they could treat them as peons.

The laws in regard to the freedmen, that these masters passed with the support of the President, were infamous. They were spiteful and inhuman. Had there been no friendly and powerful hand ready to interfere, had the slaves freed by the war been left wholly, as the Democratic party and the President desired, to the tender mercies of their late masters, and had some bold leader appeared among them, as undoubtedly he would, they would not have submitted without a desperate struggle to the doom intended for them.

Conscience and common-sense

Is it the duty of the government to reconcile "hostile parties"?

The Freedmen's Bureau was the conscience and common-sense of the country stepping between the hostile parties and saying to them, with irresistible authority, "Peace!" The country had made the slaves free. It recognized them

Entitled "The Freedman's Bureau," this sketch plays on the name of the ex-slaves' protector.

as men. It had seen their unswerving and heroic fidelity to the cause of the Union, knowing it to be that of their recovered liberty. It resolved that the only way to develop manhood is to treat men as men. It therefore stood between the freedmen and starvation and cruel laws, meanwhile giving them arms and schools and civil and political equality, that they might start fair in the common race. Through the quiet force of the Bureau the hostile class at the South has felt the perpetual presence of the will and power of the American people. The Bureau charities of direct relief of food have been shared by all the destitute of every color, and meanwhile its organizing hand has helped to arrange labor upon the new basis, to compose disputes, to accustom the whole population to the new order. Its service in this respect has been incalculable.

Despised and outraged?

It must be remembered that the danger of a bloody disturbance of the settlement of the war in regard to the freedmen has never been upon the side of the late slaves, but of their masters. Despised and outraged as they have been, the anarchical element was not the race that was said to be imbruted and degraded by slavery; it was that which claimed to be the superior and master race. The crimes of the freedmen have been under the circumstances so few as scarcely to be noted. Their industry in labor and their devotion to education have been so striking as to gain perpetual honor. While the late rebels at the South were passing their black-codes intended to restore as much of slavery as possible, and the Copperheads at the North were declaiming about the barbarization and Africanization of the Southern States—as if liberty were more barbarizing than slavery—the freedmen were filling nearly four thousand schools, and themselves supporting more than a thousand of them. Old and young were busily studying; the increase of general intelligence among them has been remarkable; and as General Howard says—who, as Chief of the Bureau, and a most sagacious friend of the freedmen, and untiring worker for them, has the best opportunity of knowing— "the hopes of the warmest friends of the freedmen have been more than fulfilled. The future is full of promise for the entire race redeemed from bondage and ignorance."

Except for the Freedmen's Bureau, keeping the peace with intelligence and authority, organizing labor, establishing schools, saving the white population from the consequences

"Copperhead" was a disparaging term for a Northerner who showed sympathies with the South in the Civil War.

A career soldier, Oliver Otis Howard (1830–1909) was chief commissioner of the Freedmen's Bureau from 1865 to 1872. Go to www. bartleby.com/65/ho/ HowardO.html for a biography.

of their own ferocity, it is easy to imagine how fearful would have been the condition of the Southern States during the period between the end of the war and the establishment of loyal governments. And now that those States are resuming their old relations in the Union, and for the first time with truly Republican governments, Congress is providing that the Bureau, which was in its nature temporary, shall cease its work. It has taught the freedmen that they are citizens of a government which recognizes their equal manhood. It has taught the late master class that all men have rights which must be respected. Clad in the armed authority of the United States, it has been a true minister of peace and as the occasion for its service disappears, the Freedmen's Bureau passes into history with that highest crown of praise, the pious gratitude of the poor and unfortunate.

Set up in 1865 for one year, the Freedmen's Bureau had its life extended in 1866. The bureau closed in 1869, although its education work continued until 1872. Go to www.bartleby.com/65/fr/Freedmen.html to find out more about the bureau and its activities.

RECONSTRUCTION AND ITS FAILURE
Professor Norm Coombs

The Radical Republicans opposed lenient treatment of the defeated South. Charles Sumner (1811–1874) was their leader in the Senate. Thaddeus Stevens (1792–1868) led them in the House.

NO

At the close of the war more attention was given to the reconstruction of Southern institutions than to the elevation of the ex-slave. While a handful of the Radical Republicans, such as Sumner and Stevens, were aware that slavery had not prepared the ex-slave for participation in a free competitive society, most liberals assumed that the termination of slavery meant the end of their problems. They believed that blacks could immediately enter into community life on an equal footing with other citizens. Any suggestion that the ex-slave needed help to get started drew considerable resentment and hostility from liberals and conservatives alike. With the abolition of the peculiar institution, the anti-slavery societies considered their work finished. Frederick Douglass, however, complained that the slaves were sent out into the world empty-handed. In fact, both the war and emancipation had intensified racial hostility. The ex-slave had not yet been granted his civil rights. At the same time, he was no longer covered by property rights. Therefore he was even more vulnerable to physical intimidation than before.

Why do you think the Civil War and the freeing of the slaves had "intensified racial hostility"?

Presidential reconstruction

As the war drew to an end, Lincoln initiated a program aimed at the rapid reconstruction of the South and the healing of sectional bitterness. With only the exclusion of a few Confederate officials, he offered immediate pardon to all who would swear allegiance to the Federal Government. As soon as ten percent of the citizens of any state who had voted in 1860 had taken this oath, a state could then hold local elections and resume home rule....

The term "sectional" equates approximately to "regional." The North, South, and West, for example, are "sections" of the United States.

After Lincoln's assassination, Andrew Johnson further accelerated the pace of reconciliation. Granting personal pardons by the thousands, he initiated a plan for restoration which was even more lenient. Southern states resumed home rule, and, in the Federal election of 1866, they elected scores of Confederate officials to Congress. At the same time other Confederate officials were elected to other local posts throughout the South. One of the most urgent tasks taken up by these new home-rule governments was the determination and definition of the status of the ex-slave. State after state passed black codes which bore an amazing resemblance to those of slavery days. Blacks were not allowed to testify in court against whites. If they quit their jobs, they could be imprisoned for breach of contract. Anyone found without a job could be arrested and fined $50. Those who could not pay the fine were hired out to anyone in the community who would pay the fine. This created a new system of forced labor. At the same time, blacks could be fined for insulting gestures, breaking the curfew, and for possessing firearms.... Although the Thirteenth Amendment had made slavery unconstitutional, the South was trying to recreate the peculiar institution in law while not admitting it in name.

Congressional reconstruction

Radical Republicans in Congress were outraged both at the unrepentant obstinacy of the South and at the leniency of Johnson's plan for restoration. After refusing to seat many of the Southern delegates to Congress the Radical Republicans went on to pass civil rights legislation which was aimed at protecting the ex-slave from the black codes. President Johnson, however vetoed these bills as well as the Fourteenth Amendment. An enraged Congress passed the civil rights legislation over his veto and came within one vote of impeaching the President. Although impeachment failed, Johnson lost his leadership in the government, and Congress, within two years after the end of the war, began Reconstruction all over again. The first large-scale Congressional hearings in American history were held to investigate the conditions in the South. The investigation documented widespread poverty, physical brutality, and intimidation as well as legal discrimination....

> In fact, President Johnson was impeached when he suspended Secretary of War Edwin M. Stanton in 1867 in what Congress viewed as a violation of the Tenure of Office Act. In 1868 the Senate, sitting as a tribunal, came within one vote of removing Johnson from office.

Congress removed home rule from the Southern states and divided the area into five military districts. Even those Southerners who had already received federal pardons were now required to swear a stricter oath in order to regain their right to vote. State conventions met to draft new constitutions. These conventions were dominated by a coalition of three groups: new black voters, whites who had come from the North either to make personal fortunes or to help educate the ex-slave, and Southern whites who had never supported the Confederacy. The oath of allegiance required a citizen to swear that he was now and always had been loyal to the Federal Government. This excluded all the Confederate officials. These new Southern reconstruction governments operated under the protection of the Army

> Whites who came south after the war were referred to disparagingly as "carpetbaggers" because they often arrived carrying all they owned in carpet bags. The Southern white Republicans who helped in Reconstruction were given the derogatory name "scalawags," the origin of which is unknown.

and with the encouragement of the Federal Government. They strove to reconstruct the South economically, politically, and socially.

They established a system of public education, built many new hospitals, founded institutions for the mentally and physically handicapped, and attempted to reform the penal system. During Reconstruction blacks played a significant political role throughout the South. Besides voting in large numbers, they were elected to local, state, and federal offices. Between 1869 and 1901, two became U. S. Senators and twenty were members of the House of Representatives....

White Southern backlash

White conservatives in the South were outraged, and they were determined to have absolutely nothing to do with a government which permitted Negro participation. They spread the myth that Reconstruction governments were in the grip of intolerably stupid and corrupt black men. Although Negroes were elected to state governments in significant numbers, the fact was that at no time were they in control.... The passionate belief in white superiority and a desperate fear of black retaliation caused many whites to resort to physical intimidation to achieve their purposes. The Ku Klux Klan was the most notorious of a large number of similar organizations which spread throughout the South. Negroes and white sympathizers were beaten and lynched. Some had their property burned, and others lost their jobs if they showed too much independence....

Although Reconstruction did protect some of the political and civil rights of the Afro-American community, it achieved almost nothing in improving the social and economic situation. The concept of social and economic rights was almost nonexistent a century ago. Political rights, however, without economic security could be a mere abstraction. Meaningful freedom had to be more than the freedom to starve. This meant that the ex-slave needed land, tools, and training to provide him with an economic base that would make his freedom real. The ex-slave had limited education, limited experience, a servile slave attitude, and he was in need of social and economic training to compensate for the years of slavery. Without this he could not enter a competitive society as an equal. Emancipation was not enough.

The other hope for the advancement of the ex-slave was through the development of industrial skills.... In 1866 the National Labor Union decided to organize black workers

In 1870 and 1871 Congress enacted three enforcement laws, including the Ku Klux Klan act of April 1871, to enable the government to clamp down on intimidation. The president was empowered to use military force if necessary. Go to www.bartleby.com/ 65/ku/KuKluxKl. html to find out more about the Ku Klux Klan and its organization.

within its ranks, but by 1869 it was urging colored delegates to its convention to form their own separate organization. This resulted in the creation of the National Negro Labor Convention....

The Knights of Labor was formed in 1869, and it did seriously try to organize blacks and whites.... It employed both black and white organizers. In 1886 its total membership was estimated at 700,000 of which 60,000 were black. The following year its total membership had shrunk to 500,000, but its black membership had increased to 90,000. The early labor movement which strove to organize the mass of industrial workers was soon replaced by skilled trade unions which aimed at the organization of a labor elite....

The convention of the Colored National Labor Union, the first black national labor organization, met in Washington, D.C., on December 6, 1869.

The Freedmen's Bureau was the one federal attempt to raise the social and economic standing of the ex-slave. Along with the American Missionary Association, the Freedmen's Bureau did significant work in education. Hundreds of teachers staffed scores of schools and brought some degree of literacy and job skills to thousands of pupils. However, beyond the field of education, the bureau did little except to provide temporary help. Begun as a war measure ... after some half dozen years, the Bureau was terminated. This left the Afro-American community without the economic base necessary for competing in American society on an equal basis.

Should the government have made more effort to give blacks a secure economic base? Is that the government's role?

White power restored

The one achievement of Reconstruction had been to guarantee [the] minimum of political and civil rights to the ex-slave, but white supremacy advocates were adamant in their intention to destroy this advance. Where terror and intimidation were not successful, relentless economic pressure by landowners, merchants, and industrialists brought most of the ex-slaves into line. Year by year they exerted less influence at the voting booths. Although the country was aware of this, Northern liberals were growing weary of the unending fight to protect the freedman. Furthermore, masses of Northern whites sympathized with Southern race prejudice. While they did approve of ending slavery, they were not willing to extend social and political equality. The North had begun to put a higher priority on peace than on justice. Industrialists were expanding their businesses rapidly, and they wanted the South to be pacified, so that it would be a safe area for investment and expansion. If this meant returning power to white conservatives, they were willing to pay the price....

Why do you think these Northern whites wanted an end to slavery if they shared the South's prejudice against blacks and were not willing to give them equality?

Summary

In its editorial of July 25, 1868, *Harper's Weekly* was in no doubt that the Freedmen's Bureau had achieved much for ex-slaves during Reconstruction. Beginning with a stinging attack on the Democratic Party, which it accuses of having wished to see a race war "in the hope of the extermination of a race guilty of a colored skin," it continues by outlining the plight of the freedmen in a hostile post-Civil War South. The article then goes on to praise the work of the Freedmen's Bureau—"the conscience and common-sense of the country"—in protecting ex-slaves from "starvation and cruel laws," while providing them with the education and organization needed to make a start in the unknown environment of freedom. As a result, the ex-slaves "were filling nearly four thousand schools," and "the increase of general intelligence among them has been remarkable." The editorial concludes on an optimistic note: The Freedmen's Bureau had done its work, and a reconstructed South, having been taught that "all men have rights which must be respected," was returning to the Union.

The second piece takes a less favorable view of Reconstruction. The author argues that the lenient policies pursued by Presidents Lincoln and Johnson permitted the South to enact laws "which bore an amazing resemblance to those of slavery days." Yet the Radical Republican state governments that followed and the entry of blacks into politics only served to incense white supremacists. They succeeded in reversing any advances the ex-slaves had made through terror, intimidation, and economic pressure. According to the author, although it "guarantee[d the] minimum of political and civil rights to the ex-slave," Reconstruction did little in economic terms to enable the freedman to "enter a competitive society as an equal." Eventually, the author points out, even Northern support for Reconstruction dwindled. Industrialists needed peace in the South for business reasons, and "If this meant returning power to white conservatives, they were willing to pay the price."

FURTHER INFORMATION:

 Books:

Foner, Eric, *A Short History of Reconstruction, 1863–1877*. New York: Harper & Row, 1990.

Foner, Eric, *Reconstruction: America's Unfinished Revolution, 1863–1877*. New York: Perennial Classics, 2002.

Stampp, Kenneth M., *The Era of Reconstruction, 1865–1877*. New York: Knopf, 1965.

@ Useful websites:

http://freedmensbureau.com
Freedmen's Bureau online, featuring the agency's records.

www.impeach-andrewjohnson.com
Site dealing with Andrew Johnson's impeachment.
www.kidinfo.com/American_History/Civil_War.html
Resource site on Civil War and its aftermath.

The following debates in the Pro/Con series may also be of interest:

In this volume:
 Topic 3 Was slavery the cause of the Civil War?

WAS RECONSTRUCTION A SUCCESS?

YES: Reconstruction set up an extensive public school system for the freed slave population

TRAINING
Did Reconstruction prepare ex-slaves for life in the community?

NO: After years of slavery freedmen had limited experience and a servile attitude, which Reconstruction did little to alter

YES: Black people now took part in politics and government, some reaching the Senate

STATUS
Did Reconstruction raise ex-slaves' social standing?

NO: Ex-slaves had little economic power. A redistribution of land under Reconstruction would have helped but did not happen.

WAS RECONSTRUCTION A SUCCESS? KEY POINTS

YES: Outraged by Black Codes and the like, Congress insisted on the drafting of new constitutions in the Southern states

YES: Congress added three amendments to the Constitution, protecting black rights, and they still exist today

PROTECTION
Did Reconstruction guarantee black rights?

NO: The Republican governments elected in the Southern states provoked a backlash by whites in the shape of the Ku Klux Klan

NO: Despite Constitutional protection, the reality was that white power was restored in the South once Reconstruction ended

59

PART 2

THE UNITED STATES BEFORE 1945

INTRODUCTION

For many historians the period between Reconstruction (1865-1877) and the end of World War II (1939-1945) is one of the most important and interesting phases in U.S. history. During these years the United States experienced great change both at home and abroad and rose to become a key player in international affairs.

National pride

Most people in the 19th century considered the United States to be a land of opportunity—a place where anyone could achieve anything. To celebrate its pride in its achievements the nation held a series of world fairs in the 19th and 20th centuries, including the Centennial Exhibition (1876) and the World's Columbian Exhibition (1893) in Chicago, which attracted more than 21 million visitors. Some commentators believe that events such as the Chicago fair served another function in diverting attention away from the confusion and fragmentation that marked U.S. society in the early 1890s. Industrialization and technological advances had created social, cultural, and economic upheaval; the nation was recovering from an economic depression, violent labor strikes, and mass unemployment. The Chicago fair gave the United States an opportunity to redefine itself and to show the world the opportunities that lay ahead.

Industrialization

In the second half of the 19th century continued industrialization brought great social and economic change. Many people moved away from traditional rural farming communities to find work in factories, constructing railroads, or in industries associated with the production of iron, steel, coal, and oil. Huge numbers of new immigrants also found employment in the rapidly expanding cities.

Other countries, such as Britain, Germany, Russia, and France, were also transformed by industrialization in the 19th century. As their production increased, so did their desire to find new markets, both in which to sell goods and as sources of material. In order to secure these markets the industrialized powers often "acquired" colonies as part of their empires. Many politicians in the 19th century believed that in order for the United States to continue its development and not stagnate it had to do the same.

Foreign policy

From the end of the 19th century the United States became more overtly involved in international affairs and engaged in conflicts with foreign nations. In 1898 it annexed Hawaii and came into conflict with Spain during the Spanish-American War over Cuba. Under the Treaty of Paris that ended the war, signed in December 1898, Cuba gained independence, and Puerto Rico and Guam were ceded to the United States, which also purchased the Philippines from Spain. Although some contemporary critics objected to what they saw as U.S. imperialism, the subsequent history of U.S. foreign

by bringing more women into the labor force. Congress passed the Nineteenth Amendment, which gave women full voting rights in 1918—the first step in a long campaign to achieve equal rights.

The period was also marked by other inequities, such as race discrimination. Many of the descendants of the early colonists and settlers resented recent immigrants, who came in large numbers from regions such as southern and eastern Europe, as well as East Asia, to

---

"Those of us who study history ... understand very well that there are many truths. There are many valid points of view about a historical event ... [I]t's better to think many truths constitute the past, rather than to think of a single truth."

—DAVID J. WEBER (1940–), HISTORIAN

---

policy contains many more examples of intervention in the affairs of other nation states.

However, it also contains examples of a very different approach: a retreat from, rather than involvement in, world affairs. This isolationist approach became the dominant theme in U.S. foreign policy in the years between the world wars, and has aroused just as much controversy as the nation's interventionist actions.

An emerging society

The period between Reconstruction and the end of World War II was also a time of great social change. Although slavery had been abolished in 1865, women were still fighting for the vote. The growing suffragist movement and industrialization helped effect change

find work in the booming cities. Also, while industrialization brought wealth to some, it brought poverty to others: Much of the urban population lived in great deprivation. Their plight was worsened, and the fortune of the nation reversed, by economic collapse in 1929, and the Great Depression of the 1930s.

The topics in this section examine chronologically some of the key issues in U.S. domestic and foreign history. Topic 5 examines whether the Nineteenth Amendment improved the position of women. Topic 6 discusses if Prohibition was a success. Topic 7 assesses U.S. support of the League of Nations. Topics 8 and 9 examine Franklin D. Roosevelt's New Deal program and role in Pearl Harbor. Finally, Topic 10 looks at the dropping of the atomic bomb on Japan.

Topic 5

DID THE NINETEENTH AMENDMENT IMPROVE THE POSITION OF WOMEN IN SOCIETY?

YES

"BUSH PROCLAIMS AUGUST 25 AS WOMEN'S EQUALITY DAY"
OFFICE OF THE PRESS SECRETARY, THE WHITE HOUSE, AUGUST 16, 2002
PRESS RELEASE, THE WHITE HOUSE

NO

"21ST-CENTURY EQUAL RIGHTS AMENDMENT EFFORT BEGINS"
WWW.NOW.ORG
TWISS BUTLER AND PAULA MCKENZIE

INTRODUCTION

The Nineteenth Amendment, also known as the Susan B. Anthony Amendment after the prominent campaigner for women's suffrage (voting) Susan Brownwell Anthony (1820-1906), came into effect on August 26, 1920. It stated, "The right of citizens of the United States to vote shall not be denied or abridged by the United States or by any State on account of sex." It marked the end of over 70 years of vigorous suffrage campaigning by women.

The amendment gave women the legally and constitutionally recognized right to vote in elections—municipal, local, state, and presidential. Previously the situation had been more piecemeal. In 1848, when Elizabeth Cady Stanton (1815-1902) and Lucretia Mott (1793-1880) organized the first women's rights convention in Seneca Falls (see pages 65-66), women did not have the

right to vote in any state. As the women's suffrage movement gathered momentum, Stanton and Anthony founded the American Equal Rights Association in 1866, and in 1869 the National Woman Suffrage Association, which campaigned for an amendment to the Constitution to give women the vote. Another group, founded in 1869 by Lucy Stone (1818-1893), the American Suffrage Association, aimed to achieve the same objective by amendments to the constitutions of the various states. The two groups merged in 1890 and became the National American Woman's Suffrage Association (NAWSA). By 1918—when the Nineteenth Amendment was passed by Congress—they had succeeded in winning women equal suffrage with men in 15 states. The amendment improved women's situation by giving them full voting rights in all states and thus the theoretical power to change political, social, and economic matters.

However, while not arguing that the amendment made women's position in society worse, many women's rights campaigners—both at the time and now—believe that it was only the first step on a long road to equality with men. They believe that more measures are necessary to achieve this aim. Social and economic equality are as important as political equality.

> *"[The NAWSA] has bequeathed to American women an opportunity, a dignity, and liberty which in 1848 were a dream in the minds only of a few."*
> —CARRIE CHAPMAN CATT, NAWSA CONVENTION, CLEVELAND, OHIO (1921)

Campaigners argue that since historically women have not had equal rights and have been discriminated against, more specific constitutional measures and laws were needed to rectify the ingrained prejudices in society. In that respect there are parallels with the struggle for equality of racial minorities. Indeed, in the 19th century women had played a key role in supporting emancipation and the black vote. They formed antislavery organizations from the 1830s, and it was largely through these groups that they began to campaign for their own suffrage and equality.

Alice Paul (1885–1977) formed the National Women's Party in 1916. Paul believed that an amendment affirming the equal application of the Constitution to all citizens would bring women the equality they deserved. In 1923 she initiated the Equal Rights Amendment (ERA), also known as the Lucretia Mott Amendment in commemoration of Seneca Falls, which stated that "Men and women shall have equal rights throughout the United States and every place subject to its jurisdiction." The ERA was passed in the Senate and then in the House of Representatives, and on March 22, 1972, the proposed amendment to the Constitution was sent to the states for ratification. It has still to be ratified.

However, legislation has been introduced that addresses some of women's concerns. The Equal Pay Act was passed in 1963, and the Civil Rights Act, which bars discrimination on all grounds, including gender, came into effect in 1964. However, feminist groups like the National Organization for Women (NOW) argue that inequalities still exist in every sector of society and continue to campaign for the ERA. In the 1990s women still earned only 70 cents for every dollar earned by men, and two-thirds of workers earning the minimum wage were female. Although attitudes began to change in the 1960s, women still have prime responsibility for childcare and running the home.

The following articles assess some of the issues linked with the Nineteenth Amendment and women's position in society. In the first President George W. Bush pays tribute to the work of the early women's rights campaigners, and in the second two NOW members argue that the ERA is still needed to overcome inequality.

BUSH PROCLAIMS AUGUST 25 AS WOMEN'S EQUALITY DAY
Press Release, The White House

President Bush urged Americans to remember the important anniversary of the day—August 26, 1920—when women in the United States gained the right to vote through the ratification of the 19th Amendment to the Constitution.

In his proclamation statement, the President said that in celebrating Women's Equality Day, Americans "remember the brave and determined individuals who worked to ensure that all women have the opportunity to participate in our democracy. Their dedication to the suffrage movement improved our society, and continues to inspire women today."

FOLLOWING IS HIS STATEMENT:

The White House
Office of the Press Secretary
August 24, 2002

Women's Equality Day, 2002, by the President of the United States of America: a Proclamation

Today, American women enjoy unprecedented opportunities in business, education, politics, and countless other aspects of our society. Historically, however, women suffered grave inequalities and were denied some of the most fundamental benefits of citizenship.

Each year on August 26th, we mark the important anniversary of the day on which women gained the right to vote. In celebrating Women's Equality Day, we remember the brave and determined individuals who worked to ensure that all women have the opportunity to participate in our democracy. Their dedication to the suffrage movement improved our society, and continues to inspire women today.

When the first Women's Rights Convention was convened in Seneca Falls in 1848, women in the United States had limited financial, legal, and political power. In addition to being denied the right to vote, they also could not own property, control their wages, or claim custody of their children.

Women's Equality Day was introduced in 1971. It was the result of a bill put forward by the women's rights activist and Democrat member of Congress Bella Abzug (1920–1998). Abzug campaigned for more women to become directly involved in politics: to exercise their right to vote and to become congresswomen.

Because women now enjoy unprecedented opportunities, does it follow that they have achieved full or equal rights?

Did the Nineteenth Amendment improve the position of women in society?

Elizabeth Cady Stanton speaking at the Seneca Falls Convention, July 19–20, 1848.

COMMENTARY: The Seneca Falls Convention

The impetus for the Nineteenth Amendment began in 1848, when two reformers, Elizabeth Cady Stanton (1815–1902) and Lucretia Mott (1793–1880), organized the first women's rights convention in the United States in the town of Seneca Falls, New York. The two women had met in 1840 at the World Anti-Slavery Convention in London, where they and other female delegates had been excluded from participating in the discussions on the basis of their gender. They were allowed to listen to proceedings from behind a screen. Both women had already campaigned actively for the abolition of slavery and for improvements to women's rights, but their treatment at the London conference galvanized them to consider more carefully the position of women in society.

Both women continued their reforming activities. In 1848 Stanton circulated petitions that helped secure the passage of a New York state statute giving property rights to married women. In the same year Mott, who lived in Philadelphia, visited her sister in Waterloo, New York, and she met with Stanton in Seneca Falls, where she lived. Stanton felt that it was time to draw public attention to the inequality of women in society and to take action to redress the situation.

The Declaration of Sentiments

Stanton and Mott arranged a convention, and Stanton drafted a document listing their grievances and demands. Entitled the Declaration of Sentiments, it was based on the Declaration of Independence and took as its premise the statement that "all men and women are created equal." It listed 18 "injuries and usurpations" against this notion and 11 resolutions designed to gain rights and privileges denied to women.

Three hundred people attended the Seneca Falls Convention, which was held on July 19 and 20, 1848. Stanton's resolutions were passed unanimously, with the exception of her call for women's suffrage, which even Lucretia Mott felt to be too radical. However, after an eloquent speech in support of the motion by a former slave, Frederick Douglass (1817–1895), the resolution was adopted. Mott also added a further resolution "for the overthrowing of the monopoly of the pulpit, and for securing to women equal participation with men in the various trades, professions, and commerce." One hundred people signed the declaration.

The convention was ridiculed in the press. In an act intended to mock, the *New York Herald* printed the declaration in full. However, Stanton saw its advantages. "Imagine the publicity given to our ideas by thus appearing in a widely circulated sheet like the *Herald*. It will start women thinking, and men too; and when men and women think about a new question, the first step in progress is taken." The convention and declaration were the foundations on which the women's rights movement were built.

Courageous heroes like Carrie Chapman Catt, Alice Paul, Elizabeth Cady Stanton, and Susan B. Anthony refused to accept women's status, and began a determined struggle to gain suffrage for women. Leading active and vocal groups like the National American Woman Suffrage Association and the National Woman's Party, these women risked attack and arrest to organize marches, boycotts, and pickets, while mobilizing an influential lobbying force of millions. Finally, on August 26, 1920, the women's suffrage movement accomplished its goal through the ratification of the 19th Amendment to the Constitution, guaranteeing women the right to vote.

In Afghanistan, the Taliban used violence and fear to deny Afghan women access to education, health care, mobility, and the right to vote. Our coalition has liberated Afghanistan and restored fundamental human rights and freedoms to Afghan women, and all the people of Afghanistan. Young girls in Afghanistan are able to attend schools for the first time.

As we celebrate this day, I encourage all Americans to learn about our important achievements in equality. Looking to the future, we must remain diligent as we work to ensure the rights of all of our citizens, and to support those who struggle daily for life's basic liberties.

NOW, THEREFORE, I, GEORGE W. BUSH, President of the United States of America, by virtue of the authority vested in me by the Constitution and laws of the United States, do hereby proclaim August 26, 2002, as Women's Equality Day. I call upon the people of the United States to observe this day with appropriate programs and activities.

IN WITNESS WHEREOF, I have hereunto set my hand this twenty-third day of August, in the year of our Lord two thousand two, and of the Independence of the United States of America the two hundred and twenty-seventh.

—GEORGE W. BUSH

The president uses the opportunity to mention the harsh treatment of women in Afghanistan. The government singled out their plight as an example of the human rights violations carried out under the fundamentalist Islamic government of the Taliban that ruled Afghanistan from 1996 to 2001. The United States invaded Afghanistan in October 2001 and removed the Taliban government as part of its War on Terror following the attacks on the World Trade Center on September 11, 2001.

21ST-CENTURY EQUAL RIGHTS AMENDMENT EFFORT BEGINS
Twiss Butler and Paula McKenzie

Go to http://www.now.org/history/history.html to find out more about NOW.

Visit the International Women's Center website http://www.wic.org/miscl/history.htm for a history of women's role in society.

Women played an important part in campaigning for the abolition of slavery and for the recognition of African Americans as full citizens. Their work for this cause gave them the experience and drive to campaign for their own rights. However, during the Civil War (1861–1865) women suspended their own cause to support the Union and to push for the abolition of slavery. They were bitterly disappointed when the wording of the Fourteenth Amendment specifically excluded them from voting.

NO

EDITORS NOTE: A resolution passed at the 1993 National NOW Conference calls for members to review and consult on the Equal Rights Amendment. This commentary considers why the ERA is essential, and why it has been opposed.

In coming months, NOW activists will address another substantive question—what do we want constitutional equality for women and nondiscrimination on the basis of sex to mean? Only then can we address another strategic question—where do we go from here and how?

Discrimination against women is a fact of life and law, but women's fight to end it is not a story every schoolchild knows—even though it provides some fascinating history. For more than two centuries since this country was founded, men have deliberately refused constitutional recognition to women's legal and civil rights. [There were] three key occasions when this was done:

- In 1776, Founding Father John Adams denied his wife Abigail's demand that the constitution of the new nation "put it out of the power of the vicious and lawless to use [women] with cruelty and indignity with impunity" as English law allowed. His response? "Depend upon it," he wrote, "We know better than to repeal our Masculine systems."

- In 1868, after the Civil War, men legislators adopted the 14th Amendment which guaranteed to all "persons" the right to equal protection of the law. However in the second section, which determined the number of U.S. Representatives that each state would be due in Congress, the use of the words "male citizens" marked the specific and intentional exclusion of women for the first time in the Constitution. The 15th Amendment, passed in 1870, extended to all men—but no women—the right to vote. The fifty-year campaign to secure a guarantee of women's right to vote resulted in ratification of the 19th Amendment in 1920. This completed the 15th Amendment, but left the 14th

Alice Paul (left) with the British suffragist Emmeline Pethick-Lawrence (1867–1954).

Amendment with no counterpart for women. To remedy this gross deficiency, suffragist leader Alice Paul drafted the Equal Rights Amendment and began the campaign for ratification.

- In 1982, ratification of the Equal Rights Amendment was denied. In practical terms, the ERA is resisted for real, not "symbolic," reasons—it would invalidate men's legal power to use sex discrimination selectively when it is to their advantage to do so. Just because this legal power is not talked about in history or law books does not mean that men are unaware of it. In 1983, for example, when Justice Department attorney William Coleman Jr. argued before the Supreme Court that a college's ban on interracial dating violated the 14th Amendment, Justice Powell asked if his arguments applied to sex as well. Coleman assured him, "No. We didn't fight a Civil War over sex discrimination and we didn't pass a constitutional amendment against it."

In what ways do you think male society uses "sexual discrimination" when it wants to? Do you think it is common in the United States?

Opposition to ERA is unreasonable

Speaking about the ERA in Congress in 1971, Representative Stewart McKinney exposed both the real motive and the false excuses for opposing the ERA when he said, "Use the

COMMENTARY: Alice Paul

Alice Paul (1885–1977) played a key role in the women's suffrage movement and the subsequent campaign for equal rights for women. Influenced by the activities of the English suffragists—with whom she had campaigned during three years of graduate study in London (1906–1909)—she advocated a strategy of direct action to achieve the passage of the Nineteenth Amendment. In addition to lobbying, she organized protests and rallies to bring woman's suffrage to the forefront of public and political attention. One of the most high-profile was a parade held in Washington, D.C., on March 3, 1913, the eve of Woodrow Wilson's inauguration as president. The scale of the demonstration—some 8,000 marchers took part—and also acts of violence against the participants that went unstopped by the authorities, ensured that the women's cause hit the headlines. As a result, the suffragists secured a meeting with the president, and public sympathy for their cause began to increase.

National Woman's Party

In 1916 Paul founded the National Woman's Party. Its members picketed the White House, the Congress, and the Supreme Court on a daily basis. Many of these so-called "sentinels of liberty" were arrested and jailed. The party also organized an anti-Democratic Party campaign in the states where women could vote. Paul believed that an effective way of making politicians recognize the women's cause was to garner support against the party in power if it was doing nothing to further women's suffrage.

When the United States entered World War I in 1917, the members of the National Woman's Party continued their campaign. While they were criticized for being unpatriotic, they knew that if they stopped protesting, their cause would be forgotten, as it had been when earlier suffragists had suspended their campaigning during the Civil War (1861–1865). More suffragists were jailed, and some—including Paul—went on a hunger strike and were force-fed. Their campaign paid off. In 1918 Woodrow Wilson backed the call for women's suffrage, and with his support the Nineteenth Amendment passed the House and Senate.

Equal Rights Amendment

After the passage of the Nineteenth Amendment Paul made the ERA the focus of her campaign. She wrote the first version of the amendment in 1923—she revised it in 1943—and it was introduced in every session of Congress until it was passed in 1972—though it remains unratified by the states. In 1938 Paul founded the World Party for Equal Rights for Women, known as the World Women's Party. She was also instrumental in gaining references to sex equality in the preamble to the United Nations charter and in the 1964 Civil Rights Act.

draft for an excuse if you like. Use child care. Use anything else. We [men] are simply trying in our own little way to preserve the right to stand up and say, 'We can declare the difference.'"

Men and women are treated differently

The accuracy of McKinney's analysis is repeatedly confirmed as courts and legislatures find pretexts for treating men and women differently. Comparisons of 14th Amendment decisions since 1870 consistently show the Supreme Court judging laws which disadvantage classes of men to be unconstitutional while seeing no constitutional barrier to discrimination against women. The only exceptions are token cases, such as Reed v. Reed (1971), which affirmed that a woman had the same right as a man to administer the estate of a deceased relative.

The court tends to follow the pattern set in early decisions when it arbitrarily invoked "the laws of God and Nature" to justify denying Myra Bradwell's right to be licensed to practice law (1872) and Virginia Minor's right to vote (1874). In Fitzpatrick v. Bitzer (1976), the court found it unconstitutional to deny backpay to men state employees who had received unequal early retirement pay based on sex, but ignored this precedent in denying backpay to women in a similar pension case, Arizona v. Norris (1983).

The Equal Rights Amendment has significance beyond issues of equal access and pay. John Adams' conviction that "masculine systems" would be endangered if men could no longer abuse women with impunity holds true centuries later. A 1977 rape study found that "All unequal power relationships must, in the end, rely on the threat or reality of violence to protect themselves." In a very real sense, then, the ERA will rectify a profound constitutional imbalance that may promote violence against women.

The Equal Rights Amendment is essential because, without clear acknowledgement of women's right to equal protection of the law, sex discrimination is not unconstitutional. Legal discourse about "standards of review" ultimately must yield to the bleak reality that hard-won laws against sex discrimination do not rest on any constitutional foundation and can be enforced fully, inconsistently, or not at all.

Women seeking enforcement of these laws must not only convince the court that discrimination has occurred, but that it matters. As legal scholar Catharine MacKinnon observes, "It is not difference that is important, but what difference difference makes."

Bearing in mind that men and women are biologically different, do you think that complete equality between the sexes is practical?

Go to http://www.findlaw.com/ for full information on all the cases cited in this article.

The author argues that legal cases are judged on grounds of tradition rather than equal rights. Do you think that the ERA is the only way to stop this from happening? How have other countries dealt with the issue?

The ERA has been put before every Congress since 1993, the year when this article was written. In the 108th Congress (2003–2004) the ERA was put forward by Democrat Congress-woman Carolyn Maloney under the slogan "Eighty years is long enough." See http://www.house.gov/maloney/issues/era/overview.html for details of her campaign and the history of the ERA.

Summary

The Nineteenth Amendment, which gives women the right to vote, is often regarded as the cornerstone of women's rights to equality in American society. The two articles that discuss this theme address the effectiveness of the Nineteenth Amendment in improving women's condition. The first article is the text of a speech by President George W. Bush on August 26, 2002. The speech was a commemoration of the anniversary of the date on which the Nineteenth Amendment passed into law, giving women the right to vote. Bush's speech commends the work of the suffragists in the early part of the twentieth century and recalls their tireless contribution to the cause of women's franchise. He states that the suffragists' accomplishment has opened the doors of democracy to women so that they can, through the political process, improve the position of women's rights. He contrasts the position of American women with that of women in Taliban Afghanistan, where these advantages were not available. Twiss Butler and Paula McKenzie's article, on the other hand, represents the viewpoint of the pro-ERA group, who believe that a further amendment is needed to attain the equality of the sexes. Their article aims to show that regardless of the Nineteenth Amendment, women in the United States have faced real and symbolic discrimination in a system that is mainly masculine. They argue that a deep antiwoman sentiment pervades the political and legal systems. According to Butler and McKenzie, underlying many legal decisions is the fundamental belief that women are different from men and should be treated as such. They point out that women's rights are about more than equal access or pay; they are about ensuring constitutional protection against discrimination on the grounds of sex. The ERA is the most effective way to offer this for women in the United States.

FURTHER INFORMATION:

Books:

Tetreault, Mary Kay Thompson. *Women in America: Half of History*. Chicago, IL: Rand McNally & Company, 1978.

Useful websites:

www.questia.com/PM.qst?action=openPageViewer&docId=6861456
History of women's suffrage.
www.spartacus.schoolnet.co.uk/USApaul.htm
Extracts from pamphlets and letters relating to Alice Paul.
www.equalrightsamendment.org/era.htm
History behind the Equal Rights Amendment.
www.closeup.org/sentimnt.htm
The text of the Declaration of Sentiments.

gi.grolier.com/presidents/aae/side/wsffrg.html
Grolier women's suffrage site.

The following debates in the Pro/Con series may also be of interest:

In *Individual and Society*:

Topic 3 Are women still the second sex?

In *Human Rights*:

Topic 9 Are human rights women's rights?

DID THE NINETEENTH AMENDMENT IMPROVE THE POSITION OF WOMEN IN SOCIETY?

YES: The Nineteenth Amendment gave women equal political rights with men

YES: The Constitution recognized women as full citizens

EQUALITY
Did the vote give women equality?

DISCRIMINATION
Did the amendment stop discrimination against women?

NO: Achieving the vote was significant, but it was just one factor in a long line of things necessary for women to have equal rights

NO: Discrimination is inherent in U.S. society and cannot be ended by a simple change of law

DID THE NINETEENTH AMENDMENT IMPROVE THE POSITION OF WOMEN IN SOCIETY?

KEY POINTS

YES: Until there is specific legislation to prevent discrimination against women, prejudice will continue based on long-established behavioral practices at the individual and institutional levels

YES: A piece of legislation to ensure the equality of women is necessary to cover those areas not included in existing laws such as the Equal Pay Act

EQUAL RIGHTS ACT
Is the ERA necessary to secure equality for women?

NO: It is not necessary to amend the Constitution to specify equal treatment of women, since it is already a fundamental principle that all citizens are equal

NO: Men and women are not the same, and therefore it is not realistic to legislate equality in every sphere of their lives

Topic 6
WAS PROHIBITION A DISASTER?

YES

FROM "ALCOHOL PROHIBITION WAS A FAILURE"
CATO POLICY ANALYSIS NO. 157, JULY 17, 1991
MARK THORNTON

NO

"DRY LAW IS WORKER'S FRIEND"
PROHIBITION'S GIFT, SELECTED ARTICLES ON PROHIBITION: MODIFICATION
OF THE VOLSTEAD LAW
THE NEW YORK TIMES, JULY 31, 1923

INTRODUCTION

Webster's Dictionary contains three definitions of the word "prohibition." Generally, it is "the act of prohibiting by authority" or "an order to restrain or stop." More specifically, it is "the forbidding by law of the manufacture, transportation, and sale of alcoholic liquors except for medicinal and sacramental purposes." Several societies and countries have enforced Prohibition at some time in their history, most famously the United States between 1920 and 1933.

The Prohibition Amendment to the Constitution, or the Eighteenth Amendment, came into effect on January 29, 1920. The National Prohibition Act, commonly known as the Volstead Act—after Congressman Andrew J. Volstead (1860–1947), who drafted it—afforded the means to enforce the amendment. It became illegal to manufacture, sell, or transport drink containing more than 0.5 percent alcohol—beer, wine, and spirits—but drinking in the privacy of the home

was allowed. Legislation was directed against the supplier rather than the drinker. Prohibition was ended in 1933 by the Twenty-First Amendment, which repealed the Eighteenth Amendment.

Prohibition had its roots in the Temperance Movement of the late 19th century, which had grown out of religious ideas about sobriety. Prohibitionists regarded alcohol as a dangerous drug that destroyed lives and disrupted families and communities. They were concerned that working men spent their pay in rowdy saloon bars and returned home with little or no money for their wives and children. Employers were worried that drinking reduced productivity in the workplace. The prohibitionists said it was the government's responsibility to free citizens from the temptation of drink by barring its sale. Moreover, they believed that outlawing liquor would benefit society and the economy. The money that people saved by not drinking would be redirected into savings or spent on useful items, such as cars, thus boosting industry. There would be less absenteeism from work and less violence at home and in public places. Those arguments received widespread support until about 1923, when public opinion swung against them, and people began to question whether the Eighteenth Amendment and the Volstead Act were effective methods of tackling the problems associated with alcohol. Indeed, they claimed that Prohibition created more problems than it solved.

> *"[Prohibition has been] a great social and economic experiment, noble in motive and far-reaching in purpose."*
> —HERBERT HOOVER, PRESIDENTIAL CAMPAIGN (1928)

Saloons reopened illegally as "speakeasies"—so-called because customers were urged to speak quietly, or "easy," to avoid police detection. The price of liquor shot up and quality tumbled, often to such low levels that it was dangerous. Enforcing Prohibition required substantial extra spending on policing and customs controls—the annual budget of the Bureau of Prohibition, which enforced the ban, was about $13.4 million. At the same time, an important source of federal revenue was lost—before Prohibition alcohol had been heavily taxed.

Bootlegging, or the illegal production and distribution of liquor, became a vast enterprise run by gangsters, such as Al Capone (1899-1947), who settled their quarrels with guns and bribed officials. The growth of organized crime and corrupt officialdom was one of the most enduring results of Prohibition. In addition, the rich and powerful were usually able to get round Prohibition, making the law socially inequable.

The Eighteenth Amendment caused political turmoil. The Republican Party was dry (in favor of Prohibition), while the Democrats were divided on the issue. In the rural Southern states most Democrats were dry, but in the urban, industrial Northern states, with big immigrant populations, the majority were wet (against Prohibition). Almost all of these immigrants came from cultures in which drinking was an accepted and popular social custom.

Internal divisions had disastrous consequences for the Democratic Party in the 1928 presidential election. Their candidate, New York's Governor Alfred E. Smith (1873-1944), was a wet who aroused such hostility among the dry Democrats that the vote was split, handing victory to the Republican Herbert Hoover (1874-1964).

When the Great Depression (1929-1939) began, Prohibition lost many of its supporters. Those in favor of repealing the Eighteenth Amendment argued that legalizing alcohol would create badly needed jobs and increase tax revenue. It would also hit gangsters and bootleggers.

The first of the following articles, written in 1991, outlines today's commonly accepted view that Prohibition was a disaster. The second, dated 1923, reflects the enthusiasm with which Prohibition was first received—it was known by many as "the noble experiment."

ALCOHOL PROHIBITION WAS A FAILURE
Mark Thornton

Mark Thornton is assistant professor of economics at Auburn University, Alabama.

Do you think that the experiences and outcomes of Prohibition apply to the other substances and activities that the author lists? What are the similarities and differences between drugs and alcohol?

Does it necessarily follow that people who enjoy drinking alcohol will turn to other addictive substances if they cannot get liquor?

The author bases much of his argument on statistics taken from Fisher's book Prohibition at Its Worst *(1927) and Warburton's book* The Economics of Prohibition *(1932). How accurate do you think figures relating to illegal activities or substances might be, bearing in mind they refer to things conducted in secret or private?*

YES

… The lessons of Prohibition remain important…. They apply not only to the debate over the war on drugs but also to the mounting efforts to drastically reduce access to alcohol and tobacco and to such issues as censorship and bans on insider trading, abortion, and gambling. Although consumption of alcohol fell at the beginning of Prohibition, it subsequently increased. Alcohol became more dangerous to consume; crime increased and became "organized"; the court and prison systems were stretched to breaking point; and corruption of public officials was rampant. No measurable gains were made in productivity or reduced absenteeism. Prohibition removed a significant source of tax revenue and greatly increased government spending. It led many drinkers to switch to opium, marijuana, patent medicines, cocaine, and other dangerous substances that they would have been unlikely to encounter in the absence of Prohibition. Those results are documented from a variety of sources, most of which, ironically, are the work of supporters of Prohibition—most economists and social scientists supported it.

Did Prohibition reduce alcohol consumption?

According to its proponents, all the proposed benefits of Prohibition depended on … reducing the quantity of alcohol consumed. At first glance, the evidence seems to suggest that the quantity consumed did indeed decrease. That would be no surprise to an economist: making a product more difficult to supply will increase its price, and the quantity consumed will be less than it would have been otherwise.

Evidence of decreased consumption is provided by two important American economists, Irving Fisher (1867-1947) and Clark Warburton (1896-1979). It should be noted that annual per capita [per person] consumption and the percentage of annual per capita income spent on alcohol had been steadily falling before Prohibition and that annual spending on alcohol during Prohibition was greater than it had been before Prohibition.

The decrease in quantity consumed needs at least four qualifications–qualifications that undermine any value that a prohibitionist might claim for reduced consumption. First, the decrease was not very significant. Warburton found that the quantity of alcohol purchased may have fallen 20 percent between the prewar years 1911–14 and 1927–30. Prohibition fell far short of eliminating the consumption of alcohol.

Second, consumption of alcohol actually rose steadily after an initial drop. Annual per capita consumption had been declining since 1910, reached an all-time low during the depression of 1921, and then began to increase in 1922.... Illicit production and distribution continued to expand throughout Prohibition despite ever-increasing resources devoted to enforcement. That pattern of consumption ... is to be expected after an entire industry is banned: new entrepreneurs in the underground economy improve techniques and expand output, while consumers begin to realize the folly of the ban.

Third, the resources devoted to enforcement of Prohibition increased along with consumption. Heightened enforcement did not curtail consumption. The annual budget of the Bureau of Prohibition went from $4.4 million to $13.4 million during the 1920s, while Coast Guard spending on Prohibition averaged over $13 million per year. To those amounts should be added the expenditures of state and local governments....

The fourth qualification may actually be the most important: a decrease in the quantity of alcohol consumed did not make Prohibition a success. Even if we agree that society would be better off if less alcohol were consumed, it does not follow that lessening consumption through Prohibition made society better off. We must consider the overall social consequences of Prohibition, not just reduced alcohol consumption. Prohibition had pervasive (and perverse) effects on every aspect of alcohol production, distribution, and consumption. Changing the rules from those of the free market to those of Prohibition broke the link that prohibitionists had assumed between consumption and social evil. The rule changes also caused unintended consequences to enter the equation.

The "Iron Law" of Prohibition

The most notable of those consequences has been labeled the "Iron Law of Prohibition" by Richard Cowan. That law states that the more intense the law enforcement, the more potent the prohibited substance becomes. When drugs or alcoholic beverages are prohibited, they will become more potent, will have greater variability in potency, will be

Following World War I (1914–1918), the United States, in common with many countries, experienced economic recession. Between the years 1920 and 1921 unemployment reached 20 percent, and prices on the stock market fell dramatically.

It has been estimated that two-thirds of liquor consumed during Prohibition was smuggled in across the Canadian border; large amounts were also brought in across the Mexican border and by sea.

Richard Cowen is editor of the online periodical MarijuanaNews.com.

Much of this "poisoned liquor" was alcohol—mainly ethanol—produced for industrial uses. Under law this industrial alcohol had to be made undrinkable, which was usually done by adding methanol, a highly poisonous alcohol. However, some industrial alcohol found its way onto the black market, often without the poisons removed.

Do you think that an activity or substance becomes more attractive if it is made illegal?

In what ways could Prohibition have improved hygiene?

adulterated with unknown or dangerous substances, and will not be produced and consumed under normal market constraints. The Iron Law undermines the prohibitionist case and reduces or outweighs the benefits ascribed to a decrease in consumption.

Statistics indicate that for a long time Americans spent a falling share of income on alcoholic beverages. They also purchased higher quality brands and weaker types of alcoholic beverages. Before Prohibition, Americans spent roughly equal amounts on beer and spirits. However, during Prohibition virtually all production, and therefore consumption, was of distilled spirits and fortified wines. Beer became relatively more expensive because of its bulk …

According to Thomas Coffey, "the death rate from poisoned liquor was appallingly high throughout the country. In 1925 the national toll was 4,154 as compared to 1,064 in 1920." …

Patterns of consumption changed during Prohibition. It could be argued that Prohibition increased the demand for alcohol among three groups. It heightened the attractiveness of alcohol to the young by making it a glamour product associated with excitement and intrigue. The high prices and profits during Prohibition enticed sellers to try to market their products to nondrinkers … Finally, many old-stock Americans and recent immigrants were unwilling to be told that they could not drink.…

Prohibition was not a healthy move

One of the few bright spots for which the prohibitionists can present some supporting evidence is the decline in "alcohol-related deaths" during Prohibition. On closer examination, however, that success is an illusion. Prohibition did not improve health and hygiene in America as anticipated.…

Prohibition was criminal

The Volstead Act … had an immediate impact on crime. According to a study of 30 major cities, the number of crimes increased 24 percent between 1920 and 1921. The study revealed that during that period more money was spent on police (11.4+ percent) … But increased law enforcement efforts did not appear to reduce drinking: arrests for drunkenness and disorderly conduct increased 41 percent, and arrests of drunken drivers increased 81 percent. Among crimes with victims, thefts and burglaries increased 9 percent, while homicides and incidents of assault and battery increased 13 percent. More crimes were committed because Prohibition destroys legal jobs, creates black-market violence, diverts resources from enforcement of other laws, and greatly increases the prices people have to pay for the prohibited goods.

Instead of emptying the prisons as its supporters had hoped … Prohibition quickly filled the prisons to capacity.… The explosion in the prison population greatly increased spending on prisons and led to severe overcrowding.…

The number of violations of Prohibition laws and violent crimes against persons and property continued to increase throughout Prohibition.… The homicide rate increased from 6 per 100,000 population in the pre-Prohibition period to nearly 10 per 100,000 in 1933. That rising trend was reversed by the repeal of Prohibition in 1933, and the rate continued to decline throughout the 1930s and early 1940s.…

Not only did the number of serious crimes increase, but crime became organized. Criminal groups organize around the steady source of income provided by laws against victimless crimes such as consuming alcohol or drugs, gambling, and prostitution. In the process of providing goods and services, those criminal organizations resort to real crimes in defense of sales territories, brand names, and labor contracts. That is true of extensive crime syndicates (the Mafia) as well as street gangs.…

It was hoped that Prohibition would eliminate corrupting influences in society; instead, Prohibition itself became a major source of corruption. Everyone from major politicians to the cop on the beat took bribes from bootleggers, moonshiners, crime bosses, and owners of speakeasies. The Bureau of Prohibition was particularly susceptible and had to be reorganized to reduce corruption.…

Chicago gangster Al Capone (1899–1947) was one of many criminals to become hugely wealthy from the illegal liquor trade. His annual earnings were estimated at $60 million. His gang was involved in one of the most notorious gang wars, the St. Valentine's Day Massacre in Chicago in 1929, in which seven members of the rival Bugs Moran gang were shot dead.

Conclusion: Lessons for today

In summary, Prohibition did not achieve its goals. Instead, it added to the problems it was intended to solve and supplanted other ways of addressing problems. The only beneficiaries of Prohibition were bootleggers, crime bosses, and the forces of big government.…

In the aftermath of Prohibition, economist Ludwig von Mises wrote, "Once the principle is admitted that it is the duty of government to protect the individual against his own foolishness, no serious objections can be advanced against further encroachments." The repeal of all prohibition of voluntary exchange is as important to the restoration of liberty now as its enactment was to the cause of big government in the Progressive Era [the 1920s].

What other methods might the government have used to moderate the consumption of alcohol?

In its attempt to improve society by Prohibition did the government encroach too much on the rights of the individual? See Volume 1, Individual and Society.

DRY LAW IS WORKER'S FRIEND
The New York Times

Elbert Henry Gary
(1846–1927) was
an influential
judge, lawyer,
and businessman.

The observations
that Judge Gary
gives in support of
his argument that
Prohibition is a
success contradict
the statistics given
in Mark Thornton's
article. Which do
you think are more
reliable, and why?

Some people
thought that
Prohibition should
be modified to
legalize so-called
light beers and
wines, that is,
wines and beers
with a low
alcoholic content
of 2 or 3 percent.
Usually, beer has a
content of 3 to 8
percent, wine 10 to
20 percent, and
spirits 40 percent.

NO

Prohibition has been of incalculable benefit to the workers in American industry, particularly those in the steel industry, and their families, Judge Elbert H. Gary, chairman of the Board of the United States Steel Corporation, declared yesterday in an interview for *The New York Times* at his office, 71 Broadway.

Based on observation and reports from officials of the Steel Corporation in plants throughout the country, Judge Gary's conclusions on the effect of the Volstead Act and the various state prohibition enforcement laws furnished a convincing argument for the retention of complete prohibition. According to Judge Gary, the effects of prohibition, despite the admitted violations of law in the large cities, have included a decrease in the consumption of intoxicating liquor, a decrease in crime and poverty, an increase in the health of the workers and their families and their savings deposits.

These advantages to the workers have been coupled with an improvement in the working ability and disposition of the employees, according to Judge Gary. Even without the material and moral advantages to its employees, Judge Gary said the Steel Corporation would be for prohibition, because it pays.

Judge Gary declared himself against any modification of the prohibition laws.

Opposes wines and beers

"How do you feel about an amendment to the Volstead Act to permit the manufacture and sale of light wines and beer?" he was asked.

He replied:

I wouldn't favor it. Perhaps, if I had been called upon to express an opinion in regard to the adoption of the original law, I might have decided in favor of permitting the manufacture and sale of beer and wine with alcoholic contents small enough to make them safe under the opinion of the best medical authorities. If I should express the opinion of a layman, which, it must be

COMMENTARY: The Temperance Movement

The origins of Prohibition in the United States can be traced back to the early 1800s, when a growing number of people began to call for temperance. Temperance means moderation in a particular action, thought, or feeling, but in this context it came increasingly to mean complete abstinence from alcoholic drink. The campaign for temperance was closely related to the religious revivalism that took place in the 1820s and 1830s, and arose from a deep-felt desire to improve the human condition. Many religious groups, especially Methodists and Baptists, played a key role in promoting abstinence from liquor. The first temperance organizations were set up in Saratoga, New York, in 1808 and in Massachusetts in 1813. By 1833 there were 6,000 local societies and several national groups. At first they campaigned for local and state Prohibition, achieving a major victory in Maine, where state Prohibition was passed in 1846, followed by several other states in the years before the Civil War (1861–1865). In 1869, as the cause gathered support, the Prohibition Party was founded.

Woman's Christian Temperance Union

Women played an important role in the Temperance Movement. They had no direct political power since they were not allowed to vote, but they exerted a strong influence through voluntary organizations associated with the church. Such groups aimed their campaigns against the liquor business and all-male saloons, which they saw as destructive to family life and family values. Women from 23 states took part in the Women's Temperance Crusade of 1873, in which they entered saloons, prayed, sang hymns, and urged saloon-keepers to stop selling liquor. The following year they created the National Woman's Christian Temperance Union in Cleveland, Ohio. With dynamic leadership, particularly that of Frances E. Willard (1838–1898), the union worked to educate people about Prohibition, as well as campaigning for women's suffrage and other reforms. During the 1880s the organization spread to other countries, and in 1883 Willard founded the World's Woman's Christian Temperance Union.

Anti-Saloon League

Another key organization in the movement toward national Prohibition was the Anti-Saloon League founded in Oberlin, Ohio, in 1893. It was a nonpartisan political pressure group dedicated to Prohibition. With offices across the United States the league worked with churches and the Woman's Christian Temperance Movement and backed members of both major political parties sympathetic to its aims. In this way it gradually generated support in Congress, and in 1913 the league announced its campaign for a constitutional amendment: After seven years of intensive lobbying the Eighteenth Amendment came into effect.

Do you think that the legalization of light wines and beers would have made a difference to the effectiveness of Prohibition?

Bound by the Eighteenth Amendment and Volstead Act, individual states had their own legislation on alcohol—a few outlawed the consumption of alcohol as well as its production and distribution. The government intended Prohibition to be enforced by state agencies under state law, with federal organizations playing a secondary role.

Gary lists numerous benefits. If Prohibition could achieve them, wouldn't that make it worthwhile?

admitted, is not valuable, I should say about four per cent of alcoholic content.

However, as the law was passed in its present form, I think it would be a mistake to amend it in favor of light wines and beer.

Judge Gary said that the Steel Corporation, through its officers and plant superintendents in many parts of the country, had made a close observation of the effects of prohibition, even before the adoption of the Federal amendment and the enactment of the Volstead Act, by watching the results of prohibition laws in the states.

Of course, there are always some persons who will object to the passage or enforcement of any penal or prohibitory law and, as a rule, they are the men who do the most talking on the subject; I [Judge Gary said] *have no hesitation in saying with emphasis that the Volstead act and State laws for prohibiting the manufacture and sale of intoxicating liquors have been very beneficial to the industry of this country and to the workmen connected with it and their families.*

Says savings increase

While there have been violations of these laws, particularly in the larger cities, while there has been illicit manufacture of "hooch," so-called, and while there has been more or less boot-legging, yet as a total result of the prohibitory laws there has been a large decrease in the use of liquor, at least in the vicinity of our various plants throughout the country.

There has been a noteworthy decrease in the number of jails, asylums and hospitals. There has been an increase, and a large increase, in the bank balances of savings deposits. The health of the people has improved. The families of workmen are better clothed and better treated. The attendance of the workmen and their families at church, of the children in schools and of all of them at clean, legitimate, healthful resorts and places of amusement, has materially increased.

The sale and use of automobiles has been largely increased by the fact that a large majority of the workmen now prefer to take excursions with their families by automobile instead of spending their time at the saloons or other places and wasting their money in practices that are physically injurious instead of beneficial.

At a meeting of steel men recently, it was stated by one of those present that the families of the workmen in the steel mills would vote with practical unanimity in favor of total prohibition, although some of the husbands might, perhaps, be in favor of the sale of beer and light wines.

All in all, however, there is no doubt that a large preponderance of the workmen of this country are in favor of the prohibition of the sale and use of all intoxicants from the standpoint of good morals, good economics and peaceful social relations.

We should all remember constantly that if any one law is broken and the offender is unpunished or unprotected, some other person may decide to take the same course with respect to another law. It is a simple but important fact that the only safety of this country is found in the adoption and enforcement of laws which are calculated to protect all the people and which discriminate against none.

Do you think that most working men really were in agreement with Prohibition? Drinkers with a low income would have been more affected by the price rise in alcohol after it was made illegal.

The example of Birmingham

Judge Gary added that a striking example of the favorable effects of prohibition had been shown in the improvement in conditions in Birmingham and other steel towns in Alabama after the passage of a strict state prohibition law a year or two before nation-wide prohibition. Judge Gary said that the acquisition of the Tennessee Coal and Iron Company by the Steel Corporation had been followed by a rapid expansion of its business, the Steel Corporation expending about $150,000,000 in development and improvements.

This expansion, he said, brought about rapid increase in population, and some of the Alabama steel cities took on the characteristics of frontier mining towns. Crime increased; there were shootings in the streets and a general looseness of action on the part of many of the steel mill employees. With the passage of the Alabama state prohibition law all this changed, he said. A new jail, which had been built and filled, became empty and had been converted to other uses. The families of the workers, both white and negro, are prosperous. The children are receiving good schooling, and even a large hospital, which the corporation built in Birmingham, filled before prohibition, is now half empty.

A few countries maintain national Prohibition today. Can you think which countries they are and their reasons for adopting Prohibition? How do their beliefs and experiences differ from those of the United States in the 1920s?

Summary

Mark Thornton has no doubt that Prohibition was a failure. His article points out the lessons that he believes should be learned from this period of U.S. history by modern politicians and law enforcers who want to reduce the availability of drugs and various other commodities that society regards as undesirable. In his view, banning anything makes it more attractive. People are prepared to pay more to get it, and wherever there is a demand there will continue to be a supply, even though production is illegal. Drinkers had to trade with criminals. Those who could no longer get alcohol turned to other drugs, such as opium. Thornton quotes the "Iron Law of Prohibition," which states that the stricter the laws against a substance, the more potent (and therefore dangerous) that substance will become. He also argues that the Eighteenth Amendment and Volstead Act created serious problems of their own, particularly the growth of organized crime and corruption.

The second article was written three years after the introduction of Prohibition and reflects a positive interpretation of its effects as viewed by Judge Elbert H. Gary, chairman of the U.S. Steel Corporation. It lists the benefits of Prohibition, based on the experience of the corporation. Gary states that reduced consumption of alcohol (it is noteworthy that he does not claim that it has been eliminated altogether, even three years into the Prohibition era) has led to lower crime rates, less poverty, healthier workers, and more money invested in savings accounts. These are exactly the social benefits that the drafters of the Eighteenth Amendment had set out to achieve. In Gary's view the alcohol ban was a great success.

FURTHER INFORMATION:

Books:

Behr, Edward, *Prohibition: Thirteen Years That Changed America*. New York: Arcade Publishing, 1997.
Woodiwiss, Michael, *Crime, Crusades, and Corruption*. Lanham, MD: Rowman & Littlefield Publishing, 1988.

Useful websites:

http://prohibition.history.ohio-state.edu/Contents
Ohio University site with articles on movements and individuals associated with temperance and Prohibition.
http://www.druglibrary.org/schaffer/Library/studies/nc/nc2a.htm
Comprehensive history of temperance and Prohibition from National Commission on Marijuana and Drugs.
http://prohibition.8m.com/prohibition.html
Research paper on Prohibition and its effects on society.

The following debates in the Pro/Con series may also be of interest:

In *The Constitution*
Part 1: The Constitution, government, and the rule of law

In *Individual and Society*
Part 2: Social responsibility in a civil society

Topic 8 Should people have to obey unjust laws?

WAS PROHIBITION A DISASTER?

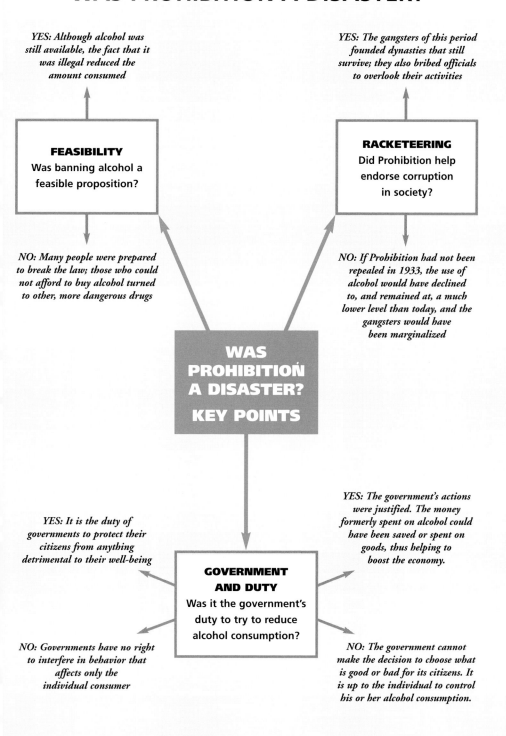

YES: Although alcohol was still available, the fact that it was illegal reduced the amount consumed

YES: The gangsters of this period founded dynasties that still survive; they also bribed officials to overlook their activities

FEASIBILITY
Was banning alcohol a feasible proposition?

RACKETEERING
Did Prohibition help endorse corruption in society?

NO: Many people were prepared to break the law; those who could not afford to buy alcohol turned to other, more dangerous drugs

NO: If Prohibition had not been repealed in 1933, the use of alcohol would have declined to, and remained at, a much lower level than today, and the gangsters would have been marginalized

WAS PROHIBITION A DISASTER? KEY POINTS

YES: The government's actions were justified. The money formerly spent on alcohol could have been saved or spent on goods, thus helping to boost the economy.

YES: It is the duty of governments to protect their citizens from anything detrimental to their well-being

GOVERNMENT AND DUTY
Was it the government's duty to try to reduce alcohol consumption?

NO: Governments have no right to interfere in behavior that affects only the individual consumer

NO: The government cannot make the decision to choose what is good or bad for its citizens. It is up to the individual to control his or her alcohol consumption.

PLAGIARISM

"A national survey published in Education Week *found that 54 percent of students admitted to plagiarizing from the Internet."*

—PLAGIARISM.ORG, 2003

Plagiarism is a serious problem that many academic institutions are trying to eradicate, although it has been made worse by widespread access to the Internet. The penalties for submitting fraudulent works are high. Not only is the plagiarist stealing another person's intellectual property, he or she is hindering the development of their own knowledge and understanding. In copying someone else's ideas verbatim, they are failing to think about issues themselves and to form their own opinions. Many students are not aware what constitutes plagiarism, and some do it unintentionally. Pleading ignorance, however, is not an acceptable excuse. Use the following guidelines to help avoid plagiarism and check your own work carefully.

How to avoid plagiarism

Plagiarism is when someone takes the ideas of another and presents them as their own. This can include writing, drawings, interviews, or diagrams. *Merriam-Webster's Dictionary* defines plagiarism as follows:

- to steal and pass off (the ideas or words of another) as one's own;
- to use (another's production) without crediting the source;
- to commit literary theft;
- to present as new and original an idea or product derived from an existing source.

The best way to avoid plagiarizing is to ensure that you cite the source of every idea that you have used. Make sure you compile a bibliography and footnotes to help list your sources accurately. When researching, keep notes of the exact location of the information you have used—this could be a webpage or the page and publication date of a journal or a book. You will need this information for your bibliography. Be sure to use quotation marks to enclose text written by someone else that you are including in your essay. State the name of your source in the main body of your text, for example, "According to Plato. ..."

Under U.S. copyright law intellectual property (ideas or information) cannot be reproduced in any way without permission. Copyright laws apply not only to written information but also to video, music, and images. Written material usually remains in copyright for 75 years after the death of the author. Not all written material is protected by copyright. Information that is general knowledge and not the result of original research, or that appears in readily available compilations, such as directories, can be used freely. If you are in doubt whether information is covered by copyright, it is always advisable to cite the source you are using.

KEY FACTS

Key words and phrases

There are certain terms that must be understood to avoid plagiarizing someone else's intellectual property.

Cite	To quote by way of an example, authority, or proof.
Source	The original or primary document or reference.
Quote	To write a passage and acknowledge the source or to cite as an illustration.
Bibliography	The list of all works referred to in a text.
Footnote	Notes giving references, explanations, or comments situated below the text at the end of a printed page.
Endnote	As above, but placed at the end of the document.
Self-plagiarism	To use your own previously produced work and submit it as new.
Paraphrase	To restate a text or passage and present it in a new form.

Quotations

When citing from a document word for word, you must use quotation marks and detail the source clearly. If it is a long passage (longer than 3 lines), start the quote on a new line, and indent and state the source with a footnote or endnote. Mention the name of the author. Use ellipses (...) to indicate omissions, and use square brackets ([]) to add your own comments or clarifications.

Paraphrasing

Paraphrasing is an essential component of an essay, especially when you are analyzing other research. The paraphrase should highlight the original ideas and meanings of other writers, but present them in an entirely different form from the original. Changing a few words around is not acceptable and constitutes plagiarism. When summarizing, remember that you must cite the source of the ideas that you have presented in your paper.

Checklist

Remember these tips to help avoid plagiarism:

- Keep all your research and rough drafts.
- Use quotations, bibliographies, and footnotes.
- Check your work for "borrowed" phrases.
- Cite all sources accurately.
- Use your own words.
- Express your own opinion.

USEFUL WEBSITES

Go to http://www.plagiarism.org/ to read about issues associated with the prevention of plagiarism from the Internet and good writing practices.

Topic 7
SHOULD THE UNITED STATES HAVE SUPPORTED THE LEAGUE OF NATIONS?

YES
"HOW THE LEAGUE OF NATIONS ENDED UP AS DEBRIS"
THE INDEPENDENT, OCTOBER 6, 2002
ROBERT FISK

NO
"SPEECH IN OPPOSITION TO THE LEAGUE OF NATIONS"
WASHINGTON, D.C., AUGUST 12, 1919
HENRY CABOT LODGE

INTRODUCTION

The League of Nations was an international organization founded after World War I (1914–1918) at the Paris Peace Conference of 1919 with the objective of maintaining peace and preventing future conflict through collective action. It was the brainchild of President Woodrow Wilson (1912–1920), who included its creation as one of the Fourteen Points he proposed in 1917 as the basis for the peace settlement to end World War I. Wilson called for "a general association of nations" based on "mutual guarantees of political independence and territorial integrity to great and small states alike."

On April 18, 1919, the delegates to the peace conference at Versailles in France unanimously adopted the draft terms for the league. These terms centered around Article X, which called for collective security as the ultimate means of keeping the peace: "The Members of the League undertake to respect and preserve, as against external

aggression, the territorial integrity and existing political independence of all Members of the League. In case of any such aggression, or in case of any threat or danger of such aggression, the Council shall advise upon the means by which the obligation shall be fulfilled." In the United States that article proved to be the most controversial element.

Wilson's problems started when Republicans gained the majority in both the House of Representatives and the Senate in the 1918 elections. That shift of power, combined with the president's failure to include any prominent Republicans in his peace delegation, ensured that he faced strong opposition to the treaty he brought home. In September 1919 Wilson launched an ambitious speaking tour across the country to win support for the league and the treaty. On September 25, after speaking in Pueblo, Colorado, he collapsed from exhaustion. A week later, back in Washington, D.C., he suffered a stroke. Bedridden, Wilson refused to compromise, urging his fellow Democrats to either stand by the original treaty or vote it down. In the final vote taken on March 19, 1920, a revised version of the treaty fell seven votes short of the two-thirds needed for ratification. As a result, the United States never ratified the Treaty of Versailles, nor did it join the League of Nations

---

"Within another generation there will be another world war if the nations of the world do not concert the method by which to prevent it."

—WOODROW WILSON,

OMAHA, NEBRASKA, 1919

Even without U.S. backing, the league had a number of successes between 1919 and 1939. It settled disputes in the Balkans and Latin America, and supervised reconstruction loans and territories such as the free city of Danzig, former German colonies, and non-Turkish areas of the Ottoman Empire. However, the league later failed to take action over major violations of the peace terms—most notably Japan's invasion of Manchuria (1932), Italy's invasion of Ethiopia (1935), and Germany's rearmament and invasion of Austria (1938), Czechoslovakia (1938–1939), and Poland (1939). In those respects many people argue that its inaction contributed to the outbreak of World War II in 1939. Some critics believe that the failure of the United States to join the league fundamentally

weakened it. Without the support of the powerful nation that had been crucial to the Allied victory, it was difficult for the organization to be an effective instrument for peace. Critics believe that the United States had a moral duty to support this international organization, and that its economic and military strength and its isolation from the political squabbles of Europe and its empires would have brought strength and fairness to the league. On the other hand, U.S. politicians who did not want to join argued that membership would compromise the nation's independence and would involve it in faraway disputes in which it had no direct concern.

Today the League of Nations is generally viewed as an ineffective attempt to promote a peaceful community of nations. The league collapsed in 1939 and was replaced in 1945 by the United Nations. Aside from the question of U.S. involvement, many factors contributed to its breakdown. They included the harsh terms of the peace treaties designed to remove power from the defeated nations through territorial changes and economic measures; increased feelings of nationalism; the absence of an army to enforce the league's decisions; and the initial exclusion of Germany and Russia from the organization.

The following texts present starkly competing answers to the question as to whether the United States should have supported the League of Nations. Robert Fisk argues that the league failed because powerful nations put self-interest before the general good. Henry Cabot Lodge (1850-1924), on the other hand, speaks out against collective security, arguing that it could entangle the United States in distant disputes and compromise its independence.

HOW THE LEAGUE OF NATIONS ENDED UP AS DEBRIS
Robert Fisk

Robert Fisk is a British political analyst, journalist, and writer, and is the Middle East correspondent for The Independent newspaper. He wrote this article in October 2002, six months before the United States invaded Iraq without UN support.

Jan Christiaan Smuts (1870–1950) was a South African soldier and statesman who became prime minister of his country in August 1919. Smuts attended the Paris Peace Conference and played an important role in setting up the League of Nations

Mandates were former German and Ottoman lands ceded to the allies after World War I. Under the auspices of the League of Nations they were administered by various allied powers in preparation for independence. Iraq was a British mandate prior to independence in 1930.

YES

So George Bush Jnr. is now an expert on the League of Nations, is he? Across America, he's been telling the folks that the United Nations is in danger of becoming no more than the old pre-Second World War organisation. A "talking shop" is how he's been referring to the League. Would that he looked at a history book now and again. He might find that the League failed the world because of the same cynicism and disregard for morality by the major powers that the United States shows today.

Wilson and 14 points

The League was formed in the aftermath of the 1914–18 war. President Woodrow Wilson of the US was one of its midwives. He wanted to protect minority rights, to give peoples independence. His "14 points" were an inspiration to all the would-be nations of the world. He demanded a new international order—shades of George Bush Snr.—and an equality of nations. "Europe is being liquidated," General Smuts announced in 1918, "and the League of Nations must be the heir to this great estate."

And so came into being a new Poland, Yugoslavia, Czechoslovakia, a reshaped Europe and, of course, a new Middle East. The modern state of Iraq (President Bush, please note) owes its creation to the League, whose British and French mandates gave us for better or worse—probably worse—Palestine and Syria and Lebanon.

Others wanted states, too. The Kurds wanted a state. The Armenians wanted to reverse their genocide by the Turks and return to homes in Turkey.

But President Wilson fell ill. The U.S. Congress declined to join the League and the U.S. turned to an isolationism from which it would only be driven after Pearl Harbor—and after (President Bush, please note again) two very profitable wartime years of neutrality.

The Americans wanted no part of the League. The future superpower, whose influence for peace would have been so beneficial to the world—and whose growing economic and

COMMENTARY: Wilson's Fourteen Points

The Fourteen Points were the basis of a peace program outlined by President Woodrow Wilson in an address he made to Congress on January 8, 1918. Wilson hoped for "peace without victory," or a negotiated settlement, and outlined the general principles and specific measures by which such an objective could be achieved. His points were designed to remove problems that had led to the conflict and to establish and maintain peace. They were the basis on which Germany and Austria–Hungary surrendered nine months later and provided the framework for the subsequent peace negotiations held in France in 1919. His points were:

1. Open diplomacy; no secret treaty making
2. Freedom of the seas in war as well as in peace
3. The removal of economic barriers to trade
4. National armaments to be reduced
5. Colonial disputes to be judged impartially, with equal weight given to the interests of subject populations and the claims of colonial governments
6. The evacuation by the Germans and Austrians of all Russian territory
7. The restoration of Belgian sovereignty
8. All occupied French territory to be restored and Alsace and Lorraine to be returned to France
9. Italy's frontiers to be readjusted along recognized lines of nationality
10. The peoples of Austria-Hungary to be given the opportunity for autonomous development
11. Romania, Serbia, and Montenegro to be restored and Serbia given access to the sea, and Balkan interstate relations to be settled on lines of allegiance and nationality
12. The non-Turkish peoples of the Ottoman Empire to be given the opportunity for autonomous development
13. The establishment of a Polish state with access to the sea
14. A general association of nations to be formed to guarantee political independence and territorial integrity to large and small states alike

Wilson's ideals and moral rigor made him immensely popular in war-torn Europe. However, the situation was extremely complex. Unlike the United States, many European countries had been devastated by the fighting, and they wanted to remove the threat of future conflict by weakening the defeated powers. Although Wilson achieved more of his points than he lost, he was also forced to compromise on many issues. However, his greatest defeat came at home. From 1918 his Republican opponents, notably Senator Henry Cabot Lodge (see pages 94–98), had campaigned against ratification of the Treaty of Versailles and its provision for the League of Nations. In 1920 they defeated the league in the Senate.

The United States' provision of supplies and participation in World War I were key factors in the allied victory. The nation was also the only major power to emerge without huge war debts. Did its power give the United States a moral responsibility to play a role in world affairs?

military might could have made Hitler revise his plans—turned its back on the League. The Kurds got no state. The Armenians never went home.

The other great powers joined the League. The French wanted it to be powerful, to have a multinational military force—not unlike today's United Nations peacekeepers—but the British, who wanted to remain the world's first superpower, turned the idea down.

The race issue

The first real test came from Japan. Our future Second World War enemy proposed a clause in the League's covenant embracing the concept of racial equality. Wilson's own adviser—for the Americans were still keen to join the League at the time—turned his back on the idea. It would "raise the race issue throughout the world," he wrote.

In the end, the "race" issue was only allowed to intrude when the League wished to demand the protection of minorities in the small and new states created after the First World War. Minorities in Poland and Czechoslovakia came under the League's care. Major states did not have to worry about such provisions. Hence when Hitler started persecuting the Jews of Germany after 1933, the League was powerless.

Do you think things could have been different regardless of the U.S. position if European powers had agreed to a multilateral army as part of the League of Nations?

In 1923—without British support for a League army—the French occupied the Rhineland to force Germany to pay wartime reparations. So individual states began to ignore the League. Italy's invasion of Abyssinia in 1935 and the Spanish civil war which began in 1936 proved its worthlessness. Under Hitler—who was certainly not interested in an "equality of nations"—Germany abandoned the League. The Soviets, surprisingly, continued to support it. Sanctions on Spain did not end their civil war. America stayed out of it.

Little nations vs. giants

Little nations tried to sway the giants. When he was president of the League's council—the forerunner of our present-day Security Council—Eamon de Valera of Ireland proposed a League multinational force to stop Italy's 1935 aggression. He was prepared to commit his own new and tiny Irish army to such a project.

Eamon de Valera was an Irish statesman and politician. A key figure in Ireland's fight for independence from Britain, he took his country out of the British Commonwealth in 1937 and renamed the country Ireland. He served three terms as Irish prime minister and was president of Ireland from 1959 to 1973.

The major powers were not interested. "We have been unable to bend our wills to sacrifice selfish advantage when it conflicts with justice to others," de Valera later complained. By 1939, he was accurately referring to the League as "debris".

Now Bush Jnr. implies that the United Nations will also be debris if it doesn't come to heel and follow America's demand to invade Iraq. He wants to use it for his project of "regime change"—which will change the map of the Middle East, produce a tide of oil wealth for U.S. companies and reduce Israel's enemies to impotence. We are supposed to believe that this is about weapons of mass destruction—and forget that the U.S. sold botulinum toxin, anthrax and vials of West Nile virus to Iraq between 1985 and 1989. For most of that time, Iraq was fighting Iran—a war which the United Nations had tried to end.

So why should Saddam have any respect for the United Nations? Why, when Israel flouts Security Council resolutions—even today—should Iraq play by the book?

The Americans care no more about Israel's failure to adhere to United Nations resolutions than Germany cared about the League when it re-entered the Rhineland, or when Italy invaded Abyssinia. It is the major powers that govern the United Nations and they will use it or abuse it as they see fit. In an odd way, the U.S. administration—which for years failed to pay its dues to the world body—is right to raise the ghost of the League. For it was the cynicism and arrogance of the major powers that destroyed it—just as America can destroy the United Nations today.

In May 2003 President George W. Bush announced victory in the U.S. military campaign in Iraq.

Is it possible to have a truly multilateral organization acting in the international interest if one nation has more economic and military power than other members? Will that nation always act independently if it sees its aims as conflicting with those of the organization, and if it doesn't need the institution's support?

SPEECH IN OPPOSITION TO THE LEAGUE OF NATIONS
Henry Cabot Lodge

NO

Mr. President:

The independence of the United States is not only more precious to ourselves but to the world than any single possession. Look at the United States today. We have made mistakes in the past. We have had shortcomings. We shall make mistakes in the future and fall short of our own best hopes. But none the less is there any country today on the face of the earth which can compare with this in ordered liberty, in peace, and in the largest freedom?

I feel that I can say this without being accused of undue boastfulness, for it is the simple fact, and in making this treaty and taking on these obligations all that we do is in a spirit of unselfishness and in a desire for the good of mankind. But it is well to remember that we are dealing with nations every one of which has a direct individual interest to serve, and there is grave danger in an unshared idealism.

Contrast the United States with any country on the face of the earth today and ask yourself whether the situation of the United States is not the best to be found. I will go as far as anyone in world service, but the first step to world service is the maintenance of the United States.

National loyalties must come first

I have always loved one flag and I cannot share that devotion [with] a mongrel banner created for a League.

You may call me selfish if you will, conservative or reactionary, or use any other harsh adjective you see fit to apply, but an American I was born, an American I have remained all my life. I can never be anything else but an American, and I must think of the United States first, and when I think of the United States first in an arrangement like this I am thinking of what is best for the world, for if the United States fails, the best hopes of mankind fail with it.

I have never had but one allegiance—I cannot divide it now. I have loved but one flag and I cannot share that devotion and give affection to the mongrel banner invented for a league. Internationalism, illustrated by the Bolshevik

Henry Cabot Lodge, who as chairman of the Foreign Relations Committee, led opposition in the Senate to Wilson's campaign to ratify the Treaty of Versailles and the League of Nations.

Cabot appeals to a long tradition of distrust for what Thomas Jefferson (1743–1826), paraphrasing George Washington (1732–1799), called "entangling alliances." When he left office, Washington had advised, "The great rule of conduct for us in regard to foreign nations is, in extending our commercial relations to have with them as little political connection as possible." After World War I such sentiments resurfaced in the policy of isolationism.

and by the men to whom all countries are alike provided they can make money out of them, is to me repulsive.

National I must remain, and in that way I like all other Americans can render the amplest service to the world.

The United States is the world's best hope, but if you fetter her in the interests and quarrels of other nations, if you tangle her in the intrigues of Europe, you will destroy her power for good and endanger her very existence. Leave her to march freely through the centuries to come as in the years that have gone.

Strong, generous, and confident, she has nobly served mankind. Beware how you trifle with your marvellous inheritance, this great land of ordered liberty, for if we stumble and fall freedom and civilization everywhere will go down in ruin.

We are told that we shall "break the heart of the world" if we do not take this league just as it stands. I fear that the hearts of the vast majority of mankind would beat on strongly and steadily and without any quickening if the league were to perish altogether. If it should be effectively and beneficently changed the people who would lie awake in sorrow for a single night could be easily gathered in one not very large room but those who would draw a long breath of relief would reach to millions.

Unrealistic ideals must be cast aside

We hear much of visions and I trust we shall continue to have visions and dream dreams of a fairer future for the race. But visions are one thing and visionaries are another, and the mechanical appliances of the rhetorician designed to give a picture of a present which does not exist and of a future which no man can predict are as unreal and short-lived as the steam or canvas clouds, the angels suspended on wires and the artificial lights of the stage.

Lodge expresses his distaste for the League of Nations by calling it a "deformed experiment" and suggests that it was a mistake to include it in the terms of the Treaty of Versailles. Do you think his scathing view was justified? And would it have been more effective to handle the treaty and the foundation of the league as two separate pieces of legislation?

They pass with the moment of effect and are shabby and tawdry in the daylight. Let us at least be real. Washington's entire honesty of mind and his fearless look into the face of all facts are qualities which can never go out of fashion and which we should all do well to imitate.

Ideals have been thrust upon us as an argument for the league until the healthy mind which rejects cant revolts from them. Are ideals confined to this deformed experiment upon a noble purpose, tainted, as it is, with bargains and tied to a peace treaty which might have been disposed of long ago to the great benefit of the world if it had not been compelled to carry this rider on its back?… no blacker care ever sat behind any rider than we shall find in this covenant of doubtful and disputed interpretation as it now perches upon the treaty of peace.

No doubt many excellent and patriotic people see a coming fulfilment of noble ideals in the words "league for peace." We all respect and share these aspirations and desires, but some of us see no hope, but rather defeat, for them in this murky covenant. For we, too, have our ideals, even if we differ from those who have tried to establish a monopoly of idealism.

Our first ideal is our country, and we see her in the future, as in the past, giving service to all her people and to the world. Our ideal of the future is that she should continue to render that service of her own free will. She has great problems of her own to solve, very grim and perilous problems, and a right solution, if we can attain to it, would largely benefit mankind.

We would have our country strong to resist a peril from the West, as she has flung back the German menace from the East. We would not have our politics distracted and embittered by the dissensions of other lands. We would not have our country's vigour exhausted or her moral force abated, by everlasting meddling and muddling in every quarrel, great and small, which afflicts the world.

Our ideal is to make her ever stronger and better and finer, because in that way alone, as we believe, can she be of the greatest service to the world's peace and to the welfare of mankind.

The troubles to which Cabot refers are strikes—in 1919 strikes included ship workers in Seattle, police in Boston, and steelworkers and coal miners nationwide—and a campaign of parcel bombs and pamphlets directed against members of the government. This series of events was linked with the feared spread of communism, known as the "Red scare."

Summary

British journalist Robert Fisk argues that the debate over whether the United States should have joined the League of Nations is not merely of historical interest. He draws direct parallels with foreign policy toward Iraq in 2002. His article discusses fundamental issues of national sovereignty, the role of international institutions, and multilateral versus unilateral action. According to Fisk, the League of Nations, with the support of the United States and the world's other powerful nations, might have stopped the aggression that ultimately resulted in World War II. He argues against the actions of powerful nations when they put self-interest before wider moral obligations of international peace. The United States should learn from its past mistake and commit itself to the United Nations to preserve peace throughout the world.

In a speech made in Washington in 1919 Senator Henry Cabot Lodge takes the opposing view, as he rallies opposition to Wilson's campaign for the ratification of the Treaty of Versailles. He emphasizes his patriotism and argues that nothing should come before his obligation to his nation, which he considers the greatest embodiment of peace and freedom. Lodge also expresses reservations about the motives of European countries, questioning whether they can ever be compatible with noble ideals for maintaining a just peace. While accepting the United States' responsibility to promote peace and the welfare of mankind, he insists that this is best achieved by not becoming entangled in "the intrigues of Europe." A league of nations that binds the United States to the interests and quarrels of other nations would, he predicts, "destroy her power for good and endanger her very existence."

FURTHER INFORMATION:

Books:

Clements, Kendrick A., *Woodrow Wilson: World Statesman*. Boston, MA: Twayne Publishers, 1987.
Knock, Thomas K., *To End All Wars*. Princeton, NJ: Princeton University Press, 1995.
Kuehl, Warren F., *Keeping the Covenant: American Internationalists and the League of Nations, 1920–1939*. Kent, OH: Kent State University Press, 1997.

Useful websites:

http://odur.let.rug.nl/~usa/E/league/leaguexx.htm
Detailed critical analysis of the background and history of the League of Nations.
http://www.firstworldwar.com/source/leagueofnations.htm
The covenant, or written terms, of the League of Nations.
http://www.firstworldwar.com/source/fourteenpoints.htm
Wilson's speech to Congress containing his 14 Points.

The following debates in the Pro/Con series may also be of interest:

In *U.S. Foreign Policy*:
Topic 1 Does the United States have a duty to protect democracy and freedom overseas?

Topic 2 Is U.S foreign policy too interventionist?

Topic 4 Should the United States show a stronger commitment to the United Nations?

SHOULD THE UNITED STATES HAVE SUPPORTED THE LEAGUE OF NATIONS?

YES: Maintaining international peace, justice, and law depends on the full and voluntary involvement of all nations in peacekeeping institutions such as the league, which place international good before national gain

YES: The Senate failed to ratify the league largely for party political reasons rather than moral objections. The league was closely identified with the Democrats, and the Republicans exploited people's fears of foreign involvement to oppose President Wilson.

INTERNATIONALISM
Was it morally right for the United States to remain actively involved in world affairs?

PARTY POLITICS
Was ratification of the Treaty of Versailles and the league prevented by party politics?

NO: For its own good and that of the world the United States must be strong and independent. It is wrong for it to involve itself in disputes that do not directly affect its well-being.

SHOULD THE UNITED STATES HAVE SUPPORTED THE LEAGUE OF NATIONS?
KEY POINTS

NO: Political maneuvering by the Republicans and Wilson's refusal to amend any of the league's terms did increase opposition to U.S. involvement, but that opposition would have prevailed regardless

YES: The involvement of this economically powerful nation could have maintained the power balance in Europe as established in the peace treaties of 1919

YES: Its support would have afforded the league strong moral guidance that transcended the deep-seated disputes of Europe

WORLD WAR II
If the United States had supported the league, could war have been avoided?

NO: The terms of the peace treaties were too harsh and sought too much retribution from the defeated powers, making future conflict inevitable

NO: The European allies thought that it was practically—and morally—right to limit the power of their enemies and would always have felt that U.S. principles were too idealized

Topic 8
WAS THE NEW DEAL "NEW"?

YES
FROM "NEW DEAL"
HTTP://GI.GROLIER.COM/PRESIDENTS/EA/SIDE/NEWDEAL.HTML
THE AMERICAN PRESIDENCY
JAMES T. PATTERSON

NO
"FRANKLIN D. ROOSEVELT'S NEW DEAL"
HTTP://WWW.STUDYWORLD.COM/FRANKLIN_D_ROOSEVELT'S_NEW_DEAL.HTM
WWW.STUDYWORLD.COM

INTRODUCTION

Franklin D. Roosevelt (1882-1945) was president from 1933 until 1945. The New Deal is the name given to a series of legislation passed by President Roosevelt between his election in 1933 and around 1938 to counter the worst effects of the Great Depression by initiating economic recovery and reform in the United States. The program's popular name came from FDR's acceptance speech when he won the Democratic nomination for president in 1932: In a phrase that proved a popular electioneering slogan, FDR promised "a New Deal for the American people."

The slogan helped FDR win a sizable majority over his Republican opponent, President Herbert Hoover. The idea of new opportunity appealed to Americans who for three years had been suffering the effects of the worst economic depression the country had ever known. Manufacturing had declined, throwing millions of Americans out of work at a time when official welfare did not exist. They relied on charity. The stock market had crashed, international trade had fallen, and on the weekend FDR was inaugurated in March 1933, the country's banking system was in danger of collapse as anxious investors rushed to withdraw their savings.

Many Americans blamed Herbert Hoover for their plight, and he earned an undeserved reputation for hardheartedness. Hoover's essential policy followed economic orthodoxy: The government should not interfere with the workings of the market. The economy would sort itself out.

FDRs' response took shape in the so-called Hundred Days, the first period of his presidency. He pushed 15 major new laws through Congress, reforming the banking system and setting up new federal planning for agriculture and industry. The Tennessee Valley Authority was set up to oversee economic regeneration of one of the country's poorest regions. There was increased unemployment relief, and job creation plans were overseen by the Public Works Administration. The National Recovery Administration aimed to coordinate government, industry, and labor in the best approaches to economic recovery. Later, in 1935 Roosevelt also launched attacks on business monopoly and proposed the creation of a comprehensive social insurance program, with old-age pensions and unemployment insurance.

"I see one-third of a nation ill-housed, ill-clad, ill-nourished."

—FRANKLIN D. ROOSEVELT, INAUGURAL ADDRESS, 1937

The New Deal was popular with the electorate, who reelected FDR in 1936. However, within only 18 months the program of legislation was over. In 1935 the Supreme Court ruled the National Recovery Administration (NRA) unconstitutional on the grounds that it gave the executive illegal power to make law through code. FDR found himself facing a recession in fall 1937, with unemployment rising again. Conservatives in Congress delayed his proposed legislation. Finally, FDR himself was distracted by events in Europe, where Germany was involved in military expansion that would lead to World War II (1939–1945).

How new was the New Deal? At the time radicals believed that it did not make enough of the president's mandate to introduce sweeping reforms of the U.S. system. Industries soon

came to dominate the agencies set up to regulate them; the New Deal's agricultural provisions aided large farming concerns rather than individual farmers. Black Americans did not benefit from the government programs as much as whites. Poverty relief was also limited.

Other critics of FDR pointed out that far from representing an unprecedented level of government interference in the economy, the labor creation programs of the New Deal were an extension of earlier policies. Herbert Hoover, they say, had himself introduced work creation projects at the start of the Great Depression, including the building of Hoover Dam in Nevada. The agencies FDR established echoed those created during World War I (1914–1918) to run the war economy.

Defenders of the New Deal, who included most Americans in the 1930s and the majority of historians since, claim that it was new because it made the government more responsive to the needs of a wider range of groups and social problems than ever before. Although they concede that full employment only returned to the United States with the economic boom triggered by World War II, they argue that the New Deal's political achievements restored faith in the American system of government at a time of potentially great crisis.

The two articles that follow give different interpretations of the New Deal. The first lists many of its measures to argue that it was improvised and innovative. The second piece, from studyworld.com, argues that in fact the legislation was a carefully thought-out program based on the earlier work of economists such as John Stuart Mill and John Maynard Keynes.

NEW DEAL
James T. Patterson

✓ New Deal, the phrase, never exactly defined, that became the label for the antidepression measures of Franklin D. Roosevelt's first two terms as president. In accepting the Democratic presidential nomination in 1932, Gov. Roosevelt of New York told the cheering delegates, "I pledge you, I pledge myself, to a new deal for the American people." To Roosevelt's admirers the New Deal signified the most imaginative burst of federal domestic legislation in U.S. history. To his critics it was a miscellany of alphabetical agencies that failed to end the Great Depression.

One of the key features of the New Deal was an increase in federal government organizations. Roosevelt believed that it was necessary to rejuvenate the economy by employing people to work for these organizations.

When Roosevelt took office in March 1933, the nation faced an economic crisis. Most of the country's banks, weakened by withdrawals of funds by frightened depositors, were closed. Between 13 and 15 million people were unemployed. To attack this crisis, Roosevelt thought, he would have to experiment in order to find the most practical approaches. For this reason his New Deal program lacked a consistent economic philosophy. It was opportunistic rather than theoretical in its approach to problems. But it was consistent in some ways. It possessed humanitarian goals, an openness to new ideas, and a willingness to expand federal powers to achieve its ends. It proposed to provide relief for the needy, recovery for the nation at large, and long-range reform of some economic institutions.

Relief policies

The gold standard is a monetary system that backs currency with a reserve of gold and allows currency holders to convert their currency into gold. The United States joined the gold standard in 1900. However, during the Depression many countries left the gold standard in order to devalue their currency and thereby boost their exports.

The relief policies of the New Deal led to the establishment of a host of administrative agencies between 1933 and 1935. The Civilian Conservation Corps (CCC) ultimately employed 2.5 million young men on conservation and reforestation projects. The Federal Emergency Relief Administration (FERA) and Civil Works Administration (CWA), both headed by Harry Hopkins, a dedicated social worker, spent more than $2 billion on doles and work relief between 1933 and 1935. The Home Owners Loan Corporation (HOLC) assisted thousands of property owners and lending institutions throughout the decade. The Roosevelt administration also took the nation off the gold standard in 1933 and resorted to mildly inflationary monetary policies in 1933 and 1934.

COMMENTARY: FDR and the Great Depression

Franklin Delano Roosevelt was one of America's foremost presidents—the only one to serve four terms, from 1933 until 1945. During his term of office he had to cope with two of the 20th century's most significant events: the Great Depression and World War II (1939–1945).

Roosevelt was born into a wealthy New York family in 1882. He attended Harvard and Columbia Law School before qualifying as a lawyer. By 1910 he had entered politics as a Democrat in the New York State Senate. From 1913–1920 he was assistant secretary of the Navy under President Woodrow Wilson. In 1921 his political career was cut short when he contracted polio and was paralyzed from the waist down. For seven years he left politics to recuperate. In 1928 he was elected governor of New York, and in 1930 he became the Democratic candidate for the presidential election of 1932. At the time of his nomination the United States was entering the Great Depression, and the economic catastrophe was to play a key part in Roosevelt's political future.

The Great Depression

The Great Depression was a time of severe decline in business activity. The 1920s had witnessed an unprecedented economic boom fed by new technology. Textiles, oil, steel, and construction all prospered, helped by the rise of the electric and automobile industries and the development of new sources of power. The era was dominated by Republican presidents who advocated a laissez-faire economic philosophy allowing markets to operate without government interference. A year before the Wall Street Crash in 1929 industries began to contract as the capacity to produce overtook the capacity to consume. By the time of the crash there was a massive surplus of goods on the market. By 1932 there were more than 13 million people unemployed as the economic depression worsened.

The New Deal

Roosevelt outlined his idea of a New Deal in the runup to the 1932 presidential election. Unlike his Republican predecessors, he wanted the federal government to have a much stronger role in running the economy. To help his candidacy, Roosevelt gathered together a group of noted economists and academics to act as policy advisers. This group, which became known as the Brain Trust, helped develop many of the ideas that became the New Deal.

After his inauguration address on March 4, 1933, Roosevelt immediately started to put his New Deal into action. The New Deal achieved many things: It regulated the stock market, insured bank deposits, employed millions of people in public projects, established old-age pensions, abolished most child labor, and encouraged workers' unions.

What do you think the author means when he says "that enriched the nation's cultural life"? Look at http://www.pbs. org/wgbh/amex/ dustbowl/ peopleevents/ pandeAMEX10. html, and see if you can find examples.

These efforts gave some relief to debtors. The most important relief agency of the New Deal was the Works Progress Administration (WPA), created in 1935 and also headed by Hopkins. During the next eight years it built or improved more than 2,500 hospitals, 5,900 school buildings, and nearly 13,000 playgrounds. It provided funds for federal theater, arts, and writers projects that enriched the nation's cultural life. The WPA's National Youth Administration gave financial aid to more than 2 million high school and college students and to 2.6 million young people who were not in school. Most of the WPA's money, some $11 billion in all by 1943, went for short-term, make-work projects to assist the unemployed. At peak periods the WPA helped more than 3 million people.

These relief agencies marked an unprecedented federal involvement in welfare. The millions of Americans who benefited from them–especially blacks and other "forgotten men"–showed their gratitude by lionizing Roosevelt and by voting Democratic in subsequent elections. The relief policies of the New Deal also did much to restore confidence in the nation's political institutions, and to undercut the agitation growing since 1929 for radical solutions to hard times....

Reform legislation

[S]everal domestic reforms of the 1930s were significant. Among them were the Federal Deposit Insurance Corporation (FDIC), which helped prevent banking panics; the Securities and Exchange Commission (SEC), which made a start toward federal regulation of the stock exchanges; and the Banking Act of 1935, which increased Washington's control over monetary policy. These enactments lessened the chances of future depressions as sharp as the one of 1929–1939.

The FDIC is an independent federal agency that insures deposits in commercial banks. It was introduced to make banks more secure so that worried investors would be less likely to withdraw their money during times of economic uncertainty.

The Tennessee Valley Authority, created in 1933, was an especially significant New Deal accomplishment. A public corporation with broad powers, it engaged in the manufacture of fertilizer, in soil conservation, and in social experiments with state and local agencies. Its most striking achievement was the building of multipurpose dams to control floods and generate cheap electric power throughout the region drained by the Tennessee River and its various tributaries.

The New Deal also helped change the nature of labor-management relations. Labor leaders, encouraged temporarily by passage of the NRA in 1933, recognized that Roosevelt would not use government to crush unions. Accordingly, they staged successful organizing drives throughout the 1930s. They also agitated for the Wagner Act, passed in 1935. This important law established the National Labor Relations Board, which guaranteed to labor the right to bargain collectively on equal terms with management.

In 1938 New Dealers secured passage of the Fair Labor Standards Act, which set minimum wages and maximum hours for certain types of work and abolished child labor involved in interstate commerce. Though the act excluded many workers from coverage, it was a cautious step toward federal supervision of labor conditions. In part because of the benevolently neutral attitude of the New Deal, in part because of the leadership of militant labor leaders, union membership in the United States jumped from 3.2 million in 1932 to 9 million in 1940. This was the most important social change of the decade.

Another lasting accomplishment of the New Deal was the Social Security Act of 1935. This law, long sought by reformers, involved the federal government in programs of old-age pensions, unemployment insurance, and assistance to needy blind and disabled persons, and to dependent children. The law was conservative in many ways: regressive payroll taxes paid for old-age pensions; many workers were not covered; and states were expected to provide most of the money for the blind, disabled, and dependent. Nonetheless, the Social Security Act became a basis for later expansion of federally assisted social services.

Legacies of the New Deal

The New Deal also helped to change politics and political institutions. Democrats, previously an awkward coalition of disparate elements, became the proponents of urban liberalism and swept to power in much of the North and Midwest. Afterward, the Democratic Party enjoyed majority status in the United States. Under the New Deal the executive branch, and the presidency in particular, also became much more activist and innovative than before. The states and localities themselves grew in the course of administering federal programs and appropriating funds for matching-grant programs. Interest groups, which were already strong before 1933, broadened their lines of contact with these expanding governmental entities. In these ways the New Deal, though of dubious value economically, set in motion long-range trends toward governmental expansion and modernization.

Collective bargaining is a method of negotiation that allows employees to use unions to represent them in talks with their management to discuss pay and working conditions.

The author argues that an increase in union membership was "the most important social change of the decade." What other important social changes do you think happened during this period?

FRANKLIN D. ROOSEVELT'S NEW DEAL
www.studyworld.com

NO

The crash of the stock market brought many hard times. Franklin D. Roosevelt's New Deal was a way to fix these times. John Stuart Mill and John Maynard Keynes were two economists whose economic theories greatly influenced and helped Franklin D. Roosevelt devise a plan to rescue the United States from the Great Depression it had fallen into. John Stuart Mill was a strong believer of expanded government, which the New Deal provided. John Maynard Keynes believed in supply and demand, which the New Deal used to stabilize the economy.

Franklin D. Roosevelt's New Deal is the plan that brought the U.S. out of the Great Depression. It was sometimes thought to be an improvised plan, but was actually very thought out. Roosevelt was not afraid to involve the central government in addressing the economic problem. The basic plan was to stimulate the economy by creating jobs. First Roosevelt tried to help the economy with the National Recovery Administration. The NRA spread work and reduced unfair competitive practices by cooperation in industry. Eventually the NRA was declared unconstitutional. Franklin D. Roosevelt then needed a new plan. Keeping the same idea of creating jobs he made many other organizations devoted to forming jobs and in turn helping the economy. One of those organizations was the Civilian Conservation Corps. This corps took men off the streets and paid them to plant forests and drain swamps. Another of these organizations was the Public Works Administration. This organization employed men to build highways and public buildings. These were only some of the organizations dedicated to creating jobs. Creating jobs was important because it put money in the hands of the consumer. This directly affected the supply and demand. The more money they had the more they could spend. This would slowly start a chain reaction and bring the economy back to the way it was before the depression. By the end of the 1930's this plan had lowered unemployment to 17.2%. To make these organizations it was going to take money.

Roosevelt had to deficit spend, which is when the government spends more than their budget in one year, in order to obtain this money. Of course these ideas of supply

The National Recovery Agency (NRA) was declared unconstitutional by the Supreme Court in 1935 because it gave legislative powers to the executive branch of government. Do you think that the economic welfare of the country is more important than upholding the Constitution?

This cartoon from the 1930s shows General Hugh Johnson (1882–1942), head of the National Recovery Administration (NRA), with a kite representing the organization. Johnson also designed the symbol of the blue eagle and came up with the slogan "We do our part."

and demand and active government didn't just come to him. He was influenced by John Maynard Keynes and John Stuart Mill. Their philosophies were the basis of the New Deal. John Stuart Mill, who began studying economics at age 13, was one of the most influential political thinkers of the mid-Victorian period. He believed in empiricism and utilitarianism. Empiricism is the belief that legitimate knowledge comes only from experience. Utilitarianism is the belief by which things are judged right or wrong. It is judged according to their consequences. In a way he was a hypocrite. When the economy was good he believed in laissez-faire, which means "hands off." If the economy was bad, though, he believed in an extended role of government. This simply meant that the government should take part in the economy and try to make it better. The New Deal was a very active government plan because it had the government working directly to make jobs and fix the economy. Mill died in 1873 and would never had a chance to talk to Franklin D. Roosevelt.

"Laissez-faire" is a term used to describe an economy with no government regulation of business activity.

Influences on Roosevelt

The author quotes directly from Franklin D. Roosevelt. Does this make his argument more convincing?

In a press conference Franklin D. Roosevelt once said, "I brought down several books by English economists and leading American economists, I suppose I must have read different articles by fifteen different experts." This writing indirectly steered Roosevelt towards a plan which expanded the role of government. Mill gave Franklin D. Roosevelt the basis of the plan, but it needed to be elaborated on. John Maynard Keynes was the man to do this. John Maynard Keynes, one of the most influential economists of the 20th century. For many years he was an active voice in economics. In 1929 he wrote *We Can Conquer Unemployment* and in 1930 he wrote his *Treatise on Money*. Ten years before he died he wrote his *General Theory of Employment, Interest and Money*. Above all he believed in supply and demand. This was an indirect way to let the economy balance itself. In order for this system to work people needed money. This could only be done by creating jobs. Keynes also believed that to reduce unemployment the government needed to increase the aggregate demand. The aggregate demand is the total amount of goods being demanded. The government could do this by creating jobs. These jobs would provide people with money to spend on products. The ability to pay and the increase desire to spend would increase the demand for goods. The demand for goods would rise and the demand for workers would rise. This would slowly reduce the unemployment rate and put the economy back where it was before the crash of the stock market.

In Arthur M. Schlesinger Jr.'s book *The Politics of Upheaval* it's stated that Franklin D. Roosevelt and Keynes communicated on several occasions such as, letters, English tea meetings, and messages delivered via mutual friends. Although Franklin D. Roosevelt never publicly embraced Keynes' theories, and at times voiced disagreement with parts of his theories, there were many similarities between the works of the two men. Franklin D. Roosevelt took these philosophies and created the New Deal, which eventually brought the United States out of the Great Depression. John Stuart Mill gave Franklin D. Roosevelt the idea of an active government and John Maynard Keynes showed him how to do it. Although Franklin D. Roosevelt never really liked economists it appears that the work of many economists showed up in his New Deal. Although Mill did not directly influence FDR his philosophies were present in Franklin D. Roosevelt's plan. Also, Keynes theories were disagreed on time and time again by FDR, but in the end the New Deal was almost a perfect example of Keynes' theories.

John Stuart Mill (1806–1873) was a British philosopher, economist, and politician. Mill was prominent in the reforming age of the 19th century, when he wrote Principles of Political Economy *(1848). He believed in expanded government, the rights of the individual against the state, and in "the greatest happiness of the greatest number."*

Summary

Was the New Deal new? In the first article James T. Patterson argues that the legislation introduced by Franklin D. Roosevelt in the first half of the 1930s was not only new but was in fact a spontaneous and improvised reaction to the economic crisis facing the country. FDR did not propose a coherent program, he argues, but introduced a whole series of measures and new agencies, each aimed at fixing different parts of the problem. Taken as a whole, Patterson suggests, the New Deal legislation represented a new level of government involvement in welfare provision. It also revised ways to provide social security and established settled relations between labor, employers, and the government. This marked a new approach to government in the United States and also changed the political landscape, enabling the Democratic Party to emerge as a unified and powerful political force that was associated with urban working-class Americans.

The No article, written by studyworld.com for students, explores the roots of the New Deal in economic thought. Although the legislation seems ad hoc, it argues, in fact it reflected a coherent economic philosophy. This was based on accepted economic principles established by, among others, John Stuart Mill in the 19th century. While an economy was thriving, Mill argued, it should be left alone; when it got into trouble, it was the government's role to create jobs and stimulate economic activity. In the early 20th century, the article says, the British economist John Maynard Keynes became a strong advocate of similar government intervention. Keynes's thinking laid the groundwork for the New Deal.

FURTHER INFORMATION:

Books:

Allen, Frederick Lewis, *Since Yesterday: The 1930s in America, September 3, 1929–September 3, 1939*. New York: HarperCollins, 1986.

Badger, Anthony J., *The New Deal: The Depression Years, 1933–40*. Chicago, IL: Ivan R. Dee Inc., 2002.

Schlesinger Jr., Arthur Meier, *The Politics of Upheaval, The Age of Roosevelt*. New York: Houghton Mifflin, 1974.

Useful websites:

www.bergen.org/AAST/Projects/depression/
Successes and failures of the New Deal programs.

http://newdeal.feri.org/speeches/1933a.htm
Roosevelt's inaugural address March 4, 1933.

http://newdeal.feri.org/chat/chat02.htm
Roosevelt's fireside chats.

The following debates in the Pro/Con series may also be of interest:

In this volume:
Topic 9 Did Franklin D. Roosevelt provoke Pearl Harbor?

In *Economics*:
Topic 1 Is the free market the best form of economic organization?

Topic 5 Does government intervention do more harm than good?

WAS THE NEW DEAL "NEW"?

YES: Its various measures and agencies reflected similar goals and were based on common economic principles

YES: Job creation programs, deals with labor and employers, new government agencies, and social security legislation all reflected unprecedented government involvement

NEW DEAL
Was the New Deal ever a coherent program of legislation?

GOVERNMENT
Did the New Deal mark a new level of government involvement in the economy?

NO: The legislation of the New Deal was a mixture of ad hoc solutions to specific problems. FDR had no fixed economic principles.

NO: Many of the approaches FDR tried reflected those that had been tried in emergencies such as World War I. Herbert Hoover had begun to institute job creation programs in 1930 and 1931.

WAS THE NEW DEAL "NEW"? KEY POINTS

YES: It helped the United States avoid the political extremism that was the reaction to the Great Depression in many other countries

YES: Its provisions gave work to millions of Americans and helped them through the worst parts of the Great Depression

POLITICS
Did the New Deal reshape U.S. politics?

EFFECTIVE
Did the New Deal work?

NO: The liberalism that underlay the New Deal was effectively stopped by conservative forces in the Supreme Court and in Congress

NO: The provisions of the New Deal did not bring economic recovery to the United States; that only came with the outbreak of World War II

Topic 9
DID FRANKLIN D. ROOSEVELT PROVOKE PEARL HARBOR?

YES

FROM "FDR'S INFAMY: PEARL HARBOR, 60 YEARS LATER"
WWW.CHRONICLESMAGAZINE.ORG, FRIDAY, DECEMBER 7, 2001
SRDJA TRIFKOVIC

NO

FROM "PART V. CONCLUSIONS AND RECOMMENDATIONS"
REPORT OF THE JOINT COMMITTEE ON THE INVESTIGATION
OF THE PEARL HARBOR ATTACK, JULY 20, 1946

INTRODUCTION

On the morning of December 7, 1941, Japanese warplanes attacked the U.S. Pacific Fleet, moored in Pearl Harbor, Hawaii, wreaking devastation. Planes from six Japanese aircraft carriers sank or seriously damaged 18 of some 90 U.S. ships at anchor and destroyed or disabled 347 American planes. The casualties were horrific: 2,403 Americans died, and 1,178 more were wounded. The attack outraged the United States, and the next day President Franklin D. Roosevelt (1882-1945) declared war on Japan. Yet although Japan's assault on Pearl Harbor arrived unannounced, was it really unexpected, or did Roosevelt see it coming, even engineer it?

Supporters of the view that Roosevelt provoked the Pearl Harbor attack argue that the president wanted to bring the United States into World War II (1939-1945) against Hitler's Germany. At the time around 80 percent of the U.S. population opposed entry into

what was seen as primarily Europe's war. Roosevelt's critics argue that the president believed an attack on the United States would dramatically alter that opinion. Also, if war broke out between the United States and Japan, the latter's allies, Germany and Italy, would enter the conflict under the terms of the Tripartite Pact of September 1940, freeing the way for American involvement in Europe.

Subscribers to this "backdoor to war" theory interpret Roosevelt's actions from the fall of 1939 as a gradual buildup to war. They point to measures such as the approval of the country's first-ever peacetime draft in 1940 and the 1941 Lend–Lease Act, which enabled aid programs to U.S. allies, as evidence of the president's agenda.

According to this theory, Roosevelt's 1940 decision to transfer the U.S. Fleet from the West Coast of the United States to Pearl Harbor was made to provide Japan with a tempting target.

Likewise, the freezing of Japanese assets in the United States and the embargo on selling Japan oil, both imposed after Japan's July 1941 invasion of Indochina (modern Vietnam, Laos, and Cambodia), are viewed as acts of provocation.

"Yesterday, December 7, 1941, a date that will live in infamy—the United States of America was suddenly and deliberately attacked by naval and air forces of the Empire of Japan."

—FRANKLIN D. ROOSEVELT,

32ND PRESIDENT (1933–1945)

Not only did Roosevelt angle for a Japanese attack, so the argument goes, he also knew it was coming and failed to warn the military commanders in Hawaii. Allegedly the United States received many warnings via various channels that Japan was planning to strike at Pearl Harbor on December 7. Besides, U.S. intelligence had broken the Japanese diplomatic and navy codes and supposedly knew of the attack in advance from intercepted radio traffic.

Opponents of the "backdoor to war" theory argue that far from trying to provoke Japan, Roosevelt wanted to avoid war. According to this view, the president believed that conflict with Japan would restrict the quantity of war aid he could send to Britain and lengthen the war against Germany. As for the accusation that the fleet was transferred to Hawaii as a lure for the

Japanese, these commentators maintain that the presence of the fleet was more of a deterrent to a Japanese attack than an invitation. Not only that, they say, Roosevelt simply could not have sanctioned the level of losses suffered at Pearl Harbor. Critics retort that the sacrifice had to be large enough to make the United States seem beatable, otherwise Hitler might have gone back on the Tripartite Pact, and Roosevelt's scheme would have been in vain.

Those who reject the "backdoor to war" idea also refute the allegation that the president knew the precise details of the Japanese strike in advance. First, they ask, how much did the United States really know at the time? True, the Americans had broken the Japanese codes, but decryption carried a low priority in peacetime, and numerous critical signals may not have been decoded then and there. Second, the information that was available appeared, it is claimed, to indicate a Japanese attack farther south than Hawaii, perhaps on Singapore. In short, the U.S. government probably knew that an attack was coming around December 7, but only with hindsight was it possible to pinpoint where.

In the first of the two articles that follow, Srdja Trifkovic argues that Roosevelt did all he could, short of declaring war, to provoke Japan into attacking Pearl Harbor. Also, he alleges that the president made sure news of the impending strike was kept from his naval and army commanders in Hawaii, so the attack would be successful and turn U.S. opinion away from isolationism. The counterargument, an excerpt from the congressional report of 1946 on Pearl Harbor, concludes that the attack succeeded because of failures on the part of the American military.

FDR'S INFAMY: PEARL HARBOR, 60 YEARS LATER
Srdja Trifkovic

YES

✓ … Roosevelt knew that provoking Japan into war against the United States was just about the only option he had in 1941 to overcome the powerful America First non-interventionist movement led by Charles Lindbergh. Most Americans wanted nothing to do with "Europe's War," but their president was determined to force them into it. During the Atlantic Conference (August 14, 1941) FDR entered into an illegal and unconstitutional agreement with Churchill that America would go to war if Japan attacked British territory in the Far East. He said: "I may never declare war; I may make war. If I were to ask Congress to declare war they might argue about it for three months." This was an impeachable offense. He allowed undercover British agents to operate freely and illegally within the United States. After the Atlantic Conference Churchill noted the "astonishing depth of Roosevelt's intense desire for war."

The author uses quotations from key personalities—FDR (Franklin Delano Roosevelt) and British Prime Minister Winston Churchill—to reinforce his argument.

Systematic and deliberate provocation

Roosevelt systematically and deliberately provoked the Japanese into attacking the United States, but Japan was merely "collateral damage" in his grand design. His real target was Hitler. Roosevelt expected the German dictator to abide by the Tripartite Pact—the mutual assistance treaty signed by Germany, Italy, and Japan on September 27, 1940—and declare war on America if Japan were to attack it. He hoped that Hitler's decision would be facilitated by a display of America's apparent vulnerability in the initial Japanese attack. He was aware of the impending attack on Pearl Harbor, he let it happen and was relieved, even pleased, when it did.

Only a week after the signing of the Tripartite Pact, Lieutenant Commander Arthur McCollum, a U.S. Naval officer in the Office of Naval Intelligence (ONI), suggested a strategy to counter the U.S. isolationist movement by provoking Japan into attacking the U.S., triggering the mutual assistance provisions of the Tripartite Pact, and bringing America into World War II. Summarized in McCollum's now famous secret memo dated October 7, 1940, the ONI proposal called for

The McCollum Memo was declassified in 1994. Visit http://whatreally happened.com/ McCollum to read it.

eight provocations aimed at Japan. Its centerpiece was keeping the might of the U.S. Fleet based in Hawaii as a lure for a Japanese attack.

The evidence is circumstantial, of course, and … its more important elements proceed as follows:

1. In the summer of 1940 Roosevelt ordered the Pacific [Fleet] to relocate from the West Coast to Hawaii. When its commander, Admiral Richardson, protested that Pearl Harbor offered inadequate protection from air and torpedo attack he was replaced.

The Pacific Fleet transferred from San Diego, California, to Pearl Harbor in May 1940.

2. On October 7 1940 Navy IQ analyst McCollum wrote an eight-point memo for Roosevelt on how to force Japan into war with [the] U.S., including an American oil embargo against Japan. All of them were eventually accomplished.

3. On 23 June 1941—one day after Hitler's attack on Russia—Secretary of the Interior and FDR's Advisor Harold Ickes wrote a memo for the President in which he pointed out that "there might develop from the embargoing of oil to Japan such a situation as would make it not only possible but easy to get into this war in an effective way. And if we should thus indirectly be brought in, we would avoid the criticism that we had gone in as an ally of communistic Russia."

4. On 18 October Ickes noted in his diary: "For a long time I have believed that our best entrance into the war would be by way of Japan."

5. The U.S. had cracked key Japanese codes before the attack. At least 1,000 Japanese military and diplomatic radio messages per day were intercepted by monitoring stations operated by the U.S. and her Allies, and the message contents were summarized for the White House. The intercept summaries were clear: Pearl Harbor would be attacked on December 7, 1941, by Japanese forces advancing through the Central and North Pacific Oceans. Nevertheless, on November 27 and 28, 1941, Admiral Kimmel and General Short were ordered to remain in a defensive posture for "the United States desires that Japan commit the first overt act." The order came directly from President Roosevelt.

Admiral Husband E. Kimmel and Lieutenant General Walter Short were the military commanders in Hawaii at the time of the Pearl Harbor attack. To read more about them, see page 119.

6. FDR received "raw" translations of all key messages. On 24 September 1941 Washington deciphered a message from the Naval Intelligence HQ in Tokyo to Japan's consul-general in Honolulu, requesting grid [references] of exact locations of U.S. Navy ships in the harbor. Commanders in Hawaii were not warned. (Sixty years later the U.S. Government still refuses to identify or declassify many pre-attack decrypts on the grounds of "national security"!)

7. On November 25 Secretary of War Stimson wrote in his diary that FDR said an attack was likely within days, and asked "how we should maneuver them into the position of firing the first shot without too much danger to ourselves. In spite of the risk involved, however, in letting the Japanese fire the first shot, we realized that in order to have the full support of the American people it was desirable to make sure that the Japanese be the ones to do this so that there should remain no doubt in anyone's mind as to who were the aggressors."

8. On November 25 FDR received a "positive war warning" from Churchill that the Japanese would strike against America at the end of the first week in December. This warning caused the President to do an abrupt about-face on plans for a time-buying modus vivendi with Japan and it resulted in Secretary of State Hull's deliberately provocative ultimatum of 26 November 1941 that guaranteed war.

9. On November 25, 1941 Japan's Admiral Yamamoto sent a radio message to the group of Japanese warships that would attack Pearl Harbor on December 7. Newly released naval records prove that from November 17th to 25th, the United States Navy intercepted eighty-three messages that Yamamoto sent to his carriers. Part of the November 25 message read: "the task force, keeping its movements strictly secret and maintaining close guard against submarines and aircraft, shall advance into Hawaiian waters, and upon the very opening of hostilities shall attack the main force of the United States fleet in Hawaii and deal it a mortal blow."

10. On November 26 Washington ordered both US aircraft carriers, the *Enterprise* and the *Lexington*, out of Pearl Harbor "as soon as possible." This order included stripping Pearl of 50 planes or 40 percent of its already inadequate fighter protection. On the same day Cordell Hull issued his ultimatum demanding full Japanese withdrawal from Indochina and all China. U.S. Ambassador to Japan called this "The document that touched the button that started the war."

11. On November 29 Hull told United Press reporter Joe Leib that Pearl Harbor would be attacked on December 7. *The New York Times* reported on December 8 ("Attack Was Expected," p. 13) that the U.S. knew of the attack a week earlier.

12. On December 1 Office of Naval Intelligence, ONI, 12th Naval District in San Francisco found the missing Japanese fleet by correlating reports from the four wireless news services and several shipping companies that they were getting signals west of Hawaii.

Admiral Isoroku Yamamoto (1884–1943) was commander in chief of the Japanese combined fleet and the architect of the Pearl Harbor attack. He was shot down and killed on a visit to the Solomon Islands in 1943. The task force that attacked Pearl Harbor was under the command of Vice Admiral Chuichi Nagumo (1887–1944).

The author is referring to the "Outline of Proposed Basis for Agreement between the United States and Japan," handed to Japanese Ambassador Nomura on November 26, 1941. Go to www.ibiblio.org/pha/timeline/411126bpw.html to read the document.

13. On 5 December FDR wrote to the Australian Prime Minister, "There is always the Japanese to consider. Perhaps the next four or five days will decide the matters."

President unsurprised

Particularly indicative is Roosevelt's behavior on the day of the attack itself. Harry Hopkins, who was alone with FDR when he received the news, wrote that the President was unsurprised and expressed "great relief." Later in the afternoon Harry Hopkins wrote that the war cabinet conference "met in not too tense an atmosphere because I think that all of us believed that in the last analysis the enemy was Hitler … and that Japan had given us an opportunity." That same evening FDR said to his cabinet, "We have reason to believe that the Germans have told the Japanese that if Japan declares war, they will too. In other words, a declaration of war by Japan automatically brings …"—at which point he was interrupted, but his expectations were perfectly clear. CBS newsman Edward R. Murrow met Roosevelt at midnight and was surprised at FDR's calm reaction. The following morning Roosevelt stressed to his speechwriter Rosenman that "Hitler was still the first target, but he feared that a great many Americans would insist that we make the war in the Pacific at least equally important with the war against Hitler."…

Churchill later wrote that FDR and his top advisors "knew the full and immediate purpose of their enemy": "A Japanese attack upon the U.S. was a vast simplification of their problems and their duty. How can we wonder that they regarded the actual form of the attack, or even its scale, as incomparably less important than the fact that the whole American nation would be united?"

To summarize

Ever the pragmatist prepared to deploy immoral means in pursuit of what he believed to be a worthy end, President Franklin D. Roosevelt provoked Japan into an "overt act of war" directed at Hawaii. He had been told of Japan's military plans in advance but concealed [them] from the Hawaiian military commanders, Admiral Husband E. Kimmel and Lieutenant General Walter Short, so they would not interfere with the overt act. The real target, Adolf Hitler, duly walked into the trap on December 10, 1941, thus committing the greatest blunder of his career and ensuring Germany's eventual defeat.

The rest, as they say, is history.…

Harry L. Hopkins (1890–1946) held numerous posts under Roosevelt, including Secretary of Commerce. Although he no longer held an official title in December 1941, he was the president's trusted aide and had acted as his go-between with Churchill and Soviet leader Stalin.

Should the president's calmness be a cause of suspicion?

Do you agree with the author's view that the president was a "pragmatist" who would use "immoral means" to "a worthy end"? Can you find evidence of these attitudes elsewhere in Roosevelt's political career? Go to http://gi.grolier.com/presidents/aael.bios/32proos.html for background information on Roosevelt's political career.

CONCLUSIONS AND RECOMMENDATIONS
Report of the Joint Committee on the Investigation of the Pearl Harbor Attack

NO

1. The December 7, 1941, attack on Pearl Harbor was an unprovoked act of aggression by the Empire of Japan. The treacherous attack was planned and launched while Japanese ambassadors, instructed with characteristic duplicity, were carrying on the pretense [of] negotiations with the Government of the United States with a view to an amicable settlement of differences in the Pacific.

2. The ultimate responsibility for the attack and its results rests on Japan.... Contributing to the effectiveness of the attack was a powerful striking force, much more powerful than it had been thought the Japanese were able to employ in a single tactical venture at such distance and under such circumstances.

3. The diplomatic policies and actions of the United States provided no justifiable provocation whatever for the attack by Japan on this Nation. The Secretary of State fully informed both the War and Navy Departments of diplomatic developments and, in a timely and forceful manner, clearly pointed out to these Departments that relations between the United States and Japan had passed beyond the age of diplomacy and were in the hands of the military.

4. The committee has found no evidence to support the charges, made before and during the hearings, that the President, the Secretary of State, the Secretary of War, or the Secretary of Navy tricked, provoked, incited, cajoled, or coerced Japan into attacking this Nation in order that a declaration of war might be more easily obtained from the Congress. On the contrary, all evidence conclusively points to the fact that they discharged their responsibilities with distinction, ability, and foresight and in keeping with the highest traditions of our fundamental foreign policy.

5. The President, the Secretary of State, and high Government officials made every possible effort, without sacrificing our national honor and endangering our security, to avert war with Japan.

Organizing their conclusions numerically enables the authors to set out their case clearly and concisely.

Go to www.ibiblio.org/pha/pha/invest.html for more detailed information on the hearings.

COMMENTARY: Kimmel and Short

Husband E. Kimmel (1882–1968) and Walter C. Short (1880–1949) were respectively the naval and army commanders in Hawaii at the time of the Pearl Harbor attack on December 7, 1941. Both took up their posts in February 1941. Kimmel became commander in chief of the U.S. Fleet and commander in chief, U.S. Pacific Fleet, with a promotion from rear admiral to the rank of admiral. Short became commander of the U.S. Army Hawaiian Department, advancing from major general to lieutenant general.

In the wake of the Japanese assault on Hawaii Kimmel and Short were held largely to blame. On December 16 both officers were relieved of their commands and reduced to their former ranks. In late January 1942 the Roberts Commission, under Supreme Court Justice Owen J. Roberts, accused Kimmel and Short of dereliction of duty. Just over a month later Kimmel retired from the Navy and Short left the Army.

A further seven inquiries into the Pearl Harbor attack took place during the 1940s, among them a Naval Board of Inquiry and the Army Pearl Harbor Board. Both of these investigations reported in October 1944 and found that leading up to the attack, Kimmel and Short were deprived of key information regarding deteriorating relations with Japan and Japanese intentions. Then, in 1946 the Congressional Joint Committee on Pearl Harbor overturned the accusation of dereliction of duty (see page 120).

Since that charge was expunged from the records of Kimmel and Short, efforts have been under way to have the two officers restored to their pre-Pearl Harbor ranks as a matter of honor, so that they would appear as full admiral and lieutenant general on their respective services' retired lists. As recently as 2000 Congress requested that the president posthumously advance Kimmel and Short in rank, declaring that they performed their duties in Hawaii "competently and professionally" and that the losses suffered on December 7, 1941, "were not a result of dereliction in the performance of those duties."

Key military information

As for why the two commanders did not receive the key information, the jury is still out. In 1995 a report by Under Secretary of Defense Edwin Dorn into the reinstatement of Kimmel and Short found that although Japanese diplomatic intercepts were available to Army and Navy officials in Washington, "the evidence of the handling of these messages ... reveals some ineptitude, some unwarranted assumptions and misestimations, limited coordination, ambiguous language, and lack of clarification and follow-up at higher levels." Other people, though, suspect a more sinister reason—that key information was deliberately withheld from Kimmel and Short so that the Japanese attack on Pearl Harbor would succeed and bring the United States into World War II.

6. The disaster of Pearl Harbor was the failure, with attendant increase in personnel and material losses, of the Army and the Navy [to] institute measures designed to detect an approaching hostile force, to effect a state of readiness commensurate with the realization that war was at hand, and to employ every facility at their command in repelling the Japanese.

7. Virtually everyone was surprised that Japan struck the Fleet at Pearl Harbor at the time that she did. Yet officers, both in Washington and Hawaii, were fully conscious of the danger from air attack; they realized this form of attack on Pearl Harbor by Japan was at least a possibility; and they were adequately informed of the imminence of war.

8. Specifically, the Hawaiian commands failed—

(a) To discharge their responsibilities in the light of the warnings received from Washington, other information possessed by them, and the principle of command by mutual cooperation.

(b) To integrate and coordinate their facilities for defense and to alert properly the Army and Navy establishments in Hawaii particularly in the light of the warnings and intelligence available to them during the period November 27 to December 7, 1941.

(c) To effect liaison on a basis designed to acquaint each of them with the operations of the other, which was necessary to their joint security, and to exchange fully all significant intelligence.

(d) To maintain a more effective reconnaissance within the limits of their equipment.

(e) To effect a state of readiness throughout the Army and Navy establishments designed to meet all possible attacks.

(f) To employ the facilities, materiel, and personnel at their command, which were adequate at least to have greatly minimized the effects of the attack, in repelling the Japanese raiders.

(g) To appreciate the significance of intelligence and other information available to them.

9. The errors made by the Hawaiian commands were errors of judgment and not derelictions of duty.

10. The War Plans Division of the War Department failed to discharge its direct responsibility to advise the commanding general he had not properly alerted the Hawaiian Department when the latter, pursuant to instructions, had reported action taken in a message that was not satisfactorily responsive to the original directive.

"Command by mutual cooperation" requires commanders from different services to coordinate the actions of their forces to achieve a common goal while each remains in command of his or her force. The alternative system, unified command, places a supreme commander from one of the services in charge of all forces.

In 1941 the War Department handled the affairs of the Army and the Air Force. In 1947 it divided into the Department of the Army and the Department of the Air Force. The Navy had long had its own department.

11. The Intelligence and War Plans Divisions of the War and Navy Departments failed:

(a) To give careful and thoughtful consideration to the intercepted messages from Tokyo to Honolulu of September 24, November 15, and November 20 (the harbor berthing plan and related dispatches) and to raise a question as to their significance. Since they indicated a particular interest in the Pacific Fleet's base this intelligence should have been appreciated and supplied [to] the Hawaiian commanders for their assistance, along with other information available to them, in making their estimate of the situation.

(b) To be properly on the qui vive to receive the "one o'clock" intercept and to recognize in the message the fact that some Japanese military action would very possibly occur somewhere at 1 p. m., December 7. If properly appreciated, this intelligence should have suggested a dispatch to all Pacific outpost commanders supplying this information, as General Marshall attempted to do immediately upon seeing it.

12. Notwithstanding the fact that there were officers on twenty-four hour watch, the Committee believes that under all of the evidence the War and Navy Departments were not sufficiently alerted on December 6 and 7, 1941, in view of the imminence of war.…

> *The "one o'clock intercept" refers to a signal picked up by the Americans. It instructed Japan's ambassador to deliver his country's decision to break off negotiations with America to the U.S. Department of State at 1:00 P.M. Washington time on December 7. This time equated to 8:00 A.M. Hawaiian time. The air raid on Pearl Harbor began at 7:55 A.M.*

Summary

Srdja Trifkovic argues that President Franklin D. Roosevelt was "determined" to bring the United States into World War II against Germany. However, faced with massive public support for nonintervention, he could not do so without a pretext. Thus, Trifkovic alleges, Roosevelt deliberately provoked Japan into attacking the United States. Any American retaliation against Japan would automatically bring the United States and Germany into conflict because of the mutual assistance pact between Japan and Germany. According to Trifkovic, Roosevelt knew about the planned attack on Pearl Harbor and took no measures to prevent it. Indeed, he welcomed it. In evidence the author cites the fact that Japanese codes had been broken, messages indicating the date and location of the Japanese attack had been intercepted, and 40 percent of Pearl Harbor's fighter aircraft had been withdrawn. In conclusion he describes Roosevelt as being "prepared to deploy immoral means in pursuit of what he believed to be a worthy end."

In contrast, the congressional investigation into Pearl Harbor, the report of which was submitted in 1946, concluded that the attack was "an unprovoked act of aggression" by Japan, that U.S. "diplomatic policies and actions" were in no way responsible for provoking it, and that there was no evidence that President Roosevelt or his cabinet "tricked, provoked, incited, cajoled, or coerced Japan into attacking." The report concluded that responsibility for "the disaster of Pearl Harbor" rested not with the president but with the U.S. military commands in Hawaii, which failed to prepare for the attack despite being "adequately informed of the imminence of war," and with the War and Navy Departments, which failed to appreciate the significance of intercepted messages and pass on their contents to Hawaii.

FURTHER INFORMATION:

Books:

Prange, Gordon W., *At Dawn We Slept: The Untold Story of Pearl Harbor*. New York: Penguin, 2001.
Stinnett, Robert B., *Day of Deceit: The Truth about FDR and Pearl Harbor*. New York: Free Press, 2001.

Useful websites:

www.geocities.com/Pentagon/6315/pearl.html
Mother of All Conspiracies site, presenting detailed evidence that Roosevelt provoked Pearl Harbor.
www.history.navy.mil/faqs/faq66-1.htm
Naval Historic Center Pearl Harbor Attack site.
http://plasma.nationalgeographic.com/pearlharbor/
National Geographic Pearl Harbor site with links.

The following debates in the Pro/Con series may also be of interest:

In this volume:
 Topic 8 Was the New Deal "new"?

 Pearl Harbor timeline, pages 124–125

In *The Constitution*:
Topic 4 Should the president be able to lead the country into war?

DID FRANKLIN D. ROOSEVELT PROVOKE PEARL HARBOR?

YES: The freezing of Japanese assets and the imposition of trade embargoes, plus Secretary of State Hull's ultimatum, pushed Japan toward war

YES: Roosevelt needed to hand the Japanese a significant victory so that Hitler would believe the United States to be vulnerable and join the war on Japan's side

BACKDOOR TO WAR
Did Roosevelt use foreign policy to goad Japan into attacking?

SACRIFICE
Did Roosevelt transfer the fleet to Hawaii as a target for Japan?

NO: Roosevelt's actions were aimed at avoiding war with Japan, since it would hinder his aid plans to Britain and extend the war in Europe

NO: Roosevelt moved the fleet to Pearl Harbor as a deterrent. Besides, he could not have tolerated sacrificing so many personnel and ships.

DID FRANKLIN D. ROOSEVELT PROVOKE PEARL HARBOR?

KEY POINTS

YES: Evidence suggests that the president must have known from intercepted Japanese messages and other sources

YES: The commanders at Pearl Harbor were not given vital intelligence. For example, news of the imminent attack was sent by commercial telegram.

FOREWARNING
Did Roosevelt know the time and place of the Japanese attack?

INFORMATION
Was Pearl Harbor taken by surprise because it was denied information?

NO: It is not known how much traffic had been decoded. Roosevelt may have suspected an attack was coming but been ignorant of exactly when and where.

NO: The Hawaiian commands had received a "war warning" and were not at a high enough state of readiness

PEARL HARBOR TIMELINE

"Yesterday, December, 7, 1941—a date which will live in infamy—the United States of America was suddenly and deliberately attacked by naval and air forces of the Empire of Japan."

—FRANKLIN D. ROOSEVELT, PEARL HARBOR SPEECH, DECEMBER 8, 1941

Shortly before 8:00 on December 7, 1941, the Japanese launched a devastating attack on the U.S. naval base at Pearl Harbor on the Hawaiian island of Oahu. They did so without declaring war and while diplomatic negotiations were still taking place between the two countries. The talks concerned Japan's invasion of China and its territorial ambitions in Southeast Asia as part of its plan to establish a so-called "Greater East Asia Co-Prosperity Sphere." The attack on Pearl Harbor resulted in the entry of the United States into World War II (1939–1945).

1937 July: The Japanese army invades North China. The United States condemns the action. **December:** Japanese aircraft attack the gunboat USS *Panay* in Chinese waters. It is unclear whether the incident is an accident. Japan apologizes.

1939 February 10: Japan occupies the Chinese island of Hainan, a strategic site for the control of supply lines. **September 1:** Germany invades Poland. **3:** Britain, France, Australia, and New Zealand declare war on Germany. **5:** The United States proclaims neutrality. **10:** Canada declares war on Germany. The Battle of the Atlantic begins.

1940 spring: The U.S. Pacific fleet makes Pearl Harbor, on the Hawaiian island of Oahu, its permanent base. The Japanese view this as a threat. **July:** Roosevelt places an embargo on all aviation fuel, steel, and scrap-iron exports to Japan. **August:** Experts working in intelligence operation "Magic" break the Japanese diplomatic code. **September 4:** The United States warns Japan against attacking French Indochina. **September 27:** Japan joins the Tripartite Pact with Germany and Italy.

1941 January 7: In secret talks with Britain the United States decides that if Japan supports Nazi Germany, and the United States enters the war, Germany is to be defeated before Japan. **27:** The U.S. ambassador to Japan, Joseph C. Grew, wires Washington, D.C., that Japan is planning an attack on Pearl Harbor if U.S–Japanese relations break down, but most U.S. officials believe that Japan will attack the Philippines first. **March 11:** Congress passes the Lend–Lease Act, which supplies material to governments fighting the Axis powers. **April 13:** Japan signs a five-year neutrality pact with the Soviet Union, which enables Japan to concentrate on its southward expansion, its northern flank secure. **May:** Kichisaburo Nomura, the Japanese ambassador in Washington, D.C., informs his superiors that Americans are reading Japanese coded messages. His superiors do not believe him and take no action.

May 27: Roosevelt declares the United States to be in an unlimited state of national emergency. **July 2:** Japan decides to continue its expansion southeastward, even if it means war with the United States and Britain. **21:** Vichy France permits Japan to occupy French Indochina. **28:** Roosevelt places an embargo on oil sales, freezes assets, and closes ports to Japanese vessels. **November:** Japanese diplomats attempt to secure U.S. agreement for the empire's southern expansion. If unsuccessful, they are ready to go to war. **5:** Isoroku Yamamoto, commander in chief of the Imperial Japanese Navy, issues Top Secret Order No.1, which details the attack on Pearl Harbor. **10:** Britain states that it will declare war on Japan should Japan attack the United States. **26:** U.S. Secretary of State Cordell Hull informs Nomura that the United States requires the Japanese to withdraw from China and Indo-China. A Japanese fleet under Vice-Admiral Nagumo Chuichi leaves the Kurile Islands for Hawaii. It includes six aircraft carriers, two battleships, three cruisers, and eleven destroyers. The fleet maintains radio silence and takes a northerly route to avoid detection. **27:** The U.S. Navy alerts its commanders in the Pacific to an imminent Japanese attack. **December 1:** Leaders at an imperial conference in Tokyo decide that Japan should go to war against the United States, Britain, and the Netherlands. **6:** Japan sends a 14-part coded message to Nomura in Washington, D.C., breaking off negotiations with the United States; it is intercepted by U.S. intelligence, which decodes it and passes it to Roosevelt.

December 7 07:20: The last part of the decoded message reaches Roosevelt. It indicates an imminent Japanese attack. A warning is relayed to U.S. bases; a delay in communications means that headquarters at Oahu does not receive the release until noon, after the attack has begun. **08:50:** A further communication from Tokyo to Nomura is intercepted. It orders him to submit the 14-part plan to Hull by 13:00. **06:00 Hawaiian time** (11:30 Washington time): The first wave of 183 Japanese planes takes off from carriers located 275 miles north of Oahu. They head in the direction of Pearl Harbor. **07:02:** Two army operators at Oahu's northern shore radar station detect aircraft approaching. A junior officer disregards the information—the aircraft are assumed to be 12 U.S. planes due to arrive from San Francisco. **07:15:** The second wave of 167 Japanese planes takes off. Since it is Sunday morning, many U.S. servicemen are ashore or relaxing. The U.S. fleet docked in Pearl Harbor comprises 70 combat vessels and 24 auxiliaries, including 8 battleships, 2 heavy cruisers, 6 light cruisers, 29 destroyers, and 5 submarines—the three aircraft carriers attached to the Pacific Fleet are not in port. **07:53:** Flight commander Mitsuo Fuchida sounds the battle cry "Tora! Tora! Tora!" ("Tiger, Tiger, Tiger"), and the first Japanese assault begins: 40 torpedo bombers, 50 high-level bombers, and 43 Zero fighters take part. Simultaneous attacks are made on air bases at Hickam, Wheeler, Ford Island, Kaneohe, and Ewa Fields to neutralize U.S. air power. **08:20:** The battleship USS *Arizona* is torpedoed and sinks; more than 1,100 service men are killed. U.S. forces mount antiaircraft fire and manage to get some 38 planes airborne. **08:50:** Nomura delivers the war message to Hull. **09:15:** The second strike force of Japanese planes arrives. **09:45:** The bombing raid ceases. Four U.S. battleships have been sunk and four more damaged. Three light cruisers, three destroyers, and three smaller vessels have been lost, along with 188 aircraft. Total U.S. military casualties amount to more than 3,400, with more than 2,300 killed. The Japanese lose 29 aircraft, 5 midget submarines, and about 100 airmen.

December 8: The United States and Britain declare war on Japan.

Topic 10
WAS IT NECESSARY TO DROP THE ATOMIC BOMB?

YES

FROM "IF THE ATOMIC BOMB HAD NOT BEEN USED"
THE ATLANTIC MONTHLY, DECEMBER 1946
KARL T. COMPTON

NO

"WAS HIROSHIMA NECESSARY TO END THE WAR?"
50 YEARS SINCE THE BOMB: A PACKET FOR LOCAL ORGANIZERS
GAR ALPEROVITZ

INTRODUCTION

On August 6, 1945, *Enola Gay*, a lone U.S. B-29 bomber, dropped a single atomic bomb over the Japanese city of Hiroshima. The weapon was the most destructive ever used, with a force equivalent to that of 15 kilotons of conventional explosives. The explosion and consequent fireball devastated 4 square miles of the city; around 66,000 people died instantly, nearly a fifth of the population. Some 69,000 more were injured; many later died of severe burns and the effects of radiation sickness.

Three days after the Hiroshima attack a second nuclear bomb was dropped on the city of Nagasaki. This bomb was even more powerful— equivalent to 21 kilotons of TNT—but its effects were limited by the city's geography. Some 39,000 people died, with 25,000 injured.

The two nuclear weapons remain the only ones ever to have been detonated in conflict. While some people believe that the power of the atom bomb made

the world a safer place by making war almost inconceivably damaging, others think that its very existence makes the world a more dangerous place.

The decision of President Harry S. Truman to use the weapon has remained the subject of controversy ever since. The main point of the debate has been whether it was necessary to use the atom bombs.

By August 1945 U.S. forces had seized islands within bombing range of the Japanese homeland. The Navy and Air Force were strangling Japan's supply routes. Japan could no longer win the war it had started at Pearl Harbor in December 1941. What was not known, however, was what it would take to defeat Japan. Experience in the Pacific had suggested that the Japanese would fight on rather than surrender, even in the face of certain defeat. U.S. military planners forecast that an invasion of the Japanese homeland—the ultimate aim of U.S. strategy in the Pacific—would be costly in terms of both U.S. troops and Japanese military and civilian defenders. Truman in his memoirs later estimated that the use of the bomb had possibly saved up to half a million potential U.S. casualties in an invasion of Japan.

The accepted view of Truman and many others since was that the atom bomb was the best way of shortening a costly war by showing the Japanese the futility of fighting on in the face of overwhelming power. The bomb was built to be used, they say, in the same way that other more conventional weapons had been used in the war. In U.S. raids on the Japanese capital, Tokyo, in March 1945 incendiary bombs had started fires that killed about 100,000 people and left a million as refugees. The atom bomb, for all its power, was no more or less moral than any other weapon in a conflict in which all sides considered civilians as legitimate targets.

"I am become death, the destroyer of worlds."

—J. ROBERT OPPENHEIMER, ON SEEING THE TEST OF THE FIRST ATOMIC BOMB, JULY 16, 1945

The so-called Revisionists question this official policy. Japan was already defeated, they argue, so the use of the atom bomb was unnecessary. The Japanese had made peace overtures to the Americans via the Russians, but the Americans had failed to respond because the Japanese had not offered the unconditional surrender demanded by the Americans.

Even in such circumstances U.S. troops would not have needed to risk a costly invasion of Japan. Time and the blockade of Japan would have eventually achieved surrender without the civilian casualties of the atom bombs. The Revisionists point to support for their theory from many of the U.S. military and political personnel at the time, including General Douglas MacArthur and former President Herbert Hoover. Even some of the scientists who had built the bomb were against its use. It had been developed to defeat Germany, they argued, which might have produced its own atomic weapon. But Germany had surrendered in May 1945, and Japan had no prospect of developing a similar weapon itself.

Revisionists look for further motives for Truman's support for the bomb. They argue that the bomb's secret development by the Manhattan Project had cost so much money that the government felt that it had to be used. They also suggest that Truman was more interested in demonstrating U.S. power not to Japan, which was already defeated, but to the Soviet Union. The end of the war in Europe left Russia in command of the countries of the east of the continent. The lines of the Cold War were already being drawn up between the U.S. and the Soviets.

The articles that follow sum up both sides of the debate. In the Yes article physicist Karl T. Compton, writing in 1946, argues that the bomb saved many American lives. Gar Alperovitz, writing for local organizers of the antiwar War Resisters League, however, explores the idea that the Japanese were already defeated and that an invasion of Japan was unnecessary. He suggests that Truman had other motives for his momentous decision.

IF THE ATOMIC BOMB HAD NOT BEEN USED
Karl T. Compton

Karl T. Compton (1887–1954) was an American physicist who directed the scientific team that developed the first nuclear reactor between 1942 and 1945. This is extracted from an essay published in The Atlantic Monthly in December 1946—see pages 216–217 for the full citation.

To make his case for the use of the atomic bomb, the author compares the losses suffered because of the atomic bombs and those in conventional bombing raids. Is he convincing?

The author asks a question and supplies the answers from different points of view. This is a good way of sticking to the argument.

YES

... I believe, with complete conviction, that the use of the atomic bomb saved hundreds of thousands—perhaps several millions—of lives, both American and Japanese; that without its use the war would have continued for many months; that no one of good conscience knowing, as Secretary Stimson and the Chiefs of Staff did, what was probably ahead and what the atomic bomb might accomplish could have made any different decision. Let some of the facts speak for themselves.

Was the use of the atomic bomb inhuman? All war is inhuman. Here are some comparisons of the atomic bombing with conventional bombing. At Hiroshima the atomic bomb killed about 80,000 people, pulverized about five square miles, and wrecked an additional ten square miles of the city, with decreasing damage out to seven or eight miles from the center. At Nagasaki the fatal casualties were 45,000 and the area wrecked was considerably smaller than at Hiroshima because of the configuration of the city.

Compare this with the results of two B-29 incendiary raids over Tokyo. One of these raids killed about 125,000 people, the other nearly 100,000.

Of the 210 square miles of greater Tokyo, 85 square miles of the densest part was destroyed as completely, for all practical purposes, as were the centers of Hiroshima and Nagasaki; about half the buildings were destroyed in the remaining 125 square miles; the number of people driven homeless out of Tokyo was considerably larger than the population of greater Chicago. These figures are based on information given us in Tokyo and on a detailed study of the air reconnaissance maps. They may be somewhat in error but are certainly of the right order of magnitude.

Was Japan already beaten before the atomic bomb? The answer is certainly "yes" in the sense that the fortunes of war had turned against her. The answer is "no" in the sense that she was still fighting desperately and there was every reason to believe that she would continue to do so; and this is the only answer that has any practical significance.

General MacArthur's staff anticipated about 50,000 American casualties and several times that number of Japanese casualties in the November 1 operation to establish the initial beachheads on Kyushu. After that they expected a far more costly struggle before the Japanese homeland was subdued. There was every reason to think that the Japanese would defend their homeland with even greater fanaticism than when they fought to the death on Iwo Jima and Okinawa. No American soldier who survived the bloody struggles on these islands has much sympathy with the view that battle with the Japanese was over as soon as it was clear that their ultimate situation was hopeless. No, there was every reason to expect a terrible struggle long after the point at which some people can now look back and say, "Japan was already beaten."

A month after our occupation I heard General MacArthur say that even then, if the Japanese government lost control over its people and the millions of former Japanese soldiers took to guerrilla warfare in the mountains, it could take a million American troops ten years to master the situation.

Lieutenant General Kuribayashi was the Japanese commander at Iwo Jima (February 1945). The Japanese strategy at Iwo Jima was unique for three reasons: 1. The Japanese fought the battle entirely from beneath the ground. They dug 1,500 rooms into the rock, connected by 16 miles of tunnels. 2. The strategy called for "no Japanese survivors." They planned not to survive. 3. The strategy was for each soldier to kill ten American soldiers before they themselves were killed.

The Japanese surrender

That this was not an impossibility is shown by the following fact, which I have not seen reported. We recall the long period of nearly three weeks between the Japanese offer to surrender and the actual surrender on September 2. This was needed in order to arrange details: of the surrender and occupation and to permit the Japanese government to prepare its people to accept the capitulation. It is not generally realized that there was threat of a revolt against the government, led by an Army group supported by the peasants, to seize control and continue the war. For several days it was touch and go as to whether the people would follow their government in surrender.

The bulk of the Japanese people did not consider themselves beaten; in fact they believed they were winning in spite of the terrible punishment they had taken. They watched the paper balloons take off and float eastward in the wind, confident that these were carrying a terrible retribution to the United States in revenge for our air raids.

We gained a vivid insight into the state of knowledge and morale of the ordinary Japanese soldier from a young private who had served through the war in the Japanese Army. He had lived since babyhood in America, and had graduated in 1940 from Massachusetts Institute of Technology. This lad, thoroughly American in outlook, had gone with his family to

Between November 1944 and April 1945 the Japanese launched some 9,000 balloon bombs to attack the United States. Made from paper and rubberized silk, they carried antipersonnel and incendiary bombs. Experts estimate that about 1,000 balloon bombs reached the United States, although only about 285 were reported.

The battle of Iwo Jima, a strategically important island 700 miles from mainland Japan, took place in February 1945. The 36-day assault resulted in the loss of approximately 19,000 Japanese military personnel. The battle of Okinawa saw the bloodiest fighting in the Pacific. The 86-day campaign, which began in April 1945, resulted in severe losses on both sides. The Japanese lost around 100,000 men, with a further 7,000 captured.

visit relatives shortly after his graduation. They were caught in the mobilization and he was drafted into the Army.

This young Japanese told us that all his fellow soldiers believed that Japan was winning the war. To them the losses of Iwo Jima and Okinawa were parts of a grand strategy to lure the American forces closer and closer to the homeland, until they could be pounced upon and utterly annihilated. He himself had come to have some doubts as a result of various inconsistencies in official reports. Also he had seen the Ford assembly line in operation and knew that Japan could not match America in war production. But none of the soldiers had any inkling of the true situation until one night, at ten-thirty, his regiment was called to hear the reading of the surrender proclamation.

Did the atomic bomb bring about the end of the war? That it would do so was the calculated gamble and hope of Mr. Stimson, General Marshall, and their associates. The facts are these. On July 26, 1945, the Potsdam Ultimatum called on Japan to surrender unconditionally. On July 29 Premier Suzuki issued a statement, purportedly at a cabinet press conference, scorning as unworthy of official notice the surrender ultimatum, and emphasizing the increasing rate of Japanese aircraft production. Eight days later, on August 6, the first atomic bomb was dropped on Hiroshima; the second was dropped on August 9 on Nagasaki; on the following day, August 10, Japan declared its intention to surrender, and on August 14 accepted the Potsdam terms.

On the basis of these facts, I cannot believe that, without the atomic bomb, the surrender would have come without a great deal more of costly struggle and bloodshed.

The role of the atomic bomb

Compton concedes that vital information remains unknowable. Does that make the whole debate irrelevant?

Exactly what role the atomic bomb played will always allow some scope for conjecture. A survey has shown that it did not have much immediate effect on the common people far from the two bombed cities; they knew little or nothing of it. The even more disastrous conventional bombing of Tokyo and other cities had not brought the people into the mood to surrender.

The evidence points to a combination of factors.
1) Some of the more informed and intelligent elements in Japanese official circles realized that they were fighting a losing battle and that complete destruction lay ahead if the war continued. These elements, however, were not powerful enough to sway the situation against the dominating Army organization, backed by the profiteering industrialists, the

peasants, and the ignorant masses. 2) The atomic bomb introduced a dramatic new element into the situation, which strengthened the hands of those who sought peace and provided a face-saving argument for those who had hitherto advocated continued war. 3) When the second atomic bomb was dropped, it became clear that this was not an isolated weapon, but that there were others to follow. With dread prospect of a deluge of these terrible bombs and no possibility of preventing them, the argument for surrender was made convincing. This I believe to be the true picture of the effect of the atomic bomb in bringing the war to a sudden end, with Japan's unconditional surrender.

The author claims that dropping the second atomic bomb ensured the Japanese surrender by showing that the bomb dropped on Hiroshima was not a fluke. Do you agree?

If the atomic bomb had not been used, evidence like that I have cited points to the practical certainty that there would have been many more months of death and destruction on an enormous scale. Also the early timing of its use was fortunate for a reason which could not have been anticipated. If the invasion plans had proceeded as scheduled, October, 1945, would have seen Okinawa covered with airplanes and its harbors crowded with landing craft poised for the attack. The typhoon which struck Okinawa in that month would have wrecked the invasion plans with a military disaster comparable to Pearl Harbor.

The facts

These are some of the facts which lead those who know them, and especially those who had to base decisions on them, to feel that there is much delusion and wishful thinking among those after-the-event strategists who now deplore the use of the atomic bomb on the ground that its use was inhuman or that it was unnecessary because Japan was already beaten. And it was not one atomic bomb, or two, which brought surrender; it was the experience of what an atomic bomb will actually do to a community, plus the dread of many more, that was effective.

If 500 bombers could wreak such destruction on Tokyo, what will 500 bombers, each carrying an atomic bomb, do to the City of Tomorrow? It is this deadly prospect which now lends such force to the two basic policies of our nation on this subject: 1) We must strive generously and with all our ability to promote the United Nations' effort to assure future peace between nations; but we must not lightly surrender the atomic bomb as a means for our own defense. 2) We should surrender or share it only when there is adopted an international plan to enforce peace in which we can have great confidence.

It is the fear of further atomic bombs, the author argues, that is a real deterrent and will assure future peace. Is this view persuasive?

WAS HIROSHIMA NECESSARY TO END THE WAR?
Gar Alperovitz

NO

"It is my opinion that the use of this barbarous weapon at Hiroshima and Nagasaki was of no material assistance in our war against Japan. The Japanese were almost defeated and ready to surrender...in being the first to use it, we...adopted an ethical standard common to the barbarians of the Dark Ages."

—*Fleet Admiral William D. Leahy, Chair of the Joint Chiefs of Staff during World War II*

> Using a quotation from a senior military figure lends great authority to the author's argument.

There is a widespread belief among Americans, particularly soldiers who were serving in the Pacific Theatre in the summer of 1945, that an invasion of Japan would cost as many as a million American lives, and the use of the atomic bomb at Hiroshima and Nagasaki brought the war to an end, with enormous saving of lives, both Japanese and American.

The reality is that in the months just prior to the August bombings, most of Japanese shipping, rail transport, and industrial production had been wiped out by an extraordinary series of air attacks. (More people died in one night in the fire bombing of Tokyo than died in the bombing of Hiroshima.) Millions were homeless. By July of 1945 both the Japanese and American military knew the war was lost.

Yet the myth persists that the use of nuclear weapons was necessary—Ted Koppel repeated it in a Nightline broadcast—that "What happened over Japan...was a human tragedy...But what was planned to take place in the war between Japan and the United States would almost certainly have been an even greater tragedy."

> The author states that if it was unnecessary to use atomic bombs, then the United States was guilty of committing war crimes. Is anything acceptable in a just war?

War crimes

The question of whether use of the bomb was necessary haunts us because if the bombs were not necessary they were war crimes, something painful for Americans to consider. It is true that by the end of World War II the lines between waging war and simply killing people in large

Captain Paul W. Tibbets waves from the cockpit of the Enola Gay, the B-29 SuperFortress that dropped the first atomic bomb on the Japanese city of Hiroshima on August 6, 1945.

The allied bombing of the medieval German city of Dresden during World War II (1939–1945) remains extremely controversial. Many people believed that the city had little strategic importance during the war and was therefore not a legitimate target. Over three days (February 13–15, 1945) incendiary bombs were dropped on the city creating firestorms. Dresden was almost completely destroyed; the number of victims has never been established but has been estimated at between 135,000 and 250,000—more than the immediate deaths following the dropping of the bomb on Hiroshima. The attack was ordered by British Air Marshall Arthur Harris, but he was never held accountable for breaches of the Geneva Conventions or for war crimes.

numbers had been largely erased. The earlier strategy of air attacks had been to pinpoint strategic targets, but in Europe, by early 1945 the air attacks had assumed a different character—as if whatever sense of moral restraint had existed when the war began had vanished. The bombing of Dresden was not a military target. The fire bombing of that city created a fire storm resulting in a terrible loss of civilian life. What was the real situation regarding Japan? The Japanese were concerned about whether the Emperor would be able to remain on his throne if they surrendered. As a result of the air attacks, and their steady isolation by U.S. sea power, the Japanese military were aware the war could not be won. In 1946 the official U.S. Strategic Bombing Survey concluded:

Certainly prior to 31 December 1945, and in all probability prior to 1 November 1945, Japan would have surrendered even if the atomic bombs had not been dropped, even if Russia had not entered the war, and even if no invasion had been planned or contemplated.

Not known to the general public until after the war, Japan had begun to put out feelers about surrender by May of 1945. On May 12, 1945, William Donovan, Director of the Office of Strategic Services (which later became the CIA) reported to President Truman that Shinichi Kase, Japan's minister to Switzerland, wished "to help arrange for a cessation of hostilities." He believed one of the few provisions the Japanese would "insist upon would be the retention of the Emperor." A similar report reached Truman from Masutaro Inoue, a Japanese official in Portugal. In mid-June Admiral William D. Leahy concluded that "a surrender of Japan can be arranged with terms that can be accepted by Japan and that will make fully satisfactory provision for America's defense against future trans-Pacific aggression."

Japanese request for peace

Meanwhile, the U.S. learned through intercepted diplomatic cables (the U.S. had broken Japanese codes early in the war) that the emperor of Japan wished to send Prince Konoye to Moscow as his personal representative to "ask the Soviet Government to take part in mediation to end the present war and to transmit the complete Japanese case in this respect." In President Truman's handwritten journal, only released in 1979, he noted in July of 1945 that Stalin had reported "a telegram from Jap Emperor asking for peace."

The most generous explanation would be that Truman did not fully understand what the atomic bomb would do, that he saw it as simply "another weapon". However, his military advisers knew it was in a different category. Even those favouring its use urged that it be used against a clearly military target with advance warning to civilians to leave the area. It is also possible that, being a politician, Truman wanted to justify the huge expense of the special crash program to develop the bomb—using it would prove to taxpayers that their funds had been well spent.

The cost of the development of the atomic bomb has been estimated at two billion dollars. Was that value for money?

Opening shots of the Cold War

Historians now tend to believe that there was another explanation, which was that Hiroshima and Nagasaki were the opening shots fired in the Cold War. The Soviet Union did not fully convey to Truman the Japanese interest in surrender—because the Soviets wanted to enter the war and secure a place at the bargaining table. (Keep in mind that technically the Soviet Union remained an ally of Japan throughout World War II, and no state of war existed between them. The Soviets actually declared war on Japan August 8th, two days after the first atomic bomb was exploded.)

The Soviet Union was the United States's enemy during the Cold War. Might that affect this suspicion of Soviet motives?

The United States, acting on the advice of conservative political advisers—not on the advice of its military leaders—dropped the first atomic bomb without responding to any of the Japanese peace feelers. Then, three days later, and after the Soviet entry in the war had made immediate Japanese surrender inevitable, the second bomb was dropped on Nagasaki. The first bomb was dropped after Japan had already begun the process of seeking the terms of surrender. The second bomb was dropped when it was clear no U.S. invasion of the Japanese home islands was needed. Are crimes of war only those actions committed by the nation which committed aggression? Was it not a crime to use the nuclear bomb without exploring the Japanese peace feelers? Fifty years will have passed this August 6, 1995, and the question remains why anyone still believes the use of the nuclear bomb was necessary. Opposing evidence is overwhelming. It is as if, to shield ourselves from knowledge of what we did, we refuse to examine the history of that period.

Fifty years after the event, at a time of peace, is it really possible to judge the attitudes of people who had been engaged in war for three and a half years?

Crimes committed without consultation

In closing it must be noted that neither the U.S. Congress nor the general public was even aware that a nuclear weapon was being developed, let alone that it would be used. As happens in war, morality vanished, secrecy prevailed, and great crimes were committed without consultation.

Summary

Writing in *The Atlantic Monthly*, Karl T. Compton argues that the atom bomb was no more inhuman than other forms of "conventional" bombing. He agrees that Japan was in effect defeated, but argues that the Japanese themselves were likely to fight on. He notes that even General Douglas MacArthur, an outspoken critic of the decision to drop the bomb, acknowledged a worst-case scenario in which the occupation of Japan would take a million U.S. troops up to ten years. He reports interviewing a young Japanese soldier at the end of the war who remained convinced that Japan would be victorious until the final surrender. Compton argues that the evidence of the first, and especially the second, atom bomb gave new force to the arguments of those Japanese who were ready to surrender in their power struggle with Japan's military hawks. Finally, he says that without the bombs the United States would have launched a costly invasion of Japan in October 1945.

The War Resisters' League use extracts compiled from the author Gar Alperovitz, president of the National Center for Economic Alternatives, to argue that the United States knew by July 1945 that the Japanese were defeated. It quotes the opinion of military leaders such as Fleet Admiral William D. Leahy, chair of the Joint Chiefs of Staff during World War II, that the atomic bomb was unnecessary. It reports evidence of Japanese peace overtures to the United States and argues that the decision to drop the bomb was based on political, not military, arguments. President Harry S. Truman, it says, had to justify the cost of building the bomb by using it and was also eager to demonstrate the military might of the United States to the Soviet Union at the start of the Cold War.

FURTHER INFORMATION:

 Books:

Alperovitz, Gar, *The Decision to Use the Atomic Bomb and the Architecture of an American Myth*. New York: Knopf, 1995.

Bird, Kai, and Lawrence Lifschultz (eds.), *Hiroshima's Shadow*. Stony Creek, CT: Pamphleteers Press, 1998.

Maddox, Robert James, *Weapons for Victory: The Hiroshima Decision Fifty Years Later*. Columbia, MO: University of Missouri Press, 1995.

Newman, Robert P., *Truman and the Hiroshima Cult*. East Lansing. MI: Michigan State University Press, 1995.

Wainstock, Dennis D., *The Decision to Drop the Atomic Bomb*. Westport, CT: Praeger, 1996.

Walker, J. Samuel, *Prompt and Utter Destruction: Truman and the Use of Atomic bombs against Japan*. Chapel Hill, NC: University of North Carolina Press, 1997.

 Useful websites:

www.atomicmuseum.com/tour/manhattanproject.cfm
The National Atomic Museum.
www.trumanlibrary.org
Information on the decision to drop the atomic bomb.

The following debates in the Pro/Con series may also be of interest:

In this volume:
Topic 9 Did Franklin D. Roosevelt provoke Pearl Harbor?

WAS IT NECESSARY TO DROP THE ATOMIC BOMB?

YES: Conventional bombing raids had devastated Japan's infrastructure, and the U.S. blockade was strangling its supply routes. Surrender was only a matter of time.

YES: President Truman had to justify the cost of developing the bomb; he was also eager to show the USSR America's power

DEFEAT
Was Japan already defeated by August 1945?

POLITICAL
Was the decision to drop the atomic bomb more political than military?

NO: Despite the fact that the tide of war had turned against them, the Japanese were prepared to fight to the death to defend their homeland

WAS IT NECESSARY TO DROP THE ATOMIC BOMB?

KEY POINTS

NO: Although some military leaders were against using the bomb, many others believed it far preferable to the planned invasion of Japan, which might have cost hundreds of thousands of lives

YES: The destructive power of the bomb meant that many nations rushed to develop their own atomic weapons. The result was a proliferation of weapons of mass destruction.

YES: It was a weapon of war, like other weapons of war. By 1945 all sides accepted that civilian casualties were an inevitable part of the war.

ATOMIC AGE
Did dropping the atomic bomb make the world a more dangerous place?

MORALITY
Was dropping the bomb morally justifiable?

NO: The devastation caused by the bombs ensured that for another 50 years nations refrained from major conflicts, knowing the destruction they could suffer

NO: No other weapon inflicted such huge devastation on the civilian population; all attacks on civilians are immoral

PART 3
AFTER 1945

The most recent period in U.S. history examined in this volumes dates from the end of World War II (1939-1945) to the terrorist attacks on New York City and Washington, D.C., on September 11, 2001. Many of the key events of this time happened within living memory, and some, such as 9/11, were watched by millions across the world as they occurred. These factors give students a different perspective since it is impossible to possess the same degree of distance or hindsight as when examining earlier events.

Superpowers and Cold War

In the period following World War II the United States quickly emerged as an economic and political superpower. Its relationship with the Soviet Union, another superpower, also deteriorated. Between 1947 and 1989 both nations fought for supremacy in a period known as the Cold War.

The United States considered the international spread of communism promoted by the Soviet Union as one of the biggest problems faced by the international community. It directed much of its foreign policy toward eliminating the influence of communism and to this end became involved in conflicts abroad, such as those that took place in Korea (1950-1953) and in Vietnam (1955-1977), among others. Some people view the space race between the United States,

the Soviet Union, and China as another dimension of the Cold War.

International opinion was divided over U.S. involvement in these overseas campaigns. The country was praised by some for championing democracy but also criticized for interfering in the affairs of foreign nation states—sometimes, it seemed, for economic rather than democratic reasons. At home critics argued that the billions of dollars expended on foreign military action would be better spent on domestic policies. Governments were also criticized for sacrificing millions of young American men and women for reasons that appeared to have no direct relevance to the United States. These arguments have emerged again in recent years, particularly with regard to the U.S. military action against Afghanistan (2001) and Iraq (2003).

The "Red Scare"

Domestic policy of the 1950s, in line with foreign policy, was directed at routing out suspected communists. The government believed that the nation was threatened by communism, and it investigated people from all walks of life—politicians, writers, actors, and teachers—suspected of communist connections. The arrest in 1950 of the German-born physicist Klaus Fuchs (1911-1988), who had worked on the Manhattan Project to develop the atomic bomb, and his subsequent confession that he had leaked information to the Soviet Union fueled the fight against communism spearheaded by Senator Joseph McCarthy (1908–1957). Evidence of an alleged Soviet spy ring emerged, and many people were arrested—including husband and wife Ethel and Julius Rosenberg, whose case received much publicity. In 1951 the Rosenbergs were found guilty of espionage and sentenced to death. After two years of appeals and protest they were executed in 1953. Some commentators believe

Martin Luther King, Jr. (1929–1968) led the Civil Rights Movement in a nonviolent campaign to end segregation against black Americans, particularly in the South. In 1964 Congress passed the Civil Rights Act, which ended discrimination based on race, color, religion, or national origin. The effect of the movement was profound, both in the United States and abroad, motivating minorities to seek equality. Similarly the U.S. feminist movement of the 1970s and 1980s also had a strong influence on global women's rights.

> *"Throughout history, freedom has been threatened by war and terror; it has been challenged by the clashing wills of powerful states and the designs of tyrants; and it has been tested by widespread poverty and disease.... Today, humanity holds in its hands the opportunity to further freedom's triumph over all its age-old foes. The United States welcomes its responsibility to lead in this great mission."*
>
> —GEORGE W. BUSH, 43RD PRESIDENT (2001–)

that their case sums up an age of mass hysteria and witch-hunts stirred up by McCarthy. Others argue that the Rosenbergs were guilty and deserved their punishment; they claim that the executions were essential to show the U.S. commitment to eliminating an ideology that it considered destructive to both its own and world stability.

The Civil Rights Movement

The United States has had a huge influence on the world in many other ways in the postwar period. From the mid-1950s the baptist minister Dr.

The topics in this section ask some key questions about post 1945 U.S. history. Topic 11 looks at whether the United States overestimated the threat of communism in the 1950s. Topic 12 and 13 look at civil rights issues, questioning whether the Civil Rights Movement really helped blacks, and whether the FBI persecuted Dr. King. The last three topics look at foreign policy issues. Topic 14 asks if the Vietnam war was avoidable. Topic 15 questions if the Persian Gulf war was about oil, and Topic 16 examines what role U.S. imperialism played in 9/11.

Topic 11
DID THE UNITED STATES OVERESTIMATE THE THREAT OF COMMUNISM IN THE 1950S?

YES
FROM "INTRODUCTION: CONFRONTATION WITH MCCARTHYISM"
THE DOCUMENTARY HISTORY OF THE TRUMAN PRESIDENCY, VOL. 25, *PRESIDENT TRUMAN'S CONFRONTATION WITH MCCARTHYISM*, 2000
DENNIS MERRILL

NO
FROM "SPEECH AT WHEELING, WEST VIRGINIA"
FEBRUARY 9, 1950
SENATOR JOSEPH MCCARTHY

INTRODUCTION

While the end of World War II (1939–1945) brought peace and prosperity to the United States, it also resulted in heightened tensions in the nation's relationship with the Soviet Union. At first President Truman (1945–1953) alternated between cooperating with the Soviet Union and trying to threaten it into acting less aggressively. However, many politicians viewed the USSR as a hostile force that was trying to expand its empire and spread communism.

Anticommunists saw a number of events as evidence that the Soviet Union intended to spread communism to other nations. These events included disagreements over the composition of the Polish government in 1945, a communist-led insurgency in Greece, a communist coup in Czechoslovakia and blockade of Berlin in 1948, the communist takeover of China and Soviet detonation of an atomic bomb in 1949, and the breakout of war in Korea, backed by communist China and the Soviet Union.

The United States centered its foreign and domestic policy on containing communism. To this end it involved itself in conflicts abroad and pursued a policy of exposing communists at home, particularly those in positions of power. But while some commentators believe that America was justified in its anticommunist drive, others argue that it overreacted, and that communism, at least at home, was not as big a problem as Americans thought.

The "Red Scare," or fear of the spread of communism, dated back to World War I (1914–1918) and its immediate aftermath. During these years many people feared that bolshevism would spread from Russia to the United States.

Anti-immigrant feeling increased, as did fear of left-wing organizations such as labor unions. Under the direction of men such as Alexander Mitchell Palmer, who was attorney general from 1919 to 1920, hundreds of people who belonged to these organizations were arrested, imprisoned, or deported.

> *"The junior senator from Wisconsin [McCarthy], by his reckless charges, has so preyed upon the fears and hatreds and prejudices of the American people that he has started a prairie fire which neither he nor anyone else may be able to control."*
> —J. WILLIAM FULBRIGHT, SENATOR FOR ARKANSAS (1954)

Fear of left-wing organizations— particularly unions—was renewed in the Depression of the 1930s. After World War II Congress passed the Taft–Hartley bill, which called for union officials to sign an affidavit stating that they were not communists. Although President Truman vetoed the act, he established the Loyalty Review Board in March 1947, which allowed the Federal Bureau of Investigation (FBI) to investigate communism among federal government employees. The review continued until 1952, examined 3.2 million people, and resulted in some 2,700 people being dismissed from their posts. During the investigations the board refused to present evidence or allow its informants to be questioned or even identified. Successful legal appeals against its findings eventually destroyed the board's credibility.

Similarly, in 1947 the House Un-American Activities Committee (HUAC), which had been formed in 1938 to investigate people thought to be disloyal to the United States, began new proceedings. It launched extensive investigations to find suspected communists, notably in the movie business. In 1950 HUAC sponsored a bill requiring communists to register as foreign agents. In so doing, it was influenced by the militant anticommunism of Senator Joseph McCarthy (1908–1957).

McCarthy came to prominence with a speech in February 1950 (see pages 147–151) in which he alleged that 57 communists had infiltrated the State Department. Although unable to substantiate this claim, he received support from people concerned about communist interest in Korea, Eastern Europe, and China. McCarthy continued to accuse and name people as communists when he became chairman of the Government Committee on the Operations of the Senate in 1952. He was, however, discredited in 1954 during a hearing on his charges of subversion in the Army.

While the influence of communism increased after 1945 globally, some people argue that the U.S. response to the communist threat was extreme. Government agencies did identify cases of internal communist infiltration, but critics argue that "McCarthyism" was little more than a witch hunt in which thousands of innocent people were made to suffer. The following two extracts look at the issue further.

INTRODUCTION: CONFRONTATION WITH MCCARTHYISM
Dennis Merrill

YES

…A pervasive feeling of economic insecurity … accompanied the end of the war. While many feared that military victory would bring a return of the depression conditions of the 1930s, the war's cessation instead brought an economic boom accompanied by a new financial worry: double-digit inflation. Shocked by the rapidly rising cost of living, American workers, many of them unionized during the 1930s, struck for higher wages. Business interests and conservatives often tagged union activists as "radicals" in a ploy to arouse public opposition to the work stoppages. They also railed against New Deal labor reform and welfare programs, which, they insisted, smacked of socialism. The anti-union Taft-Hartley Act, passed by the Republican Congress in 1947, required union officials to sign an anticommunist affidavit. Although Truman vetoed Taft-Hartley, he too engaged in the politics of fear. Facing a challenge from the liberal Democrat Henry Wallace in 1948, Truman attempted to discredit the former vice president by calling him a "parlor pink."

The Taft–Hartley Act, passed over Truman's veto, forbade unions from making contributions to political parties. This was widely seen as a Republican attempt to cut off the Democratic Party's funding. The anticommunist affidavit was resented since it assumed that union members were automatically suspect and had to prove their loyalty.

Cold-War pressures

The souring of U.S.–Soviet relations and the onset of the cold war intensified the nation's anxieties. … Truman established in March 1947 the Loyalty Review Board to investigate federal government employees and to ferret out communists and communist sympathizers, popularly known as "fellow travelers." The first loyalty program ever created by a U.S. president, the review board unleashed the Federal Bureau of Investigation (FBI) to conduct background checks on thousands of U.S. citizens. The procedures of inquiry allowed the FBI to maintain the confidentiality of its sources, thereby denying the accused the right to a thorough defense prior to dismissal from employment. The review, which continued well into the Eisenhower presidency, resulted in the dismissal of 2,700 federal employees.…

One person who lost his position, representative of many liberals who were active in public life, was Yale professor John Peters. Go to http://info.med.yale.edu/yjbm/issues/yjbm_75_1/roraback_peters_2914.PDF to read more about his case and see the methods by which the Loyalty Review Board operated.

In the Republican-led House of Representatives, the House Committee on Un-American Activities (HUAC), originally established in 1938, redoubled its investigation of communists on the homefront. On August 3, 1948, a committee witness named Whittaker Chambers, an editor of *Time* magazine and an admitted former Soviet spy, dropped a bombshell when he testified that Alger Hiss, president of the prestigious Carnegie Endowment for International Peace and former assistant secretary of state who had accompanied President Franklin Roosevelt to Yalta in 1945, had also once been a Soviet agent. Truman referred to the charge as a "red herring," and long-time friend Secretary of State Dean Acheson rushed to Hiss's defense. But when a grand jury convicted Hiss of perjury in January 1950, for falsely denying his former communist connections under oath, the administration came under fierce partisan attack. The episode propelled a young congressman and HUAC member, Republican Richard M. Nixon of California, to national prominence. HUAC soon expanded its inquiry and launched highly publicized probes into communist influence in unions, universities, and the Hollywood film industry.

Alger Hiss (1904–1996) served most of a five-year sentence, being released in 1954. In 1992 he asked the Russian historian Dimitry Volkogonov to check the declassified archives of the KGB for any references to him. Volkogonov found no evidence that Hiss had ever been a Soviet spy or agent. See http://homepages.nyu.edu/~th15/home.html for full background on the Hiss case.

McCarthy: visionary or demagog?

The Hiss case, Chiang Kai-shek's final collapse in China, and news of the Soviet Union's atomic detonation, all coming within weeks of each other, set the stage for Senator Joseph McCarthy's bravado performance in Wheeling, West Virginia, in February 1950. Another blow came when Scotland Yard arrested the nuclear physicist Klaus Fuchs, who had worked on the Manhattan Project, and charged him with espionage. Within days of his speech in West Virginia, McCarthy sent Truman a telegram demanding the immediate opening of State Department loyalty review files. "Failure on your part to do so will label the Democratic Party as being the bedfellow of international Communism," he blustered. Truman unequivocally denied McCarthy's assertions. At a press conference on February 16, the president declared: "There was not a word of truth in what the Senator said." On March 30 he went further: "I think the greatest asset that the Kremlin has is Senator McCarthy." Still, the pressure mounted and the burden of proof fell on those who dared question the accuser.

Once the president's direct denials failed, the White House decided to work with Democrats on Capitol Hill to refute the charges. The Senate Foreign Relations Committee created a special subcommittee chaired by Maryland Democrat Millard E. Tydings, a conservative anticommunist, to conduct its own review. Despite the strong reservations of the Justice

The Manhattan Project was the allied operation to construct a nuclear bomb during World War II. Klaus Fuchs (1911–1988), a German-born British physicist and longtime communist, passed nuclear information to the Soviet Union from 1943 onward.

Can you think of other times and places where the burden of proof has fallen on the people defending themselves rather than on those making the accusation?

The number of names on McCarthy's list has been the subject of confusion. In his original speech he used the number 205, but in the written version he later prepared (see following pages) he changed this to 57. See www.crimsonbird.com/history/mccarthy.htm for an explanation of where these numbers came from.

The "Fair Deal" was Truman's continuation of ideas from Roosevelt's "New Deal," which had tackled the Depression in the 1930s. Go to http://odur.let.rug.nl/~usa/H/1994/ch11_p10.htm for more information.

The "China hands" were diplomats and officials in the State Department who had dealings with Chinese leaders—both the communist Mao Zedong and the nationalist Chiang Kai-Shek. See www.state.gov/r/pa/ho/time/cwr/17383.htm for further information.

Department … Truman agreed to provide the committee with the controversial loyalty files that McCarthy had demanded earlier. Pressed in turn to share his evidence, McCarthy cut his list of names from 205 to fifty-seven, most of whom were categorized as communist sympathizers rather than out-and-out "reds."…

The Tydings Committee interviewed a parade of witnesses who collectively undermined McCarthy's case. The committee's final report in July 1950 completely absolved the administration of negligence in national security. The report nonetheless failed to win the endorsement of a single Republican.

Rather than weakening, McCarthy's power grew in the ensuing months. He received strong support from Republican Party leaders in the Senate, Kenneth Wherry of Nebraska and Robert Taft of Ohio, who saw in the communist issue a means to attack a president whose domestic Fair Deal programs remained popular. Indeed, the Republicans made modest gains in the fall 1950 off-year elections, with the ranks of defeated Democrats including Millard Tydings, against whom McCarthy personally campaigned. Although a small number of moderate Republicans, led by Maine's Margaret Chase Smith, issued a "declaration of conscience" that criticized their Wisconsin colleague, most did not question any of his specific allegations. In January 1951 President Truman established a President's Commission on Internal Security and Individual Rights, headed by Fleet Admiral Chester Nimitz, and filled it with conservatives in another effort to defuse the attacks. But the Republican Congress refused to pass legislation to authorize the commission and the group was officially disbanded later in the year. …

Truman hits back

The Korean War further strengthened McCarthy, who along with other Republicans lambasted the president for dismissing General Douglas MacArthur after the famed military hero had advocated war against the People's Republic of China. McCarthy especially focused his sights on Secretary of State Dean Acheson, whose defense of Alger Hiss and the "China hands" made him an easy target for red baiting.… McCarthy also accused Truman of being a drunkard and called for his impeachment from office.

Counseled by advisers not to overreact to the smears, Truman could hold back no longer. In a nationally broadcast speech to the American Legion on August 14, 1951, the president delivered a tour de force. Without mentioning McCarthy by name, he denounced Hitler-like "big lie" tactics, "hate mongers and character assassins." "Everyone in Russia lives in fear of being called an anticommunist," he observed. Then, speaking in terms the meaning of which no one could mistake, he declared: "In a dictatorship everybody lives in fear and terror of being denounced and slandered. Nobody dares stand up for his rights." The Wisconsin senator nonetheless maintained his following, and for the remainder of Truman's term continued to be a thorn in the president's side. In the 1952 presidential campaign he savaged the Democratic candidate, Adlai Stevenson, whom he regularly made a point of accidentally calling "Alger" Stevenson.

In a democracy laws and procedures are supposed to protect people from being accused unjustly or without evidence. Equally, holding left-wing views is not a crime. Why do you think the law was not effective in protecting people during this time?

Fall from grace

Joseph McCarthy remained a national figure only briefly beyond the Truman years. Truman's successor, Republican Dwight D. Eisenhower, privately expressed contempt for McCarthy but refrained from public criticisms for fear of dividing his party. Back in charge of the Senate, Republican leaders assigned McCarthy the chairmanship of the relatively unimportant Government Operations Committee, which McCarthy used as a forum for further investigations. Throughout 1953 and the first half of 1954 he grew increasingly reckless, charging that communists had infiltrated the U.S. Information Service, the Voice of America, the Government Printing Office, and the Foreign Service. He finally overreached himself when he accused the U.S. Army of coddling communists. In the Senate's first televised hearings, McCarthy appeared crude, blustering, and out of control. A turning point came on June 9, 1954, when the Army general counsel Joseph N. Welch pointedly asked McCarthy: "Have you no sense of decency, sir?" A few months later the Senate censured McCarthy for "conduct ... contrary to the Senate traditions." McCarthy died of acute alcoholism in 1957, embittered and isolated.

The Army/McCarthy hearings were among the first to be televised. See www.museum.tv/ archives/etv/A/ html/A/army-mccarthy/army-mccarthy.htm for an assessment of the effect of the broadcasts on the public's perception of McCarthy.

Although Senator McCarthy represented only one manifestation of McCarthyism, the most overt anticommunist hysteria subsided following his fall from grace. But the dust settled only after countless individuals had paid an immense price in terms of careers ruined and reputations destroyed. The country as a whole had suffered an irredeemable loss of civil liberties and freedom of expression. The legacy of McCarthyism, a disdain for nonconformity and intolerance of dissent, remained intact until the domestic reform and antiwar movements of the 1960s....

SPEECH AT WHEELING, WEST VIRGINIA
Senator Joseph McCarthy

With this speech McCarthy launched his campaign to expose alleged communists in the State Department. His timing exploited the fear of communism generated by recent events—see Dennis Merrill's article on page 142.

This is a paraphrase of a speech made by Abraham Lincoln in 1838. See http://showcase.netins.net/web/creative/lincoln/speeches/lyceum.htm for the original speech. Lincoln's birthday, February 12, was the occasion chosen for McCarthy's speech —although it was actually given on February 9.

NO

Six years ago, at the time of the first conference to map out the peace—Dumbarton Oaks—there was within the Soviet orbit 180,000,000 people. Lined up on the antitotalitarian side there were in the world at that time roughly 1,625,000,000 people. Today, only six years later, there are 800,000,000 people under the absolute domination of Soviet Russia—an increase of over 400 percent. On our side, the figure has shrunk to around 500,000,000. In other words, less than six years ago the odds have changed from nine to one in our favor to eight to five against us. This indicates the swiftness of the tempo of Communist victories and American defeats in the cold war. As one of our outstanding historical figures once said, "When a great democracy is destroyed, it will not be because of enemies from without, but rather because of enemies from within."

The truth of this statement is becoming terrifyingly clear as we see this country each day losing on every front.

Traitors in our midst

At war's end we were physically the strongest nation on earth and, at least potentially, the most powerful intellectually and morally. Ours could have been the honor of being a beacon in the desert of destruction, a shining living proof that civilization was not yet ready to destroy itself. Unfortunately, we have failed miserably and tragically to arise to the opportunity.

The reason why we find ourselves in a position of impotency is not because our only powerful potential enemy has sent men to invade our shores, but rather because of the traitorous actions of those who have been treated so well by this Nation. It has not been the less fortunate or members of minority groups who have been selling this Nation out, but rather those who have had all the benefits that the wealthiest nation on earth has had to offer—the finest homes, the finest college education, and the finest jobs in Government we can give.

This is glaringly true in the State Department. There the bright young men who are born with silver spoons in their mouths are the ones who have been worst.

Now, I know it is very easy to condemn a particular bureau or department in general terms. Therefore, I would like to cite one rather unusual case—the case of a man who has done much to shape our foreign policy.

When Chiang Kai-shek was fighting our war, the State Department had in China a young man named John S. Service. His task, obviously, was not to work for the communization of China. Strangely, however, he sent official reports back to the State Department urging that we torpedo our ally Chiang Kai-shek and stating, in effect, that communism was the best hope of China.

Later, this man—John Service—was picked up by the Federal Bureau of Investigation for turning over to the Communists' secret State Department information. Strangely, however, he was never prosecuted. However, Joseph Grew, the Under Secretary of State, who insisted on his prosecution was forced to resign. Two days after Grew's successor, Dean Acheson, took over as Under Secretary of State, this man—John Service—who had been picked up by the FBI and who had previously urged that communism was the best hope of China, was not only reinstated in the State Department but promoted, and finally, under Acheson, placed in charge of all placements and promotions.

Today … this man Service is on his way to represent the State Department and Acheson in Calcutta—by far and away the most important listening post in the Far East…

Another interesting case was that of Julian H. Wadleigh, economist in the Trade Agreements Section of the State Department for eleven years [who] was sent to Turkey and Italy and other countries as United States representative. After the statute of limitations had run so he could not be prosecuted for treason, he openly and brazenly not only admitted but proclaimed that he had been a member of the Communist Party … that while working for the State Department he stole a vast number of secret documents... and furnished these documents to the Russian spy ring of which he was a part.

Fifty-seven cases

This, ladies and gentlemen, gives you somewhat of a picture of the type of individuals who have been helping to shape our foreign policy. In my opinion the State Department, which is one of the most important government departments, is thoroughly infested with Communists.

I have in my hand fifty-seven cases of individuals who would appear to be either card-carrying members or

John Service, who spoke Chinese and lived for many years in China, reported that Chiang's government was corrupt and its army demoralized, and that U.S. support for Mao was the best way to ensure friendly relations with postwar China. See http://edition.cnn. com/SPECIALS/cold. war/episodes/06/ interviews/service/ for an interview with Service.

What might have attracted Americans to become communists? Would the political system benefit from the existence of a radical left-wing party?

McCarthy uses "infested," a word usually only applied to rats and other vermin.

certainly loyal to the Communist Party, but who nevertheless are still helping to shape our foreign policy.

One thing to remember in discussing Communists in our Government is that we are not dealing with spies who get thirty pieces of silver to steal the blueprints of a new weapon. We are dealing with a far more sinister type of activity because it permits the enemy to guide and shape our policy....

This brings us down to the case of one Alger Hiss who is important not as an individual any more, but rather because he is so representative of a group in the State Department. It is unnecessary to go over the sordid events showing how he sold out the Nation which had given him so much. Those are rather fresh in our minds.

However, it should be remembered that the facts in regard to his connection with this international Communist spy ring were made known to the then Under Secretary of State Berle three days after Hitler and Stalin signed the Russo-German alliance pact....

Under Secretary Berle promptly contacted Dean Acheson and received word in return that Acheson (and I quote) "could vouch for Hiss absolutely"—at which time the matter was dropped....

Again in 1943, the FBI had occasion to investigate the facts surrounding Hiss's contacts with the Russian spy ring. But even after that FBI report was submitted, nothing was done.

Then late in 1948—on August 5—when the Un-American Activities Committee [HUAC] called Alger Hiss to give an accounting, President Truman at once issued a Presidential directive ordering all Government agencies to refuse to turn over any information whatsoever in regard to the Communist activities of any Government employee to a congressional committee....

If time permitted, it might be well to go into detail about the fact that Hiss was Roosevelt's chief adviser at Yalta when Roosevelt was admittedly in ill health and tired physically and mentally ... and when, according to the Secretary of State, Hiss and Gromyko drafted the report on the conference....

Of the results of this conference, Arthur Bliss Lane of the State Department had this to say: "As I glanced over the document, I could not believe my eyes. To me, almost every line spoke of a surrender to Stalin."

The people will rise up

As you hear this story of high treason, I know that you are saying to yourself, "Well, why doesn't Congress do something

In fact, in an interview with Berle on September 1, 1939, the former Soviet spy Whittaker Chambers merely said that Hiss was the type of person whom the communists were trying to recruit. Go to http://homepages. nyu.edu/~th15/ berlmemo.html for more background.

At the Yalta conference in February 1945 Roosevelt, Churchill, and Stalin met to map out the future of a postwar world. With 12 million Soviet soldiers in Eastern Europe Roosevelt and Churchill had little choice but to accept that those countries fell within the Soviet "sphere of influence."

about it?" Actually, ladies and gentlemen, one of the most important reasons for the graft, the corruptions—one of the most important reasons why this continues is lack of moral uprising on the part of the 140,000,000 American people. ...

As you know, very recently the Secretary of State [Acheson] proclaimed his loyalty to a man guilty of what has always been considered as the most abominable of all crimes—of being a traitor to the people who gave him a position of great trust. The Secretary of State in attempting to justify his continued devotion to the man who sold out the Christian world to the atheistic world, referred to Christ's Sermon on the Mount as a justification and reason therefore, and the reaction of the American people to this would have made the heart of Abraham Lincoln happy.

When this pompous diplomat in striped pants, with a phony British accent, proclaimed to the American people that Christ on the Mount endorsed communism, high treason, and betrayal of a sacred trust, the blasphemy was so great that it awakened the dormant indignation of the American people.

He has lighted the spark which is resulting in a moral uprising and will end only when the whole sorry mess of twisted, warped thinkers are swept from the national scene so that we may have a new birth of national honesty and decency in Government.

Dean Acheson (1893–1971) was assistant secretary, then undersecretary in the State Department before becoming secretary of state in 1949. He is now generally regarded as one of the 20th century's most distinguished holders of that office.

Acheson had stood by Hiss, quoting Christ's saying "I was in prison and ye came unto me" to explain his loyalty.

Summary

Did the United States overestimate the strength of communism in the 1950s? Certainly the United States pursued a vigorous anticommunist policy both at home and abroad after World War II (1939–1945). The preceding two documents look at the debate. In the first, an extract from *The Documentary History of the Truman Presidency*, the author focuses on Senator Joseph McCarthy. He argues that anticommunist feeling existed in the United States, as shown by the existence of HUAC and as enunciated by the Truman Doctrine of 1947, but that McCarthy was able to take advantage of certain events and jump on the anticommunist bandwagon. This led to a period of intense anticommunist feeling and scaremongering. While the progress and danger of communism abroad were real, the author suggests that the danger of communists at home was greatly overinflated. Rather, in his view, the issue became a convenient weapon for extreme conservatives trying to reverse the marginalization they had suffered during the Roosevelt era.

The second article is Senator Joseph McCarthy's famous speech of February 9, 1950, at Wheeling, West Virginia, which argues that communists have infiltrated the State Department and asserts that the government has not done enough to deal with the problem. He argues that these people are selling out the nation and that they have to be dealt with. He notes that those he singles out for attack were people who had the greatest advantages in life.

FURTHER INFORMATION:

Books:

Campbell, Gordon A., *The Home Front: The Cold War in the United States*, San Diego, CA: Lucent, 2003.
Fried, Albert (ed.), *McCarthyism: The Great American Red Scare: A Documentary History*, New York: Oxford University Press, 1997.
Schrecker, Ellen (ed.), *The Age of McCarthyism: A Brief History with Documents*. New York: Palgrave, 2002.

Useful websites:

www.gpo.gov/congress/senate/senate12cp107.html
United States Congress site offering transcripts of the Army/McCarthy hearings.
www.spartacus.schoolnet.co.uk/USAred.htm
Spartacus site with links to profiles of the people involved and the background to events.
www.cnn.com/SPECIALS/cold.war/
CNN's resource site derived from its award-winning 1995 television documentary series *Cold War*.

http://home.earthlink.net/~neuhausj/1950s/paranoia.html
Page that looks at aspects of communism in the 1950s.

The following debates in the Pro/Con series may also be of interest:

In this volume:
 Topic 14 Was the Vietnam war avoidable?

In *Arts and Culture*:

 Topic 14 Should the politics of artists matter?

 The House Un-American Activities Committee (HUAC), pages 188–189

DID THE UNITED STATES OVERESTIMATE THE THREAT OF COMMUNISM IN THE 1950S?

YES: After 1945 the Soviet Union became involved in many conflicts, especially in Eastern Europe, supporting communist-led insurgencies

YES: Truman sent troops to Korea as part of a United Nations action after it became apparent that the Soviet Union was supporting North Korea

SOVIET UNION
Was the Soviet Union really a threat to democracy?

KOREA
Was the United States justified in getting involved in the Korean War?

NO: Many politicians used it as a scapegoat in order to get involved in other countries' affairs

NO: It was a conflict in Southeast Asia. It was a waste of money, troops, and lives.

DID THE UNITED STATES OVERESTIMATE THE THREAT OF COMMUNISM IN THE 1950S?

KEY POINTS

YES: Senator McCarthy jumped on the anticommunist bandwagon in 1949 and quickly rose to prominence as a result. His popularity then grew, as did anticommunist sentiment.

YES: Government investigations uncovered a number of spies such as Klaus Fuchs and Whittaker Chambers, and it is likely that many more went undiscovered

MCCARTHYISM
Did Senator McCarthy use anticommunist feeling for his own ends?

COMMUNISTS
Were there many secret communists in the United States?

NO: McCarthy's sentiments were valid. He was worried about the influence of communism in the federal government.

NO: Only a few people were proved to be communists. Thousands of innocent people were persecuted by HUAC and McCarthy.

Topic 12

DID THE CIVIL RIGHTS MOVEMENT IMPROVE THE POSITION OF BLACKS IN SOCIETY?

YES

FROM "INTERVIEW WITH ROSA PARKS"
HTTP://TEACHER.SCHOLASTIC.COM/ROSA/INTERVIEW.HTM, JANUARY–FEBRUARY 1997
SCHOLASTIC WEBSITE

NO

FROM "WHICH WAY FOR BLACKS IN THE USA—BLACK NATIONALISM
OR SOCIALIST REVOLUTION?"
HTTP://WWW.MARXIST.COM/USA/BLACKS.HTML, FEBRUARY 1999
ROB SEWELL

INTRODUCTION

The position of African Americans, who in 2000 numbered some 36.4 million, or 12.9 percent, of the U.S. population, has been among the longest-running unresolved issues in U.S. society. Evidence of improvements in the wealth and status of black Americans—symbolized by the emergence of figures such as Secretary of State Colin Powell and National Security Adviser Condoleezza Rice—is balanced by the fact that the group as a whole is still disproportionately poor (more than 22 percent live in poverty) and undereducated (only 5 percent are holders of graduate degrees).

The civil rights movement that began in the mid 1950s was only the latest stage in a struggle whose first major milestone was the abolition of slavery in the U.S. in 1865. Following this, the Fourteenth Amendment in 1868 guaranteed all Americans "equal protection under the law," and in 1870 the Fifteenth Amendment prohibited any infringement of a citizen's right to vote "on account of race, color, or previous condition of servitude."

But the legislation had little effect for almost a century, especially in the South, where state laws were enacted to get around the new amendments by introducing new conditions for voters such as literacy and property tests that while not explicitly racially based, had the effect of preventing blacks from voting. These new laws were backed up by strong social pressures and the frequent use of physical violence, most notoriously lynchings, to keep the black population intimidated. There was no real change until 1954, when the Supreme Court ruled in the case of *Brown v. Board of Education of*

Topeka, Kansas that segregation in public schools was unconstitutional because separate facilities were inherently unequal.

That decision began to inspire action against other examples of inequality, such as the law in some Southern states that a black person could not sit down on public transportation if a white person was standing. In 1955 that situation changed when a black woman named Rosa Parks (1913–) refused to surrender her seat to a white man on a bus in Montgomery, Alabama, precipitating the 381-day bus boycott that resulted in a 1956 Supreme Court order outlawing discriminatory practices on public transportation.

"Civil Rights: What black folks are given in the U.S. on the installment plan."
—DICK GREGORY, CIVIL RIGHTS ACTIVIST AND COMEDIAN (1972)

Parks's historic act of defiance was both a symptom and a cause of a new civil rights movement that aroused national opinion against segregation. The leader of the movement soon became Dr. Martin Luther King, Jr.

Numerous acts were passed in an effort to guarantee black people voting rights, access to housing, and equal opportunity in employment. However, every step along the road to equality was met with resistance. President John F. Kennedy introduced ambitious legislation to end discrimination in public facilities, desegregate public schools, and protect black voters. But Southern conservatives blocked the bill in Congress, and it was not until July 2, 1964, that the Civil Rights Act was signed into law by Kennedy's successor, Lyndon B. Johnson.

Even after this event progress remained slow. By 1965 desegregation had been accomplished in only 1,160 of the 3,028 Southern school districts that contained white and black pupils. Only about 10 percent of blacks were attending schools with whites.

Unskilled and poor blacks regarded the 1964 act as a mockery. Urban riots in 1967 left nearly 100 people dead. More militant wings of the movement, such as the Black Panthers, sought to move beyond civil rights, claiming that it was first essential for African Americans to develop a more positive image of themselves.

One success of the civil rights movement was to increase the number of blacks elected to public office, from mayors of major cities to congressional elections. Meanwhile, Supreme Court decisions in the 1970s condemned racially discriminatory hiring practices, awarded back pay to victims of job discrimination, and supported race-conscious affirmative action by private employers.

But civil rights were again threatened when the Reagan administration tried to limit school busing for the purposes of integration and denounced the use of numerical quotas in affirmative-action programs.

In the first article Rosa Parks—the inspiration of the Montgomery bus boycott—says that blacks are better off today than before the civil rights movement. The second article, by Rob Sewell, lists some of the injustices and privations that are still endured by African Americans.

INTERVIEW WITH ROSA PARKS
Http://Teacher.Scholastic.com/Rosa/
Interview/htm

YES

Life before civil rights

Q: How do you feel about the way black Americans used to be treated?

A: I always felt badly because our people were not treated fairly. We should have been free and given the same opportunities others had.

Q: How did it feel not to have civil rights?

A: Of course it felt like we should all be free people and we should have the same rights as other people. In the South, at that time, there was legally enforced segregation. There were places black people couldn't go, and rights we did not have. This was not acceptable to me. A lot of other people didn't disobey the rules because they didn't want to get into trouble. I was willing to get arrested—it was worth the consequences....

Go to www.achievement. org/autodoc/ page/par0bio-1 for a brief biography of Rosa Parks and her place in the civil rights movement.

Q: How do you feel about the people who treated you so unfairly?

A: I don't think well of people who are prejudiced against people because of race. The only way for prejudiced people to change is for them to decide for themselves that all human beings should be treated fairly. We can't force them to think that way....

Role in civil rights

Q: What made you decide on December 1, 1955, not to get up from your seat?

A: That particular day that I decided was not the first time I had trouble with that particular driver. He evicted me before, because I would not go around to the back door after I was already onto the bus. The evening that I boarded the bus, and noticed that he was the same driver, I decided to get on anyway. I did not sit at the very front of the bus; I took a seat with a man who was next to the window—the first seat that was allowed for "colored" people to sit in. We were not disturbed until we reached the third stop after I boarded the

In segregated Montgomery black people were obliged to sit at the back of the bus and to enter by the rear door. Twelve years earlier the same driver had made Rosa Parks leave the bus and get on by the rear door because she entered by the front door.

bus. At this point a few white people boarded the bus, and one white man was left standing. When the driver noticed him standing, he spoke to us (the man and two women across the aisle) and told us to let the man have the seat. The other three all stood up. But the driver saw me still sitting there. He said would I stand up, and I said, "No, I will not." Then he said, "I'll have you arrested." And I told him he could do that. So he didn't move the bus any further. Several black people left the bus.

Two policemen got on the bus in a couple of minutes. The driver told the police that I would not stand up. The policeman walked down and asked me why I didn't stand up, and I said I didn't think I should stand up. "Why do you push us around?" I asked him. And he said, "I don't know. But the law is the law and you are under arrest." As soon as he said that I stood up, the three of us left the bus together.

One of them picked up my purse, the other picked up my shopping bag. And we left the bus together. It was the first time I'd had that particular thing happen. I was determined that I let it be known that I did not want to be treated in this manner. The policemen had their squad car waiting, they gave me my purse and bag, and they opened the back door of the police car for me to enter.

The law at that time gave bus drivers the right to assign passengers a particular seat or order them to give up their seat. See http://home.att.net/ ~reniqua/code1.htm for the the text of the law.

Q: Did you think your actions would have such a far-reaching effect on the Civil Rights movement?
A: I didn't have any idea just what my actions would bring about. At the time I was arrested I didn't know how the community would react. I was glad that they did take the action that they did by staying off the bus.

Q: What was it like walking all those miles when the bus boycott was going on?
A: We were fortunate enough to have a carpool organized to pick people up and give them rides. Of course, many people walked and sometimes I did too. I was willing to walk rather than go back to the buses under those unfair conditions. Very shortly after the boycott began, I was dismissed from my job as a seamstress at a department store. I worked at home doing sewing and typing. I don't know why I was dismissed from the job, but I think it was because I was arrested.

Four days after Rosa Parks's arrest the African American population of Montgomery, who made up some 75 percent of bus passengers, began boycotting the city's bus network and walking or organizing carpools instead.

Q: What did your family think about what happened?
A: After I was in jail I had the opportunity to call home and speak to my mother. The first thing she asked me was if they had attacked me, beat me. That's what they used to do to

The National Association for the Advancement of Colored People is a nonviolent civil rights organization, founded in 1909. See www.naacp.org/ for more details.

people. I said no, that I hadn't been hurt, but I was in jail. She gave the phone to my husband and he said he would be there shortly and would get me out of jail.

There was a man who had come to my house who knew I had been arrested. He told my husband he'd give him a ride to the jail. Meantime, Mr. E.D. Nixon, one of the leaders of the NAACP, had heard about my being arrested from a friend of mine. He called to see if I was at the jail. The people at the jail wouldn't tell him I was there. So Mr. Nixon got in touch with a white lawyer named Clifford Durr. Mr. Durr called the jail, and they told him that I was there. Mr. Nixon had to pick up Mr. Durr before he could come get me. Mr. Durr's wife insisted on going too, because she and I were good friends. Mr. Nixon helped release me from jail.

Q: Were you scared to do such a brave thing?
A: No, actually I had no fear at that particular time. I was very determined to let it be known how it felt to be treated in that manner—discriminated against. I was thinking mostly about how inconvenienced I was—stopping me from going home and doing my work—something I had not expected. When I did realize, I faced it, and it was quite a challenge to be arrested. I did not really know what would happen. I didn't feel especially frightened. I felt more annoyed than frightened.

Can you think of a situation in this country today in which you might choose to be arrested because you were following a moral principle or protesting an unjust law?

Q: Did you know that you were going to jail if you didn't give up your seat?
A: Well, I knew I was going to jail when the driver said he was going to have me arrested. I didn't feel good about going to jail, but I was willing to go to let it be known that under this type of segregation, black people had endured too much for too long.

Q: How did you feel when you were asked to give up your seat?
A: I didn't feel very good about being told to stand up and not have a seat. I felt I had a right to stay where I was. That was why I told the driver I was not going to stand. I believed that he would arrest me. I did it because I wanted this particular driver to know that we were being treated unfairly as individuals and as a people.

Q: What were your feelings when you were able to sit in the front of the bus for the first time?
A: I was glad that the type of treatment—legally enforced

segregation—on the buses was over ... had come to an end. It was something rather special. However, when I knew the boycott was over, and that we didn't have to be mistreated on the bus anymore, that was a much better feeling than I had when we were being mistreated.

Q: How do you feel about being called the "Mother of the Civil Rights Movement"?
A: I accept the title quite well. I appreciate the fact that people feel that way about me. I don't know who started calling me that.

Civil rights today

Q: What one lesson would you like to leave with students?
A: I always encourage children to stay in school, get good grades, and to believe in themselves. Of course they should take care of their health and keep themselves from certain things that would be detrimental to them either physically or mentally. They should be sure to get the best education that they can and choose careers that they can be progressive in as they go into their adulthood. In our Pathways to Freedom Institute and our Institute for Self Development, we take young people on trips and give them opportunities to meet many civil rights leaders. We teach them to be good citizens and do what they can do to help other people as they become successful themselves. I urge children to have a spiritual awareness in their lives. If children work towards a positive goal in life, it will help them be successful when they become adults....

Do you think the relationships between the different races are where they should be today?

There is still as much racism among some people. It still exists, but we are not under the legally enforced segregation that we used to be. There are still people who are prejudiced because of race. The Rosa and Raymond Parks Institute accepts people of any race. We don't discriminate against anyone. We teach people to reach their highest potential. I set examples by the way I lead my life....

Civil rights leaders always stressed the importance of education in helping African Americans advance in U.S. society. Do you agree with this emphasis? Do you think this advice is being widely followed today?

Do you think changes in the law have helped young people escape the racist attitudes of some people in earlier generations?

WHICH WAY FOR BLACKS IN THE USA—BLACK NATIONALISM OR SOCIALIST REVOLUTION?
Rob Sewell

NO

X   The United States is the richest and most powerful country on the planet. Yet despite this, the poison of racism remains an integral part of America. Blacks, together with the other racial minorities, remain the most exploited section of society, mostly employed in the lowest-paid and menial jobs. … Today, despite all the "reforms" of the last thirty-odd years, blacks continue to suffer from lynchings and violence at the hands of the state, racist organisations and individuals, as well as being forced to live under conditions of mass poverty and oppression. The recent gruesome murder of a black man in Texas who was dragged to death behind a truck is a vivid reminder of American racism. Black youth are faced with daily harassment and intimidation by the police.

James Byrd, Jr., was murdered on June 7, 1998 near the town of Jasper, Texas. Three men were convicted of the murder in separate trials in 1999.

Separate and unequal

Thirty years ago, a commission headed by Otto Kerner, the governor of Illinois, found that America was "moving towards two societies, one black, one white, separate and unequal." Today, despite all the promises from successive Administrations, a follow-up report claims the situation has grown far worse for the mass of blacks.

The "Report of the U.S. National Advisory Commission on Civil Disorders," headed by Otto Kerner, was issued on March 1, 1968

The new report, which comes from the Milton S. Eisenhower Foundation, while conceding that the black middle class has grown, and that black high-school graduation rates have risen, points to the fact that unemployment in a large number of black inner-city neighbourhoods is at "Depression levels" of 50 percent or more. Unemployment amongst blacks is twice the rate for whites.

Go to www. eisenhower foundation.org/ aboutus/media/ WashPostKerner ProphecyMar1.html for a summary of the report's findings.

America's child-poverty rate is four times higher than Western Europe, and the rate of incarceration for black men is four times higher than in the days of apartheid South Africa. Figures from the Justice Department show that between 1985 and 1995, as the number of white men sentenced to more than a year in gaol rose by 103 percent, the number of black male convicts grew by 143 percent.

In 1997, the number of black Americans in poverty was 9.1 million while the number of poor Hispanics was 8.3 million. For children, the situation is horrific. Black infant mortality is twice that of whites. Forty-five percent of black children live below the poverty line compared with 16 percent of white children. These are the kind of figures you would expect in a third world country.

In the U.S., blacks earn only 58 percent of whites' earnings. In 1979, a black worker was likely to earn 10.9 percent less than a white in a similar job, but by 1989 that differential had grown to 16.4 percent. According to the book "The State of Working America 1992-93" by Mishel and Bernstein, "This 'black–white earnings gap' jumped up 50 percent from 1979 to 1989... Education-wise, the greatest increase in black–white earnings gap was among college graduates, with minimal 2.5 percent differential in 1979 exploding to 15.5 percent in 1989." While the black middle class has grown, affirmative action and quotas have not prevented this deterioration for the mass of blacks.

At the same time, the class divide has never been greater. The rich got richer, while the position of the majority has deteriorated. Corporate America has made a bonanza. Bill Gates has an income equal to the combined income of 115 million Americans.

Divide and rule?

The poison of racism is deliberately fostered by the ruling class as a means of keeping the working class divided, and diverting attention away from the real problems of American capitalism. This policy of "divide and rule" on racial, national or religious lines, has been a common feature of the ruling class internationally. As the Black Panther, Bobby Seale correctly wrote: "Racism and ethnic differences allow the power structure to exploit the masses of workers in this country, because that's the key by which they maintain their control. To divide the people and conquer them is the objective of the power structure..." This situation also confirms the words of Malcolm X, "You cannot have capitalism without racism."...

Years of racism, police harassment and terrible social conditions has produced an explosive mix within the inner cities, especially amongst the black and Latino youth. This has periodically erupted in riots, most recently in Los Angeles, one of the richest cities in the USA. But riots have no perspective and arise spontaneously out of poverty conditions. If the labour leaders offered a real fighting

Apart from racial divisions, what other reasons can you think of for the growing gap between rich and poor in the United States?

Do you agree that racism is deliberately fostered by people in power? Give examples to back up your answer, whether yes or no.

Malcolm X linked the beginnings of racism with the rise of the African slave trade in the 16th century. Given that slavery has a long history that predates capitalism, do you agree with this assessment? Or do you think earlier slavery was nonracial in character?

"Jim Crow laws" is the collective term for all the state and local laws that, in open defiance of federal law, were passed by Southern states after the Civil War in an attempt to segregate blacks and whites and to ensure the continued subjugation of black people. Jim Crow was the name of a character in a minstrel show of the 1830s who represented the "typical" black slave.

The author implies that the same people supported both the Civil Rights Act (1964) and the Voting Rights Act (1965), on the one hand, and the murder of Martin Luther King and Malcolm X on the other. Do you agree?

The Black Panther Party was founded in 1966 "to serve the needs of the oppressed people in our communities and defend them against their oppressors." Bobby Seale was one of its founding members. See www. blackpanther.org/ for more information.

alternative, then the energies of these youth could be harnessed in a positive direction.

In the 1950s and 1960s, the revolt of the blacks against their discrimination and social position shook the ruling class to its foundations. Despite the oppression and the violence unleashed against the civil rights movement, the black revolt defeated the Jim Crow laws. This movement, if it had been linked to the struggle of the working class as a whole, could have been a massive force for social change. Unfortunately, the labour leaders, who looked to the pro-capitalist Democratic Party, were incapable of leading this movement against racism and the oppression and of uniting all workers on a class basis.

The need for unity

As a result, the ruling class, in order to control the situation, made some concessions on voting rights and civil rights in the south. It sought to confine the movement within the confines of capitalism by moving in the direction of affirmative action and the quota system. This strategy went hand in hand with the murder of Martin Luther King, Malcolm X and a whole number of Black Panther leaders, who sought to go beyond capitalism and the Democratic Party.…

During the height of the black revolt in the 1960s, Stokely Carmichael, one of the Black Panther leaders, first raised the slogan of "Black Power" as a rallying cry for blacks to unite and challenge white society. In so far as it represented a break at the time from the white liberals of both the Democratic and Republican parties it represented a step forward.

As the black population made up only 13 percent of the population as a whole, it was clear that blacks by themselves could never transform society. Malcolm X, who began as a black nationalist came to the conclusion that an alliance with white workers was the only way forward. He was murdered before this idea was fully developed. But it was the Black Panthers that arrived at even clearer ideas on class unity and the struggle to transform society. According to Bobby Seale: "We fight racism with solidarity. We do not fight exploitative capitalism with black nationalism. We fight capitalism with basic socialism. And we do not fight imperialism with more imperialism. We fight imperialism with proletarian internationalism."

The only way in which the socialist transformation of America can come about is through the united struggle of black and white workers and youth, and the establishment of a mass workers' party based on the trade unions and committed to a socialist programme. This does not mean that blacks have to wait before engaging in struggle. However, a revolutionary black movement needs to appeal for a united struggle with sections of radicalised white workers. Black liberation is inseparable from the liberation of the working class as a whole. Marxism has a responsibility to offer a perspective and a way forward for the movement at each stage, explaining its weaknesses and reinforcing its strengths....

Do you agree that the position of blacks in U.S. society is inseparable from the question of the position of working people generally? Or do you think racism is a quite separate issue from that of economic systems?

Explosion of the ghettos

...When the ghettos exploded in the 1960s, the movement led to the rise of the Black Muslims, the Black Panthers, the League for Revolutionary Black Workers, including the demand for black power. These movements sprang out of the brutal conditions faced by blacks. They were also inspired by the unfolding colonial revolution. Their determination to find a solution to their problems showed the revolutionary potential amongst the most oppressed layers of American society. Many, especially the Panthers, became open to the ideas of Marxism and favoured the creation of a new workers' party. In a short space of time they evolved from a largely black nationalist movement to a revolutionary movement. Unfortunately, the Panther's lack of clear perspectives or a programme served to derail the movement. Subject to vicious state repression, the Panthers went into crisis, and suffered a whole series of splits.

Do you agree that affirmative action policies were passed with the intention of undermining the civil rights movement?

On top of the policy of state repression, the ruling class made a series of concessions which served to undermine the movement. These became known as affirmative action policies, which set quotas for the number of blacks to be employed in jobs. This system, in reality, has helped only a small minority of blacks, mainly from the middle class.... In practice, affirmative action has not worked. During this period, real wages and living standards have declined and the jobs market has shrunk. The position of black workers is no better than before—in fact, it is worse. ...The problem of jobs is a central issue. Does the labour movement simply ignore discrimination at work or elsewhere? Absolutely not!...We must fight for a class alternative to affirmative action, that can draw the ranks of the working class together in common struggle....The labour movement must make it clear at all times that it is not prepared to stand for discrimination against blacks or other minorities....

Do you agree that the position of black workers is worse now than before the 1950s? Is the answer the same for all parts of the country and all kinds of work?

Summary

The first article is an interview with the activist Rosa Parks. Most of the questions relate to the incident in 1955 when she was arrested for refusing to give up her seat on a bus to a white man, as she was then legally required to do. Her action led to the bus boycott in Montgomery, Alabama, which in turn catalyzed the modern civil rights movement. The final question, however, is about the present state of relations between blacks and whites in the United States. She says that in her view, although there is "still as much racism among some people," black people no longer have to endure legally enforced segregation. The implication is that they are therefore better off than they used to be.

In the second article, from 1999, Rob Sewell takes a radically different view of the current plight of African Americans. He points out that despite the reforms of the previous 30 years, the current rate of unemployment among blacks is still twice as high as that of whites, and that those blacks who do work tend to have low-paid, menial jobs—African American earnings are running at 58 percent of white wages. Further, a higher percentage of blacks than whites is in prison, and there are still racial murders. He concludes that, since only 13 percent of the population of the United States is black, they will never be powerful enough to attain equality unless they unite with poor whites, whose real income declined by 18 percent between 1973 and 1995. Although many people believe that racism is the product of ignorance, Sewell thinks that it is a function of divide-and-rule capitalism—poor whites have been turned against poor blacks by "Corporate America."

FURTHER INFORMATION:

Books:

Chafe, William H. (ed.), *Remembering Jim Crow: African Americans Tell about Life in the Segregated South*. New York: New Press, 2001.

D'Angelo, Raymond (ed.), *The American Civil Rights Movement: Readings and Interpretations*. Guilford, CT: McGraw-Hill/Dushkin, 2001.

Morris, Aldon D., *The Origins of the Civil Rights Movement: Black Communities Organizing for Change*. New York: Free Press, 1984.

Useful websites:

www.jimcrowhistory.org/home.htm
Site based on the PBS series *The Rise and Fall of Jim Crow*, with historical background and resources for teachers.
www.stanford.edu/group/king/
The Martin Luther King, Jr., Papers Project site.

www.usccr.gov/
U.S. Commission on Civil Rights. Site of the bipartisan organization set up to monitor progress on civil rights.

The following debates in the Pro/Con series may also be of interest:

In this volume:

Topic 4 Was Reconstruction a success?

Topic 13 Did the FBI persecute Dr Martin Luther King, Jr.?

DID THE CIVIL RIGHTS MOVEMENT IMPROVE THE POSITION OF BLACKS IN SOCIETY?

YES: Segregation was outlawed; the act was like the Magna Carta for the United States

YES: There is no longer one law for whites and another for blacks

SEGREGATION
Has the 1964 Civil Rights Act achieved what it set out to do?

JUSTICE FOR ALL
Has the movement achieved equality under the law?

NO: Many people deliberately dragged their feet in implementing the new law; there is still some segregation in the 21st century

NO: In percentage terms there are far more blacks than whites in U.S. prisons

DID THE CIVIL RIGHTS MOVEMENT IMPROVE THE POSITION OF BLACKS IN SOCIETY?

KEY POINTS

YES: There is an active black caucus in Congress; there is no walk of life from which African Americans are barred

YES: Blacks have been given more job opportunities than ever before; health care is available on the same basis as for whites

SOCIAL INCLUSIVENESS
Are blacks now fully involved in, and benefiting from, all aspects of American life?

NO: Affirmative action is often poorly implemented; the percentage of African Americans in positions of power and responsibility is lower than their percentage of the population

NO: Most blacks have low-grade, badly paid jobs; black infant mortality is twice as high as that of white children

Topic 13
DID THE FBI PERSECUTE DR. MARTIN LUTHER KING, JR.?

YES

FROM "THE FBI'S VENDETTA AGAINST MARTIN LUTHER KING, JR."
THE LAWLESS STATE: THE CRIMES OF THE U.S. INTELLIGENCE AGENCIES
AS EXTRACTED ON WWW.THIRDWORLDTRAVELER.COM
MORTON HALPERIN, JERRY BERMAN, ROBERT BOROSAGE, CHRISTINE MARWICK

NO

FROM "THE BEAST AS SAINT: THE TRUTH ABOUT MARTIN LUTHER KING, JR."
SPEECH, AMERICAN DISSIDENT VOICES (RADIO PROGRAM), JANUARY 15, 1994
KEVIN ALFRED STROM

INTRODUCTION

Martin Luther King, Jr., (1929–1968) was the best-known of the leaders of the civil rights movement in the United States during the 1960s. Born to a Baptist pastor in Atlanta, Georgia, in 1929, King studied theology before becoming a preacher and setting up the first black ministry in Montgomery, Alabama, in 1955. Shortly afterward he achieved national prominence by leading the Alabama bus boycott, in which blacks refused to use buses in a protest against segregated seating. In 1959 King founded the Southern Christian Leadership Conference (SCLC), which led the civil rights movement in the 1960s.

King based his campaign on nonviolence—his tactics included protest marches, strikes, and economic boycotts—and on his gift for stirring oratory. In August 1963 he led the March on Washington, in which hundreds of thousands assembled in the capital to protest for civil liberties and hear King deliver his famous speech, "I Have a Dream."

The recipient of the Nobel Peace Prize and the Kennedy Peace Prize in 1964, King was assassinated four years later by a white drifter named James Earl Ray, who shot him in Memphis, Tennessee. Ray was sentenced to 99 years in prison, but by the end of the century King's own family had joined the growing number of people who doubted Ray's guilt, or at least his sole guilt. The assassination, like that of President John F. Kennedy, remains a favorite topic of conspiracy theorists. King's own role in shaping U.S. society was recognized in 1986, when the third Monday in January was declared Martin Luther King Day.

King's rise to prominence in the civil rights movement brought him to the attention of the Federal Bureau of Investigation (FBI) and its director,

J. Edgar Hoover (1895-1972). Among the bureau's responsibilities was monitoring possible sources of threats to the U.S. government and Constitution. The FBI was wary of the powerful leaders of the civil rights movement. That partly may have stemmed from racism, but it also reflected a concern about the possible links between civil rights campaigners and communists in the United States.

> *"We are a fact-gathering organization only. We don't clear anybody. We don't condemn anybody."*
> —J. EDGAR HOOVER, JUNE 14, 1956

At the height of the Cold War the idea that the American way of life was under grave threat seemed very real to some people. Hoover and other right-wing thinkers only served to encourage that sense of imminent danger.

In October 1963 Attorney General Robert F. Kennedy—himself a noted liberal—authorized the FBI to put King under surveillance by tapping his telephones and bugging his hotel rooms. In November 1964 Hoover publicly branded King the "most notorious liar" in America and "one of the lowest characters in the country." Hoover had gathered information relating to King's extramarital sexual affairs. The agency sent King a tape of recordings of incriminating phone calls and a letter attempting to blackmail him into committing suicide.

Some critics view such treatment as persecution. They argue that King was a national figure whose personal life had no bearing on his political life. They also argue that Hoover was motivated by an obsession with King's sex life and a determination to end his career. Some theorists take the argument even further. They claim that the FBI was complicit in King's assassination. Such speculation has been fueled by reported discrepancies between the gun fired by Ray and the bullets that killed King.

There are supporters of the FBI, however, who argue that the bureau's treatment of King was by and large acceptable judged by the standards of the time—although few deny that the letter urging King to suicide was inexcusable. At the time nobody knew that King would become a national hero: He seemed to be a potentially dangerous radical. It was not only the FBI that feared King might be dangerous: The surveillance operation was authorized by the Democratic administration of President John F. Kennedy. There was some real evidence of communist influence, albeit very limited, in the civil rights movement.

Apologists for the FBI allege that King was not just involved with communism, but also that he was embezzling funds from the civil rights movement itself. They also assert that the FBI did not comprise J. Edgar Hoover alone, though he was certainly highly influential in shaping its operations, but also other agents who were far more sympathetic to King and the civil rights cause.

In the first article that follows, Morton Halperin and his colleagues argue that the FBI took the law into its own hands in its attempts to discredit King. But Kevin Alfred Strom, in the second extract, claims that the FBI was right to treat him with suspicion.

THE FBI'S VENDETTA AGAINST MARTIN LUTHER KING, JR.
Morton Halperin, et al.

YES

The unfolding story of the civil rights protest movement and the leadership role of Martin Luther King, Jr., is a most ignoble chapter in the history of FBI spying and manipulation. As the civil rights movement grew and expanded, the FBI pinpointed every group and emergent leader for intensive investigation and most for harassment and disruption, the FBI's domestic version of CIA covert action abroad. The NAACP [National Association for the Advancement of Colored People] was the subject of a COMINFIL investigation. The Congress of Racial Equality (CORE) and the Student Nonviolent Coordinating Committee (SNCC) were listed by the FBI as "Black-Hate" type organizations and selected for covert disruption of their political activities. But the most vicious FBI attack was reserved for King and the Southern Christian Leadership Conference [SCLC]. All of the arbitrary power and lawless tactics that had accumulated in the bureau over the years were marshaled to destroy King's reputation and the movement he led. The FBI relied on its vague authority to investigate "subversives" to spy on King and SCLC; its vague authority to conduct warrantless wiretapping and microphonic surveillance to tap and bug him; its secrecy to conduct covert operations against him. ...

> COMINFIL is an acronym for communist infiltration and the FBI code-name for investigations undertaken against organizations from the Boy Scouts to the National Association for the Advancement of Colored People. The program began in March 1960 and investigated those whom FBI officials considered as being possibly under communist influence.

I have a dream

On August 28, 250,000 persons marched on Washington. The march, sponsored by a cross-section of civil rights, labor, and church organizations, was designed to support the enactment of civil rights legislation. That day, when Martin Luther King addressed the assemblage, he made his most memorable speech: "I have a dream ..." The speech brought the crowd to its feet, applauding, echoing the "Amens" that greet evangelical preaching, and shouting "Freedom Now!" The FBI reacted differently. In memoranda to the director, King's speech was characterized as "demagogic," and the presence of "200" Communists among the 250,000 marchers caused the Intelligence Division to state that it had

> A demagogue is a leader who makes use of popular prejudices and false claims and promises in order to gain power.

underestimated communist efforts and influence on American Negroes and the civil rights movement....

More ominously, the FBI suggested that "legal" efforts to deal with King might not be enough. "It may be unrealistic," the memorandum went on, "to limit ourselves as we have been doing to legalistic proofs or definitely conclusive evidence that would stand up in testimony in court or before Congressional Committees...."

On October 1, 1963, Hoover received and then approved a combined COMINFIL-COINTELPRO plan against the civil rights movement. The approved plan called for intensifying "coverage of Communist influence on the Negro." It recommended the "use of all possible investigative techniques" and stated an "urgent need for imaginative and aggressive tactics ... to neutralize or disrupt the Party's activities in the Negro field."

Imaginative and aggressive tactics

On October 10 and 21, Attorney General Kennedy gave the FBI one of those "investigative techniques" by approving the wiretaps on King. On October 18, 1963, the FBI distributed a different kind of memorandum on King, not only to the Justice Department, but to officials at the White House, the Central Intelligence Agency, the State Department, the Defense Department, and Defense Department intelligence agencies. It summarized the bureau's Communist Party charges against King and went much further. According to Assistant Attorney General Burke Marshall, it was a personal diatribe ... a personal attack without evidentiary support on the character, the moral character and person of Dr. Martin Luther King, and it was only peripherally related to anything substantive, like whether or not there was communist infiltration or influence on the civil rights movement.... It was a personal attack on the man and went far afield from the charges [of possible Communist influence].

The Attorney General was outraged and demanded that Hoover seek the return of the report. By October 28, all copies were returned. This was the first—and last—official action to deter Hoover's vendetta against King.

In November, John F. Kennedy was assassinated ....While the nation mourned, the FBI held a conference at the beginning of December to plan its campaign to destroy King and the civil rights movement. At that all-day meeting FBI officials put forward proposals that make G. Gordon Liddy's Watergate plan seem pale by comparison. Officials of the nation's number one law enforcement agency agreed to use

J. Edgar Hoover (1895–1972) was director of the Federal Bureau of Investigation (FBI) from 1924 until his death in 1972. During the 1930s he participated in the arrest of several major gangsters in his battle against organized crime. After World War II (1939–1945) he switched his attention to fighting communism. He accumulated enormous power, not least through the secret files he amassed on the private lives of public figures.

John F. Kennedy (1917–1963) was the 35th president. He was the first Catholic and the youngest person to be elected president. On November 22, 1963, he was assassinated by rifle fire while being driven through Dallas, Texas in an open car. The alleged assassin, Lee Harvey Oswald (1939–1963), was shot and killed two days later by Jack Ruby (1911–1967). Kennedy's assassination is still controversial. It is the subject of many conspiracy theories.

Entrapment is luring someone into behaving or acting in a compromising way that could be used against them later. In many countries it is illegal. Do you think the end ever justifies the means?

"all available investigative techniques" to develop information for use "to discredit" King. Proposals discussed included using ministers, "disgruntled" acquaintances, "aggressive" newsmen, "colored" agents, Dr. King's housekeeper, and even Dr. King's wife or "placing a good looking female plant in King's office" to develop discrediting information and to take action that would lead to his disgrace.

Illegal bugs

From the nature of Burke Marshall's description of the October 18 report, it is obvious that the FBI was on to something it viewed as unsavory about King's private life. The report made the charges, but as Marshall said, there was no "evidentiary" support. Now the FBI was out to get the proof. By January, the FBI had initiated … surveillance of King, deploying its most experienced personnel to gather information, and had placed the first of many illegal bugs in Dr. King's room at the Willard Hotel in Washington, D.C.

According to Justice Department regulations at the time, microphonic surveillance …, did not require the approval of the attorney general. Even under its own regulations, however, the FBI could only use this technique to gather "important intelligence or evidence relating to matters connected with national security." In this case the FBI

Do you think that taping private conversations is constitutional?

planned to use "bugs" to learn about "the [private] activities of Dr. King and his associates" so that King could be "completely discredited." It was clearly illegal.

The Willard Hotel "bug" yielded "19 reels" of tape. The FBI, at least in its own opinion, had struck pay dirt. The bug apparently picked up information about King's private extramarital and perhaps "inter-racial" sexual activities. This opened up the possibility of discrediting King as a Communist who engaged in "moral improprieties." For J. Edgar Hoover, "immoral" behavior was a crime comparable to "subversive" activity—and of equal utility.…

The authors list degrees, awards, and honors that Martin Luther King, Jr., received worldwide to emphasize that he was a highly respected citizen. But do such awards say anything about King's character?

With Kennedy and Lyndon Johnson pressing action on civil rights legislation and calling for a "War on Poverty," Martin Luther King was a man the country and the world thought worthy of honor… In 1964, while continuing his "nonviolent" activities on behalf of civil rights in St. Augustine, Florida, and other cities, King was awarded honorary degrees by universities; he was invited by Willy Brandt, the mayor of West Berlin, to speak at a ceremony honoring the memory of President Kennedy; he had an audience with Pope Paul VI in Rome; and, in October, he was named by the Nobel Prize Committee to receive the Peace Prize in December…

In April, Hoover was quoted in the press as having testified that "Communist influence does exist in the civil rights movement." King reacted sharply "…We challenge all who raise the "red" issue, whether they be newspaper columnists or the head of the FBI himself, to come forward and provide real evidence which contradicts this stand of the SCLC. We are confident that this cannot be done."

Civil rights movement and communism

… Hoover's first response was to say that it was incumbent on the civil rights movement to prove that there was no Communist influence.… Asked to respond to King's charges, Hoover, off the record, called King "one of the lowest characters in the country." On the record, he called King the most "notorious liar" in the country. Hoover's comments were widely publicized.

King's response this time was designed to dampen the controversy. "I cannot conceive of Mr. Hoover making a statement like this," King said, "without being under extreme pressure. He has apparently faltered under the awesome burden, complexities, and responsibilities of his office." King also sent Hoover a telegram stating that while he had criticized the bureau, the director's response was "a mystery to me" and expressed a desire "to discuss this question with you at length."

On November 27, Roy Wilkins was told … that if King wanted "war" the FBI was prepared to engage in one, and the two of them discussed the FBI's "derogatory" material. Wilkins told DeLoach that if the FBI made it public, it could ruin the civil rights movement. Obviously Wilkins reported this back to King, and a number of leaders, including King, agreed to take steps to set up a meeting with the director. Hoover agreed to meet with King on December 1.…

According to all accounts, the meeting was exceedingly cordial.… Only now do we know how close the FBI came to an all-out confrontation. Unknown to King or SCLC until later, the FBI, at the height of the public controversy, took its most distressing step. It mailed the "tapes" to the SCLC office in Atlanta with a covering letter urging King to commit suicide or face public revelation of the information on the tapes on the eve of the award ceremonies in Sweden.…

Although public scandal was averted at the last moment, the FBI's campaign continued. From 1965 until King's death [three years later], the covert effort of the FBI to destroy King and to topple him from "his pedestal" continued.…

For more information on the civil rights movement see Civil Rights timeline, 1942–1992, in Volume 1, Individual and Society, pages 34–35.

Do you think there is much difference between J. Edgar Hoover's comments on the record and off? What does that tell us about his opinion of Martin Luther King, Jr.?

Do you think Hoover's campaign to discredit Martin Luther King, Jr., would have been more successful if he had been less emotional in his dealings with him?

THE BEAST AS SAINT...
Kevin Alfred Strom

Why do you think the author applies the words "so-called" to King? What kind of impression does that create?

NO

...Every January, the media go into a kind of almost spastic frenzy of adulation for the so-called "Reverend Doctor Martin Luther King, Jr." King has even had a national holiday declared in his honor, an honor accorded to no other American, not Washington, not Jefferson, not Lincoln. (Washington and Lincoln no longer have holidays—they share the generic-sounding "President's Day.")

A liberal judge has sealed the FBI files on King until the year 2027. What are they hiding? Let's take a look at this modern-day plastic god....

The FBI and King

The author talks about the "controlled media." What does he mean by that term? Who is controlling it?

Lest you be tempted to believe the controlled media's lie about "racists" in the FBI being out to "get" King, you should be aware that the man most responsible for the FBI's probe of King was Assistant Director William C. Sullivan. Sullivan describes himself as a liberal, and says that initially "I was one hundred per cent for King ... because I saw him as an effective and badly needed leader for the Black people in their desire for civil rights."

The probe of King not only confirmed their suspicions about King's Communist beliefs and associations, but it also revealed King to be a despicable hypocrite, an immoral degenerate, and a worthless charlatan.

According to Assistant Director Sullivan, who had direct access to the surveillance files on King which are denied the American people King had embezzled or misapplied substantial amounts of money contributed to the "civil rights" movement. King used SCLC funds to pay for liquor, and numerous prostitutes both Black and White, who were brought to his hotel rooms, often two at a time, for drunken sex parties which sometimes lasted for several days. These types of activities were the norm for King's speaking and organizing tours.

The Lorraine Motel

The National Civil Rights Museum (NCRM) opened in 1991 on the site of the Lorraine Motel in Memphis. Visit their website: www.civilrights museum.org for more information.

In fact, an outfit called The National Civil Rights Museum in Memphis, Tennessee, which is putting on display the two bedrooms from the Lorraine Motel where King stayed the

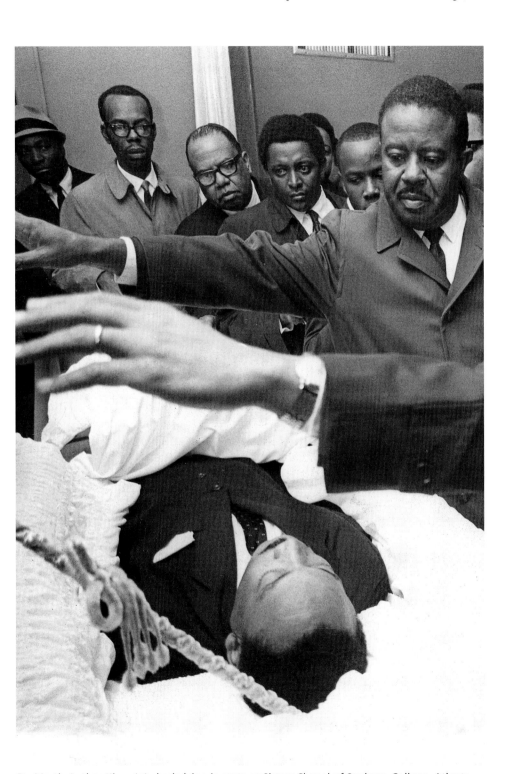

Dr. Martin Luther King, Jr.'s, body lying in state at Sisters Chapel of Spelman College, Atlanta.

COMMENTARY: COINTELPRO

COINTELPRO is an acronym for the FBI's secret counterintelligence programs that were at work from 1956 to 1971. Counterintelligence is defined as those actions by an intelligence agency intended to protect its own security and to undermine hostile intelligence operations. Techniques the FBI had employed to combat hostile foreign agents were used against domestic threats to the established social and political order. The goal of the secret programs was to "misdirect, discredit, disrupt, and otherwise neutralize specific individuals and groups." Those programs took place during the Cold War, at a time when fear and suspicion of communism were at an all-time high. The programs were exposed in 1971 and were officially ended.

The targets
The programs were aimed at five groups that the FBI considered threats to domestic tranquillity:
- Communist Party, USA (CPUSA)
- Socialist Worker's Party (SWP)
- White hate groups (targeted the Ku Klux Klan, American Nazi Party, and the National States Rights Party)
- Black nationalist hate groups (targeted Congress of Racial Equality, Nation of Islam, Student Nonviolent Coordinating Committee, Deacons of Defense and Justice, the Southern Christian Leadership Conference (SLCL), Black Panther Party, and Martin Luther King, Jr.)
- New Left program (targeted Students for a Democratic Society: SDS)

The methods
The FBI used infiltration, harrassment, forged correspondence, anonymous letters and telephone calls, and threats of violence and burglary to frighten activists and disrupt their activities. In 1971 the programs were exposed, and five years later restrictions were imposed on the FBI to curtail their surveillance programs. Following the terrorist action of September 11, 2001, however, in May 2002 Attorney General John Ashcroft once again granted the FBI powers to carry out domestic surveillance.

night before he was shot, has declined to depict in any way the "occupants" of those rooms. That according to exhibit designer Gerard Eisterhold would be "close to blasphemy." The reason? Dr. Martin Luther King, Jr., spent his last night on Earth having sex with two women at the motel and physically beating and abusing a third.

Sullivan also stated that King had alienated the affections of numerous married women. According to Sullivan, who in 30 years with the Bureau had seen everything there was to be seen of the seamy side of life, King was one of only seven people he had ever encountered who was such a total degenerate.

King and violence?

Noting the violence that almost invariably attended King's supposedly "non-violent" marches, Sullivan's probe revealed a very different King from the carefully crafted public image. King welcomed members of many different Black groups as members of his SCLC, many of them advocates and practitioners of violence. King's only admonition on the subject was that they should embrace "tactical nonviolence."

Sullivan also relates an incident in which King met in a financial conference with Communist Party representatives, not knowing that one of the participants was an infiltrator actually working for the FBI.

J. Edgar Hoover personally saw to it that documented information on King's Communist connections was provided to the President and to Congress. And conclusive information from FBI files was also provided to major newspapers and news wire services. But were the American people informed of King's real nature? No, for even in the 1960s, the fix was in the controlled media and the bought politicians were bound and determined to push their racial mixing program on America. King was their man and nothing was going to get in their way. With a few minor exceptions, these facts have been kept from the American people. The pro-King propaganda machine grinds on, and it is even reported that a serious proposal has been made to add some of King's writings as a new book in the Bible.

Ladies and gentlemen, the purpose of this radio program is far greater than to prove to you the immorality and subversion of this man called King. I want you to start to think for yourselves. I want you to consider this: What are the forces and motivation behind the controlled media's active promotion of King? What does it tell you about our politicians when you see them, almost without exception, falling all over themselves to honor King as a national hero? What does it tell you about our society when any public criticism of this moral leper and Communist functionary is considered grounds for dismissal? What does it tell you about the controlled media when you see how they have successfully suppressed the truth and held out a picture of King that can only be described as a colossal lie?

You need to think, my fellow Americans. You desperately need to wake up.

Using extreme language, examples, or anecdotes can capture your audience's attention and make your argument more convincing. It can, however, also detract from it.

The author claims that in the 1960s the media and politicians were involved in a plan to promote racial mixing. He expresses it in such language as to make it a negative thing. Why do you think that is?

Strom suggests that people lose their jobs for criticizing King, but he gives no examples. Does that weaken the case for his argument?

Summary

In their book *The Lawless State* Morton Halperin and his colleagues call the FBI treatment of Martin Luther King, Jr., "a most ignoble chapter" in the bureau's history. They argue that the surveillance of King reflected lawless and arbitrary victimization of the civil rights leader and highlight the weak basis for the FBI claim of communist involvement in the civil rights movement. They also report evidence that J. Edgar Hoover had a personal vendetta against Dr. King and suggest that attempts to entrap and spy on King were barely legal. In contrast to the honors being showered on the preacher in 1964, Halperin writes, the FBI attempted to blackmail him into suicide by threatening to reveal details of his personal behavior.

In "The Beast as Saint," originally broadcast in 1994, Kevin Alfred Strom begins by questioning the decision to seal the FBI files on King until 2027. He goes on to suggest that the decision is part of a liberal attempt to protect King's reputation. He cites the apparent sympathies of some FBI operatives with the civil rights movement but then suggests that King's financial and sexual misdeeds branded him a "degenerate." Although the FBI provided clear information about King's personality to the president and to Congress, none of its evidence ever appeared in the national media. Strom sees this as evidence of a deep malaise in the "controlled media," which has created "a colossal lie about King," and concludes with a call to Americans to "wake up."

FURTHER INFORMATION:

Books:

Churchill, Ward, and Jim Vander Wall, *The Cointelpro Papers: Documents from the FBI's Secret Wars against Domestic Dissent*. Boston, MA: South End Press, 1990.

Garrow, David J., *The FBI and Martin Luther King*. Harmondsworth and New York: Penguin, 1981.

Gentry, Curt, *J. Edgar Hoover: The Man and His Secrets*. New York: Norton, 1991.

McKnight, Gerald, *The Last Crusade: Martin Luther King, Jr., the FBI, and the Poor People's Campaign*. Boulder, CO: Westview Press, 1998.

O'Reilly, Kenneth (ed.), *Black Americans: The FBI Files*. New York: Carroll and Graf, 1994.

Perkus, Cathy (ed.), *Cointelpro: The FBI's Secret War on Political Freedom*, New York: Monad Press, 1975.

Useful websites:

www.usdoj.gov/crt/crim/mlk/part1.htm
"Department of Justice Investigation of Recent Allegations Regarding the Assassination of Dr. Martin Luther King, Jr." The report, which was released on June 9, 2000, found "no reliable evidence that Dr. King was killed by conspirators who framed James Earl Ray."
www.aclu.org/congress/kingreport.pdf
ACLU "Report on the Dangers of Domestic Spying by Federal Law Enforcement: A Case Study on FBI Surveillance of Dr. Martin Luther King," January 2002.

The following debates in the Pro/Con series may also be of interest:

In *Individual and Society*:
Civil rights timeline, 1942–1992, pages 34–35

Topic 8 Should people have to obey unjust laws?

DID THE FBI PERSECUTE DR. MARTIN LUTHER KING, JR.?

YES: Everyone in public life is open to moral scrutiny, especially someone who is not only a preacher but who also bases his message on moral grounds

YES: Although it is difficult to understand now, there was a very real fear of communism and other forms of subversion in the 1960s

FEET OF CLAY
Was Martin Luther King, Jr.'s, personal life relevant to his political life?

WITCH HUNT
Was alleged communist influence in the civil rights movement an excuse for FBI actions?

NO: Public figures are no more perfect than any other members of society. King's behavior is a matter for him, his family, and his god.

NO: There have never been many communists in the United States. The few who were involved in the civil rights movement were peripheral figures with no powers.

DID THE FBI PERSECUTE DR. MARTIN LUTHER KING, JR? KEY POINTS

YES: Details of financial and sexual scandals are contained in the FBI reports on King. The liberal establishment has sealed those records until 2027 to protect his reputation.

YES: Fingerprints on the gun used in the shooting prove that Ray fired the fatal shots. He was found guilty in a court.

EVIDENCE
Did the FBI have evidence that King had behaved improperly?

ASSASSINATION
Was James Earl Ray acting alone when he shot King dead?

NO: If evidence of King's alleged misdemeanors existed, it would have come to light. Before he was acknowledged as a national hero, many people would have been happy to destroy his reputation.

NO: Ballistic evidence suggests that the gun might not prove Ray's guilt. The FBI had King under constant surveillance: It was either complicit in the murder or knew that King was being stalked by his killers.

Topic 14
WAS THE VIETNAM WAR AVOIDABLE?

YES

FROM "VIETNAM VETERANS AGAINST THE WAR STATEMENT"
SENATE COMMITTEE ON FOREIGN RELATIONS, APRIL 23, 1971
JOHN KERRY

NO

FROM "PEACE WITHOUT CONQUEST"
ADDRESS AT JOHNS HOPKINS UNIVERSITY, APRIL 7, 1965
LYNDON B. JOHNSON

INTRODUCTION

The Vietnam War was the United States' longest armed conflict, direct American military intervention in Vietnam lasting from the mid-1960s to 1973. During that time around 3 million American service personnel were engaged in Vietnam, and more than 58,000 Americans lost their lives. But why was the United States involved militarily in Vietnam, and could the war have been avoided?

America's Vietnam War had its roots in the 1950s, and the buildup to full military involvement was gradual. From 1946 to 1954 Vietnam fought for independence from France. Together with Laos and Cambodia, Vietnam made up Indochina, which had been part of the French colonial empire since the 1800s. Resistance to France centered on the League for Vietnamese Independence—the Vietminh—an organization that had also resisted the occupying Japanese during World War II (1939–1945). The leader of the Vietminh was Ho Chi Minh (1890–1969), a Russian-trained

communist. In 1949 China, Vietnam's giant neighbor, became a communist state. Fearful that Vietnam might go the same way, to be followed, like a set of falling dominoes, by the rest of Southeast Asia, the government of President Harry S. Truman (1884–1972) provided France with aid in its fight against the Vietminh.

In May 1954, however, the Vietminh defeated the French decisively at Dien Bien Phu, bringing the eight-year anticolonial conflict to a close. The subsequent agreement, the Geneva Accords, divided Vietnam into two states at the 17th parallel. The northern state—North Vietnam—recognized Ho Chi Minh's government. South Vietnam, meanwhile, was led by Ngo Dinh Diem (1901–1963). With a communist government now in place in the north, the United States desired a strong South Vietnam. The administration of President Dwight D. Eisenhower (1890–1969) provided Diem with economic and military aid to cement his regime in place and keep the communists at bay. However, Diem's authoritarian methods and his refusal to hold elections to unite the country, as specified in the Geneva Accords, led to unrest. Foremost among the insurgents were the South Vietnamese communists, or Vietcong, who in 1960 joined with other anti-Diem groups to become the National Liberation Front (NLF).

> *"You have a row of dominoes set up, you knock over the first one, and what will happen to the last one is the certainty that it will go over very quickly."*
> —DWIGHT D. EISENHOWER, 34TH PRESIDENT (1953–1961), EXPLAINS THE DOMINO THEORY

Faced with the formation of the NLF, which Washington believed was controlled by the communist North, and heightened guerrilla activity, the United States increased its military presence in South Vietnam. In 1960 there were around 900 U.S. service personnel in the country acting as military advisers. Under President John F. Kennedy (1917–1963) the figure rose to 16,000.

It was during the tenure of Kennedy's successor, Lyndon B. Johnson (1908–1973), that the United States took the step to direct military intervention in Vietnam. The trigger was the alleged attacks by the North Vietnamese on two U.S. Navy vessels in the Gulf of Tonkin in August 1964. Days later Congress passed the Tonkin Gulf Resolution, which effectively permitted the president to go to war. Johnson ordered air strikes against North Vietnam in retaliation for the Tonkin Gulf attacks, and America's Vietnam War was under way in earnest.

So was the war avoidable? Those who say no contend that it was a necessary conflict to prevent the spread of communism in Southeast Asia and one the United States needed to enter as a leading advocate of freedom. They further point to the U.S. commitment to stand by South Vietnam, arguing that to walk away would have been a breach of trust. Not only that, such an action would have undermined American credibility in other countries potentially faced with a similar situation.

Commentators who argue that the Vietnam War was avoidable, including many Americans at the time, dismiss as paranoia the U.S. fear of the spread of communism. They also argue that it was only the corrupt government of South Vietnam that wanted U.S. assistance, not the country's population. If only the U.S. government had had the strength to admit it had made a mistake, these critics contend, America's war might never have taken place. But successive presidents had sanctioned American involvement in Vietnam, and none could face the political consequences of pulling out.

The following pieces provide two contemporary perspectives on the war. The first, a 1971 statement by John Kerry to the Senate Committee on Foreign Affairs, gives the view of the Vietnam Veterans Against the War. In the second, a 1965 presidential address, Lyndon B. Johnson explains why the war has to be fought.

VIETNAM VETERANS AGAINST THE WAR STATEMENT
John Kerry

The author, John Kerry (1943–), served as a U.S. Navy officer in the Vietnam War and later became a spokesperson for the Vietnam Veterans Against the War. In 1984 he was elected as a senator for Massachusetts.

YES

I would like to talk on behalf of all those veterans and say that several months ago in Detroit we had an investigation at which over 150 honorably discharged, and many very highly decorated, veterans testified to war crimes committed in Southeast Asia. These were not isolated incidents but crimes committed on a day-to-day basis with the full awareness of officers at all levels of command. It is impossible to describe to you exactly what did happen in Detroit—the emotions in the room and the feelings of the men who were reliving their experiences in Vietnam. They relived the absolute horror of what this country, in a sense, made them do.

Genghis Khan (1162–1227) founded the great Mongol Empire of the Middle Ages. His campaigns of conquest were notorious for the devastation they wrought.

Horrors of war

They told stories that at times they had personally raped, cut off ears, cut off heads, taped wires from portable telephones to human genitals and turned up the power, cut off limbs, blown up bodies, randomly shot at civilians, razed villages in fashion reminiscent of Genghis Khan, shot cattle and dogs for fun, poisoned food stocks, and generally ravaged the countryside of South Vietnam in addition to the normal ravage of war and the normal and very particular ravaging which is done by the applied bombing power of this country.

In The American Crisis, a series of articles on the American Revolution, political theorist Thomas Paine (1737–1809) wrote, "These are the times that try men's souls. The summer soldier and the sunshine patriot will, in this crisis, shrink from the service of their country."

Winter soldiers

We call this investigation the Winter Soldier Investigation. The term *Winter Soldier* is a play on words of Thomas Paine's in 1776 when he spoke of the Sunshine Patriots and summertime soldiers who deserted at Valley Forge because the going was rough.

We who have come here to Washington have come here because we feel we have to be winter soldiers now. We could come back to this country, we could be quiet, we could hold our silence, we could not tell what went on in Vietnam, but we feel because of what threatens this country, not the reds, but the crimes which we are committing that threaten it, that we have to speak out....

In our opinion and from our experience, there is nothing in South Vietnam which could happen that realistically threatens the United States of America. And to attempt to justify the loss of one American life in Vietnam, Cambodia or Laos by linking such loss to the preservation of freedom, which those misfits supposedly abuse, is to us the height of criminal hypocrisy, and it is that kind of hypocrisy which we feel has torn this country apart.

The Vietnam experience

We found that not only was it a civil war, an effort by a people who had for years been seeking their liberation from any colonial influence whatsoever, but also we found that the Vietnamese whom we had enthusiastically molded after our own image were hard put to take up the fight against the threat we were supposedly saving them from.

We found most people didn't even know the difference between communism and democracy. They only wanted to work in rice paddies without helicopters strafing them and bombs with napalm burning their villages and tearing their country apart. They wanted everything to do with the war, particularly with this foreign presence of the United States of America, to leave them alone in peace, and they practiced the art of survival by siding with whichever military force was present at a particular time, be it Viet Cong, North Vietnamese or American.

> To add emphasis to his argument, the author has used the same verb and sentence structure to introduce three consecutive paragraphs.

We found also that all too often American men were dying in those rice paddies for want of support from their allies. We saw first hand how monies from American taxes were used for a corrupt dictatorial regime. We saw that many people in this country had a one-sided idea of who was kept free by the flag, and blacks provided the highest percentage of casualties. We saw Vietnam ravaged equally by American bombs and search and destroy missions, as well as by Viet Cong terrorism—and yet we listened while this country tried to blame all of the havoc on the Viet Cong.

Moral breakdown

We rationalized destroying villages in order to save them. We saw America lose her sense of morality as she accepted very coolly a My Lai and refused to give up the image of American soldiers who hand out chocolate bars and chewing gum.

> The My Lai massacre was an infamous atrocity carried out by U.S. service personnel in Vietnam in 1968. See Volume 9, Criminal Law and the Penal System, Topic 4 Should soldiers be prosecuted for crimes committed during war?

We learned the meaning of free fire zones, shooting anything that moves, and we watched while America placed a cheapness on the lives of orientals.

We watched the United States' falsification of body counts, in fact the glorification of body counts. We listened while month after month we were told the back of the enemy was about to break. We fought using weapons against "oriental human beings." We fought using weapons against those people which I do not believe this country would dream of using were we fighting in the European theater. We watched while men charged up hills because a general said that hill has to be taken, and after losing one platoon or two platoons they marched away to leave the hill for reoccupation by the North Vietnamese. We watched pride allow the most unimportant battles to be blown into extravaganzas, because we couldn't lose, and we couldn't retreat, and because it didn't matter how many American bodies were lost to prove that point, and so there were Hamburger Hills and Khe Sanhs and Hill 81s and Fire Base 6s, and so many others.

Now we are told that the men who fought there must watch quietly while American lives are lost so that we can exercise the incredible arrogance of Vietnamizing the Vietnamese.

Each day to facilitate the process by which the United States washes her hands of Vietnam someone has to give up his life so that the United States doesn't have to admit something that the entire world already knows, so that we can't say that we have made a mistake. Someone has to die so that President Nixon won't be, and these are his words, "the first President to lose a war."

"Vietnamization" was the term for the U.S. handover of South Vietnam's defense to the South Vietnamese as American troops were steadily withdrawn from the country. The process began in 1969 under the government of President Richard M. Nixon (1969–1974).

More than just war and diplomacy

We are asking Americans to think about that because how do you ask a man to be the last man to die in Vietnam? How do you ask a man to be the last man to die for a mistake?… We are here in Washington to say that the problem of this war is not just a question of war and diplomacy. It is part and parcel of everything that we are trying as human beings to communicate to people in this country—the question of racism which is rampant in the military, and so many other questions such as the use of weapons; the hypocrisy in our taking umbrage at the Geneva Conventions and using that as justification for a continuation of this war when we are more guilty than any other body of violations of those Geneva Conventions; in the use of free fire zones, harassment interdiction fire, search and destroy missions, the bombings, the torture of prisoners, all accepted policy by many units in South Vietnam. That is what we are trying to say. It is part and parcel of everything.

The Geneva Conventions, not to be confused with the Geneva Accords of 1954 (see page 176), provide for the humane wartime treatment of civilians, prisoners of war, the sick, and the wounded.

An American Indian friend of mine who lives in the Indian Nation of Alcatraz put it to me very succinctly. He told me how as a boy on an Indian reservation he had watched television and he used to cheer the cowboys when they came in and shot the Indians, and then suddenly one day he stopped in Vietnam and he said, "my God, I am doing to these people the very same thing that was done to my people," and he stopped. And that is what we are trying to say, that we think this thing has to end.

We are here to ask, and we are here to ask vehemently, where are the leaders of our country? Where is the leadership? We're here to ask where are McNamara, Rostow, Bundy, Gilpatric, and so many others? Where are they now that we, the men they sent off to war, have returned? These are the commanders who have deserted their troops. And there is no more serious crime in the laws of war. The Army says they never leave their wounded. The marines say they never even leave their dead. These men have left all the casualties and retreated behind a pious shield of public rectitude. They've left the real stuff of their reputations bleaching behind them in the sun in this country....

Robert S. McNamara (1916–), Walt W. Rostow (1916–2003), McGeorge Bundy (1919–1996), and Roswell L. Gilpatric (1906–1996) were senior defense and national security figures in the Kennedy and Johnson administrations of the 1960s. They were involved in formulating American policy in Vietnam.

One last mission

We wish that a merciful God could wipe away our own memories of that service as easily as this administration has wiped away their memories of us. But all that they have done and all that they can do by this denial is to make more clear than ever our own determination to undertake one last mission—to search out and destroy the last vestige of this barbaric war, to pacify our own hearts, to conquer the hate and fear that have driven this country these last ten years and more. And more. And so when thirty years from now our brothers go down the street without a leg, without an arm, or a face, and small boys ask why, we will be able to say "Vietnam" and not mean a desert, not a filthy obscene memory, but mean instead where America finally turned and where soldiers like us helped it in the turning.

The author contrasts the individual experience of the war with that of the politicians. Which viewpoint do you think is more important in recording history?

PEACE WITHOUT CONQUEST
Lyndon B. Johnson

NO

Over this war and all Asia is another reality: the deepening shadow of communist China. The rulers in Hanoi are urged on by Peking. This is a regime which has destroyed freedom in Tibet, which has attacked India and has been condemned by the United Nations for aggression in Korea. It is a nation which is helping the forces of violence in almost every continent. The contest in Vietnam is part of a wider pattern of aggressive purposes.

Why are these realities our concern? Why are we in South Vietnam?

We are there because we have a promise to keep. Since 1954 every American president has offered support to the people of South Vietnam. We have helped to build, and we have helped to defend. Thus, over many years, we have made a national pledge to help South Vietnam defend its independence.

And I intend to keep that promise.

To dishonor that pledge, to abandon this small and brave nation to its enemies, and to the terror that must follow, would be an unforgivable wrong.

The wider picture

We are also there to strengthen world order. Around the globe from Berlin to Thailand are people whose well-being rests in part on the belief that they can count on us if they are attacked. To leave Vietnam to its fate would shake the confidence of all these people in the value of an American commitment and in the value of America's word. The result would be increased unrest and instability and even wider war.

We are also there because there are great stakes in the balance. Let no one think for a moment that retreat from Vietnam would bring an end to conflict. The battle would be renewed in one country and then another. The central lesson of our time is that the appetite of aggression is never satisfied. To withdraw from one battlefield means only to prepare for the next. We must say in Southeast Asia, as we did in Europe, in the words of the Bible: "Hitherto shall thou come, but no further."

U.S. troops cross a field in Vietnam.

Although the final defeat of South Vietnam suggests that U.S. efforts were indeed futile, Johnson made this speech when victory still seemed possible.

There are those who say that all our efforts there will be futile—that China's power is such that it is bound to dominate all Southeast Asia. But there is no end to that argument until all the nations of Asia are swallowed up.

There are those who wonder why we have a responsibility there. Well, we have a responsibility there for the same reason that we have a responsibility for the defense of Europe. World War II was fought in both Europe and Asia and when it ended we found ourselves with continued responsibility for the defense of freedom.

Our objective is the independence of South Vietnam and its freedom from attack. We want nothing for ourselves—only that the people of South Vietnam be allowed to guide their own country in their own way.

We will do everything necessary to reach that objective and we will do only what is absolutely necessary.

Response to escalation

In recent months attacks on South Vietnam were stepped up. Thus, it became necessary for us to increase our response and to make attacks by air. This is not a change of purpose. It is a change in what we believe that purpose requires.

Johnson uses another oratorical device, the repetition of key phrases and structures, to drive home what he is saying. Compare this with the similar use by John Kerry on page 179.

We do this in order to slow down aggression. We do this to increase the confidence of the brave people of South Vietnam who have bravely born this brutal battle for so many years with so many casualties. And we do this to convince the leaders of North Vietnam—and all who seek to share their conquest—of a simple fact: We will not be defeated. We will not grow tired. We will not withdraw either openly or under the cloak of a meaningless agreement.

The sustained bombing of North Vietnam began in February 1965. The campaign, called Operation Rolling Thunder, continued until 1968.

We know that air attacks alone will not accomplish all of these purposes but it is our best and prayerful judgment that they are a necessary part of the surest road to peace.

We hope that peace will come swiftly. But that is in the hands of others besides ourselves. And we must be prepared for a long continued conflict. It will require patience as well as bravery—the will to endure as well as the will to resist.

I wish it were possible to convince others with words of what we now find it necessary to say with guns and planes: armed hostility is futile—our resources are equal to any challenge—because we fight for values and we fight for principle rather than territory or colonies, our patience and our determination are unending.

Once this is clear, then it should also be clear that the only path for reasonable men is the path of peaceful settlement.

Such peace demands an independent South Vietnam—securely guaranteed and able to shape its own relationship to all others—free from outside interference—tied to no alliance—a military base for no other country.

These are the essentials of any final settlement.

We will never be second in the search for such a peaceful settlement in Vietnam.

There may be many ways to this kind of peace: in discussion or negotiation with the governments concerned; in large groups or in small ones; in the reaffirmation of old agreements or their strengthening with new ones.

We have stated this position over and over again fifty times and more to friend and foe alike. And we remain ready with this purpose for unconditional discussions.

And until that bright and necessary day of peace we will try to keep conflict from spreading. We have no desire to see thousands die in battle—Asians or Americans. We have no desire to devastate that which the people of North Vietnam have built with toil and sacrifice. We will use our power with restraint and with all the wisdom that we can command. But we will use it.

Johnson concludes his speech with a powerful statement. This is a good and memorable way to end an argument.

Summary

The Vietnam War was the longest conflict in U.S. history. To its critics the war was unjust and avoidable—a waste of lives, resources, and money. To its supporters it was a necessary war fought against the spread of communism.

The first extract is a statement made in 1971 to the Senate Committee on Foreign Relations by John Kerry on behalf of the Vietnam Veterans Against the War. Kerry states that "there is nothing in South Vietnam which could happen that realistically threatens the United States of America." He goes on to argue that that most of the people that the U.S. forces were supposed to be saving in South Vietnam "didn't even know the difference between communism and democracy" but wanted to be left alone in peace. Kerry accuses America of losing its morality and of being unable to admit it made a mistake in waging the war, which he views as driven by hate and fear.

In the second piece, an April 7, 1965, speech by Lyndon B. Johnson, the then president explains why the United States was fighting in Vietnam. He refers to the "deepening shadow of communist China" over Asia, stating that "The rulers in [the North Vietnamese capital] Hanoi are urged on by Peking." He continues by citing a pledge given by the United States "to help South Vietnam defend its independence." Johnson insists that to go back on that pledge would not only be "an unforgivable wrong" but would damage U.S. credibility in the eyes of those countries that believe "that they can count on us if they are attacked." He points to America's "continued responsibility for the defense of freedom" and explains that North Vietnam's aggression has given the Unites States little choice but to escalate the war while being ever ready to negotiate. Johnson concludes by saying, "We have no desire to see thousands die in battle—Asians or Americans.... We will use our power with restraint and with all the wisdom that we can command. But we will use it.

FURTHER INFORMATION:

Books:

Karnow, Stanley, *Vietnam, A History*. New York: Penguin, 1997.

Kimball, Jeffrey P. (ed.), *To Reason Why: The Debate about the Causes of U.S. Involvement in the Vietnam War*. New York: McGraw-Hill, 1989.

Useful websites:

www.pbs.org/wgbh/amex/vietnam
PBS Vietnam War series site.

www.spartacus.schoolnet.co.uk/vietnam.html
Extensive resource site on Vietnam and the war.

www.vietnamwar.com
Americans.net site on the Vietnam War.

The following debates in the Pro/Con series may also be of interest:

In this volume:
Topic 11 Did the United States overestimate the threat of communism in the 1950s?

In *U.S. Foreign Policy*:
Topic 1 Does the United States have a duty to protect democracy and freedom overseas?

WAS THE VIETNAM WAR AVOIDABLE?

YES: Vietnam was just the first of many Asian countries that would fall to communism if China had its way

YES: Since World War II the United States has had a responsibility for the defense of freedom in both Europe and Asia

DOMINO EFFECT
Did communism threaten to spread throughout Southeast Asia?

INTERVENTIONISM
Was the United States right to intervene in the name of freedom?

NO: Such fears within the U.S. government were nothing but paranoia

NO: The U.S. government had no business committing the nation to war over the internal affairs of a Southeast Asian country

WAS THE VIETNAM WAR AVOIDABLE?

KEY POINTS

YES: To abandon South Vietnam would have undermined U.S. trustworthiness in the eyes of other vulnerable countries

YES: The United States had made a pledge to support the independence of South Vietnam

CREDIBILITY
Was the reliability of the United States as a partner at stake in Vietnam?

NO: Maybe. But the people of South Vietnam were not concerned with being "saved," only the corrupt South Vietnamese government

NO: Successive U.S. governments were more concerned with saving political face. They did not want to be vilified as the ones who lost South Vietnam.

THE VIETNAM WAR

"The infirmities of man are such that force must often precede reason, and the waste of war, the works of peace."

—LYNDON B. JOHNSON, JOHN HOPKINS UNIVERSITY, APRIL 7, 1965

In 1945 Ho Chi Minh, leader of the Vietminh, or League for the Independence of Vietnam, declared the country's independence from French rule. The French resisted, and the Vietminh, with funding from communist China and the Soviet Union, waged a guerrilla war on the French, who were backed by the United States. A peace accord was signed on July 21, 1954, which divided the country in half along the 17th parallel. South Vietnam was led by the noncommunist, pro-American Ngo Dinh Diem; the North by the communist Ho Chi Minh. When Diem refused to participate in independent elections to unite the country in 1956, South Vietnamese communist forces opposed to his government formed the Vietcong. Diem was assassinated in a military coup on November 1, 1963, and a series of unstable administrations followed. The United States gave increasing military aid to South Vietnam, some people argue, in a bid to fight the spread of communism.

1964 August 2: The USS *Maddox*, a destroyer stationed in international waters in the Tonkin Gulf, 30 miles off the coast of North Vietnam, allegedly comes under fire from North Vietnamese patrol boats. **7:** The Gulf of Tonkin Resolution is approved by Congress. It gives President Lyndon B. Johnson the power to wage all-out war against North Vietnam.

1965 February: The Vietcong attack a U.S. base at Pleiku. The United States begins a bombing campaign on North Vietnam, dubbed Operation Rolling Thunder, which continues almost unbroken for three years. **March:** The first U.S. combat troops arrive in Vietnam. In the United States there are widespread antiwar protests. **May 15–16:** A nationally broadcast teach-in protest reaches over 100 campuses. **July 25:** Johnson increases U.S. troops in Vietnam to 125,000.

1966 February 6–9: Johnson meets with South Vietnamese Premier Nguyen Cao Ky

in Honolulu. He announces that the United States is willing to settle the conflict peacefully and withdraw from the whole of Vietnam if a stable and just government can be secured in the South. The policy becomes known as "pacification." In the meantime, Johnson pledges continued U.S. support against aggression from the North.

1967 January 8–26: In Operation Cedar Falls approximately 16,000 U.S. and 14,000 South Vietnamese troops set out to destroy Vietcong operations and supply sites near Saigon, capital of South Vietnam. An extensive system of tunnels, apparently a Vietcong command base, is discovered in an area called the Iron Triangle. **April 15:** Massive antiwar demonstrations are held throughout the United States. Protesters burn draft cards in New York's Central Park. **August:** Secretary of Defense Robert McNamara announces that U.S. bombing raids against North Vietnam have not achieved their objectives. U.S. troops in Vietnam rise to 500,000.

1968 January 30: The North Vietnamese and Vietcong launch a massive offensive during Tet, the Vietnamese festival celebrating the lunar New Year. They capture key cities and provinces in South Vietnam, including Saigon, where they invade the U.S. embassy. Within two weeks U.S. forces recapture most areas, but antiwar feeling increases in the United States. **February 28:** General Westmoreland, commander of U.S. forces in Vietnam, reports that the communists have the upper hand. His request for 200,000 more troops is denied. **March 16:** U.S. troops under the command of Lieutenant William Calley enter the village of My Lai, which they are allegedly told to "search and destroy." They kill between 200 and 500 civilians. **31:** Johnson declares an end to bombing north of the 20th parallel and announces that he will not run for president again. **May 13:** North Vietnamese and American negotiators agree to meet in Paris to discuss peace. They soon reach stalemate. **October 31:** Johnson orders a complete stop to bombing in North Vietnam. **November:** Richard Nixon is elected president.

1969 March: President Nixon authorizes the bombing of Cambodia, a sanctuary for the North Vietnamese and Vietcong. The campaign is not disclosed to Congress or the U.S. public and continues for 14 months. **May 14:** Nixon announces a peace offer. **June:** The United States institutes a policy of "Vietnamization," designed to pass the task of defense from U.S. to South Vietnamese troops. **September 2:** Ho Chi Minh dies. **November 12:** U.S. journalist Seymour Hersh writes about My Lai. **15:** More than 250,000 antiwar protesters demonstrate in Washington, D.C. **December:** Nixon begins withdrawing U.S. troops from Vietnam.

1970 May: U.S. troops invade Cambodia. **4:** National Guardsmen open fire on a crowd of student antiwar protesters at Kent State University in Ohio. Four students are killed and eleven wounded.

1971 June: *The New York Times* publishes the Pentagon Papers, a leaked report commissioned by Robert McNamara on U.S. involvement in Vietnam. The document causes a nationwide outcry and debate over the government's right to keep its conduct in the war classified.

1972 March: North Vietnamese forces invade the demilitarized zone between North and South Vietnam. **April :** Nixon orders bombing of strategic sites around Hanoi–Haiphong. **October:** A peace agreement is reached between Henry Kissinger, head of the U.S. National Security Council, and Le Duc Tho, leader of the North Vietnamese delegation. The settlement breaks down after objections from President Thieu of South Vietnam. **November 7 :** Nixon wins reelection. **December:** Nixon orders renewed bombing of North Vietnam to force concessions in peace talks acceptable to South Vietnam.

1973 January 27: A peace agreement is reached by the South Vietnamese communist forces, North Vietnam, South Vietnam, and the United States. **March 29:** The last U.S. troops leave Vietnam. **August:** The United States ends bombing campaign in Cambodia.

1974 North and South Vietnam accuse each other of breaking the peace accord. Fighting continues. **August 9:** Nixon resigns.

1975 The North Vietnamese initiate the Ho Chi Minh Campaign—a concerted effort to "liberate" Saigon. President Gerald Ford announces that as far as the United States is concerned, the Vietnam War is "finished." **April 21:** President Thieu resigns. **30:** The South Vietnamese government surrenders to North Vietnam. **July 2:** The country is united as the Socialist Republic of Vietnam.

Topic 15

WAS THE PERSIAN GULF WAR A WAR ABOUT OIL?

YES

FROM "ECONOMIC CAUSES OF THE GULF WAR"
WWW.WORLDSOCIALISM.ORG, NOVEMBER 1990
WORLD SOCIALIST MOVEMENT

NO

FROM "THE GULF WAR: ORIGINS AND MOTIVATIONS"
HTTP://WWW.USERS.QWEST.NET/~MBENJAMIN4/MYPAGES/
THOUGHTS/GULFWAR2.HTML
BENJAMIN MOSS

INTRODUCTION

Throughout American history presidents have sought to justify war in moral terms. At the start of the 20th century Woodrow Wilson led the country into World War I (1914–1918) in order to end war itself and to make the world safe for democracy. Similarly, Franklin Delano Roosevelt appealed to the defense of freedom as the country's World War II (1939–1945) rallying cry. Such justifications are consistent with America's fundamental political principles of liberty, equality, and democracy. A country dedicated to such universal principles of justice is not supposed to wage war directly for the sake of national glory, territorial aggrandizement, or mere self-interest.

The motives for military action by U.S. forces in the first Persian Gulf War may have been influenced by political and economic factors as much as by moral considerations. On August 2, 1990, 120,000 Iraqi troops backed by

850 tanks swept into the neighboring country of Kuwait, an oil-rich ally of the United States. A tiny country, Kuwait is strategically important for its location on the Persian Gulf and economically rich because of its abundant oil fields.

Saddam Hussein, the Iraqi military dictator, had mixed motives for ordering this invasion. He believed, as did most Iraqis, that Kuwait was actually an ancient province of Iraq that had been illegally carved away by British imperialists in the 1920s as part of the dismantling of the Ottoman Empire. Kuwaitis, on the other hand, did not accept this: The region of Kuwait had been ruled by the Al-Sabah dynasty since 1756.

In addition, control of Kuwait would give Hussein possession of its huge oil reserves, as well as its strategically important Persian Gulf ports. Iraq had suffered economically from Kuwait's production of oil beyond the quotas that had been set by the Organization of Petroleum-Exporting Countries (OPEC): Kuwait's overproduction sent world oil prices plummeting, which cut into Iraq's own oil profits.

"The real reason for U.S. opposition to Iraqi occupation of Kuwait is not to keep oil prices low, but to keep Washington, Wall Street, and their allies in charge of setting oil prices.... It is a greedy offensive that pursues U.S. oil advantage."

—NOAM CHOMSKY AND MICHAEL ALBERT, *Z MAGAZINE* (1991)

President George H.W. Bush quickly denounced the Iraqi invasion as "naked aggression." On August 15 he ordered U.S. forces to Saudi Arabia and the Persian Gulf. The United States also led a broad coalition in the United Nations that condemned the invasion of Kuwait. They enforced economic sanctions against Iraq to force it to withdraw from Kuwait voluntarily. In early November Bush announced a change in policy to what he called "an offensive military option," and the deployment of troops from a coalition force of 32 nations quickly increased, reaching 580,000 by January 1991.

By January 15, 1991—the deadline set by United Nations Resolution 678 for Iraqi withdrawal from Kuwait—the president had narrowly secured a

congressional endorsement of the use of force. On January 16 Bush announced the start of war, in defiance of critics who urged him to give economic sanctions more time. After 38 days of aerial bombing and four days of an allied ground offensive Iraq was driven out of Kuwait. But Saddam Hussein remained in power.

Publicly, Bush repeatedly put the case for military action in moral terms. While stressing the importance of protecting oil supplies, he also acknowledged that vital economic interests were also at stake: "Our jobs, our way of life, our own freedom, and the freedom of friendly countries around the world would all suffer if control of the world's great oil reserves fell into the hands of Saddam Hussein." And so Bush presented the issue of stopping Hussein as much in terms of protecting freedom as in protecting economic interests.

However, critics of the moral argument point out that the United States had supported and helped arm Saddam Hussein in the 1980s. They also argue that if the war was about freedom, then Bush should not have supported Kuwait, which is not a democracy but an unelected monarchy.

In his speech at the start of the war Bush said: "Saddam Hussein systematically raped, pillaged, and plundered a tiny nation, no threat to his own." War against Iraq was not only in the nation's economic interest, but it was also morally justified. Not so, according to the articles that follow. Both reject the official reason for military action against Iraq. Instead, they argue that the Gulf War was driven by motives of self-interest. They disagree sharply, however, about what exactly those motives were.

ECONOMIC CAUSES OF THE GULF WAR
World Socialist Movement

YES

☑ ...U.S. President George Bush and British Prime Minister Margaret Thatcher say that Saddam Hussein is a dictator whose expansionist ambitions must be checked in the interests of world peace. Saddam Hussein says that he has struck a blow for Arab Nationalism by eliminating a state tailor-made by Western imperialism to suit its interests. Saddam Hussein is a dictator and he has taken over a state created by Western imperialism, but it is not for these reasons that the West is preparing to go to war. The Western powers tolerate dictators when it suits their interests. In fact they tolerated, financed and armed Saddam Hussein himself when they needed someone to prevent Iran under Khomeini coming to dominate the Gulf area and threaten their oil supplies. And they tolerated the Indonesian invasion and annexation of East Timor in 1975 as they had that of Goa by India in 1961 without shrieking that world peace and order were threatened. The difference was that, while in East Timor and Goa only carrots grew, Kuwait is situated right in the middle of the world's largest and lowest-cost oilfields.

Oil and empire
British imperialism made Kuwait, which remained nominally part of the Ottoman Empire, a "protectorate" in 1899. This was done not for its oil resources, which nobody even suspected existed, but for its strategic position....

Oil, however, was soon discovered near Kuwait, first in Persia and then in Mesopotamia. Britain acquired complete control of the Persian oilfields but those of Mesopotamia had to be shared with Germany. As Turkey had entered the First World War on the side of German imperialism, the British and French imperialists made plans to carve up the Ottoman Empire amongst themselves in the event of victory. A secret agreement in 1916 gave what is now Syria, Lebanon and the northern part of Iraq to France, and Palestine and what is now Jordan and the southern part of Iraq to Britain.

Almost as soon as the agreement had been signed, someone in the British Foreign Office realised that a ghastly mistake had been made: northern Mesopotamia contained the oilfields of Mosul and Kirkuk. The French were persuaded on some pretext to agree to a rectification, and after the war the spoils were divided along the lines of today's Middle Eastern states. Iran is just as much an artificial creation of Western imperialism as Kuwait....

Kuwait remained a British protectorate when Iraq became an independent state in 1932, but the new Iraqi rulers were not happy about being deprived of a secure outlet to the Persian Gulf. A glance at a map of Iraq will show that it only has two possible outlets to the sea. The first is via the Shatt al Arab river, but this is shared with Iran. The second is via an inlet to the west, access to which is controlled by two islands belonging to Kuwait.

At one time—in the fifties when Iraq under a pro-Western king and government seemed firmly anchored in the Western camp through its membership of CENTO, the Middle Eastern equivalent of NATO—British officials considered making some concessions to Iraq on this issue, but this was blocked by the Al-Sabah dynasty. The Emir of Kuwait, which since 1946 had become an oil-producing area with huge reserves, proved to be the better judge of his interests. On 14 July 1958, the king of Iraq and his pro-western prime minister were overthrown and killed in a military coup led by pro-Nasser army officers. The British Foreign Minister, Selwyn Lloyd, rushed to Washington to discuss the crisis. On 19 July he sent a secret telegram, recently released under the thirty-year rule, to Macmillan, the Prime Minister, in which he said:

> ...One of the most reassuring features of my talks here has been the complete United States solidarity with us over the Gulf. They are assuming that we will take firm action to maintain our position in Kuwait.... They assume that we will also hold Bahrain and Qatar, come what may. They agree that at all costs these oilfields must be kept in Western hands....On balance, I feel it very much to our advantage to have a kind of Kuwaiti Switzerland where the British do not exercise physical control. (The Independent, 13 September).

This was the solution eventually adopted and in 1961 Kuwait was granted "independence" in the sense of no longer being subject to direct "physical control" by Britain. Iraq immediately moved its troops up to the border—and British troops had to be rushed in to prop up the artificial Middle Eastern "Switzerland" that their government had just set up.

Kuwait survived and ... the ruling Al-Sabah dynasty became one of the richest families in the world....

Do you think countries that win wars should be able to carve up territories and "divide the spoils," as this author suggests?

The emir of Kuwait is the constitutional monarch. He belongs to the Al-Sabah family that has ruled Kuwait since 1756.

General Gamel Abdel Nasser (1918–1970) became president of Egypt in 1956. His nationalization of the Suez Canal led to a war with Britain, France, and Israel. He became the effective leader of the Arab world during this time.

Switzerland is a small country in central Europe that has long maintained a policy of neutrality in international affairs.

The Kurds are a largely Sunni Muslim ethnic group. They were promised independence by the 1920 Treaty of Sevres, which created the modern states of Iraq, Syria, and Kuwait. But Turkey rejected the treaty in 1923 and subjugated its own Kurdish population. President Saddam Hussein tried to ethnically cleanse the Kurds of Iraq in the 1990s. They remain the world's largest ethnic group without an official homeland.

The Shatt al Arab war

Iraq meanwhile also developed its oil resources and revenues, which were mainly used to build up its armed forces so strengthening the grip of the military on the state.... [I]n 1975 a treaty was signed between Iraq and Iran under which Iraq ceded control of the eastern side of the Shatt al Arab to Iran in return for Iran withdrawing its support for the Kurdish nationalists. When, however, the Shah was overthrown in 1979 and Iran began to slip into chaos, the tables were turned. The Iraqi ruling class decided to use the occasion to attack Iran and regain control of the whole of the Shatt al Arab and perhaps more. So began, in 1980, one of the longest and bloodiest wars of modern history. The war lasted eight years and led to the death of about one million people—all for control of a strategic commercial waterway.

The Western powers were happy to let the war go on, using Iraq to block any Iranian take-over of the Gulf region. When, however, Iran began to attack shipping in the Gulf in 1987, the West was forced to send its own taskforce of warships and warplanes to the area to protect the free flow of its oil supplies.

Why Iraq invaded Kuwait

... Iraq emerged from its war with Iran with a huge financial debt and a desperate need for money to pay for reconstruction. With oil revenues as virtually its only source of income, Iraq favoured using the OPEC cartel to push up the price of oil by restricting its supply. Since this was in the interests of a number of other OPEC members, including Iran, some move in this direction was agreed. However, two countries in particular—Kuwait and the United Arab Emirates—failed to apply this. They consistently exceeded their quotas, so preventing the price of oil from rising.

The Organization of Petroleum-Exporting Countries (OPEC) is an association of the eleven major oil-producing countries. It was founded in 1960 to coordinate policies.

The reason why the emirs and sheiks and sultans of the Gulf pursued this policy was not shortsightedness or cussedness. It was because it had become in their economic interest to do so. The Al-Sabah family had not wasted all its riches on horse-racing, gambling and gold-fitted bathrooms. Most of it had been re-invested in capitalist industry and finance in the West, so much so in fact that a large part of Kuwait's income came from these investments. In other words, the Kuwaiti and other Gulf rulers had become Western capitalists themselves and not just oil rentiers—with the same interest in not having too high a price for oil.

A "rentier" is someone who lives on income from fixed investments.

Iraq regarded this refusal to take steps to raise the price of oil as a plot to prevent it recovering from the war. Combined with their long-standing claim to Kuwait as a means of obtaining a vitally-needed secure trade route to the sea, this decided the Iraqi ruling class to take military action. On the night of 1/2 August 1990 Kuwait was invaded and later annexed. As an additional bonus, the Kuwaiti oilfields when added to the Iraqi ones make Iraq potentially almost as big a producer sitting on as big reserves as Saudi Arabia.

Bush, and Thatcher who happened to be in America on a lecture tour, reacted quickly, issuing an ultimatum to Iraq not to move further down the coast and take over the Saudi oilfields and dispatching a battle fleet to the Gulf for the second time in three years.

Iraq probably had no intention of invading Saudi Arabia, but America had every interest in finding an excuse to send troops to protect the Saudi oilfields. Since 1950 these had been an American preserve: under an agreement with the King of Saudi Arabia European oil companies were excluded and US ones, grouped together as A.R.A.M.C.O., given a monopoly....

The Arabian American Oil Company (ARAMCO), formed in 1944, is the national oil company of Saudi Arabia and possesses a quarter of the world's proven oil reserves.

The Gulf, [Jimmy Carter explained in his January 23, 1980 State of the Union message] ... was of "great strategic importance" because "it contains more than two-thirds of the world's exportable oil" and because the Strait of Hormuz at its mouth is "a waterway through which much of the free world's oil must flow". At the time the immediate threat was seen as coming from Russia which had just invaded Afghanistan, but the Carter Doctrine applied equally to threats to American oil supplies from other states like Iran and now Iraq. In Britain the *Sunday Times* (12 August 1990), which has called for war since day one of the crisis, has been equally frank:

Do you think Western powers have the right to protect their oil interests in the Gulf by going to war? Or do Middle East countries have the right to dictate terms to the rest of the world?

> *The reason why we will shortly have to go to war with Iraq is not to free Kuwait, though that is to be desired, or to defend Saudi Arabia, though that is important. It is because President Saddam is a menace to vital Western interests in the Gulf, above all the free flow of oil at market prices, which is essential to the West's prosperity.*

If war breaks out in the Middle East, the issues at stake will be purely economic and commercial: access to the sea and a high price of oil, on the one side, and control of oilfields and a low price of oil, on the other. Neither of which are issues justifying the shedding of a single drop of working class blood.

Simply because the motives for war are economic, does that make them wrong? Is not oil a valid reason to go to war?

THE GULF WAR: ORIGINS AND MOTIVATIONS
Benjamin Moss

To understand why the US went to war against Iraq, one needs to examine some of the history of US Middle East policies, as well as some of the domestic context in the US. In the Middle East, one should look at the US role in Iran, in particular. For the domestic scene, there is some relevant history, as well, but it is also important to bring to bear events in the US preceding and surrounding the war.

The U.S. and the Middle East

The Gulf War was an extension of the so-called "Cold War," the essential goal of which was for the US to dominate the so-called "Third World," with rationale of fighting "commies" providing the supposed justification. Near the beginning of the "Cold War," shortly after WWII, Mossadegh and moderate, capitalist democracy arrived in Iran. Mossadegh attempted to assert local control over local resources by nationalizing Iran's oil fields. For this crime, his administration was demonized as "communist," and the CIA restored the Shah in the early 1950s. From that time until the Iranian revolution of 1979, the US used its position in Iran as one cornerstone in its policy of attempting to control the oil resources of the region.

When the Iranians finally expelled the Shah again in the 1979 revolution, the US lost one of its key means of dominating the Middle East. The US then started down the familiar path of trying to destabilize a target country (Iran, this time) through a combination of economic and military measures and covert destabilizations. The covert operations centered on attempts to engineer a coup by making overtures to elements within the military, in this case through arms sales and transfers, some of which were later revealed in the Iran–Contra scandal.

It is important to note that these arms transfers to Iran began when Reagan took office, if not before. However, the Iran–Contra committee expressly rejected examining the period before the Lebanon hostages had been taken (i.e., the early 1980s) in order to frame the "Iran" part of the

A "cold war" is a conflict that involves hostility without open armed conflict. The former Soviet Union and the Western powers were involved in a long cold war after World War II.

Mohammad Mossadegh (1880–1967) was an Iranian political leader. He was premier in Iran from 1951 to 1953. In 1953 Mossadegh was deposed from power in a coup d'état by the shah of Iran. He was put on trial and imprisoned for three years. After his release he was kept under house arrest until he died.

Go to http://gi.grolier.com /presidents/aae/side /irancont.html for more information on the Iran–Contra affair.

Iran–Contra scandal around the question of whether Reagan had been "trading arms for hostages." In so doing, the committee effectively covered up the true function and original purpose of the arms sales. Committee members wanted to hold Reagan's feet to the fire for disobeying Congressional will, but they did not want questions of actual policy to interfere with their power-play with the Executive branch. However, the arms transfers were not the only front against the mullahs. The central initiative of the direct, military destabilization of Iran was US support and promotion of the prolonged and mutually devastating Iran-Iraq war during the 1980s. In 1979, the US exploited Iraq's desire for a port by encouraging Iraq to attack Iran, not that Iraq needed a lot of coaxing. The history of Iraq's pursuit of a port also brings Kuwait and Britain into the equation....

The mullahs were the fundamentalist Muslim leaders of Iran's revolution in 1979.

The US also pressured Saudi Arabia and Kuwait to finance Iraq's attack on Iran, and it was very much in those countries' interests to harass the radical fundamentalists ruling Iran. The attack on Iran was largely enabled by US and West European arms and Saudi and Kuwaiti money. And even when an Iraqi missile struck the USS *Stark*, the US actively joined the action in the Persian Gulf on the side of Iraq, eventually shooting down an Iranian passenger airliner by "mistake."

The U.S. Navy ship USS Stark was struck by an Exocet missile fired by an Iraqi ship during the Iran–Iraq war. The missile killed 37 American sailors.

Kuwait also used the war to jockey for position. First, it used the war as a cover to move its border many miles into disputed territory with Iraq, and pumped out billions of dollars worth of oil. We might note that if Mexico were to move into Texas and start pumping oil, the US would go to war in about ten minutes. And after the Iran-Iraq war, Iraq was somewhat dismayed to find Kuwait and Saudi Arabia demanding quick repayment of the massive "loans" they had made to Iraq to finance the war. Iraq would obviously have had to use oil revenues to repay those moneys, but there followed as well a series of Kuwaiti oil market maneuvers that halved the price of Iraq's crude oil, costing Iraq further billions. Iraq protested and tried to negotiate a solution in various meetings and summits during the first half of 1990, virtually until their invasion of Kuwait. For its part, Kuwait was said to be willing to discuss everything but "territorial adjustments," and Iraq broke off talks and invaded....

So Hussein called in US ambassador April Glaspie, and asked her what the US response would be to an Iraqi military action against Kuwait. She repeatedly said that the US had "no opinion on ... conflicts such as your border disagreement with Kuwait," adding that she had "direct instruction from the President" on this point. In addition, top State Department officials were then publicly stating that the US "was not obligated to come to Kuwait's aid if it were attacked." In diplomatic terms, this was a clear green light for Hussein to invade Kuwait....

There are two basic reasons that the US used Hussein and then turned on him. First, Hussein started to represent a threat to US hegemony in the region. He asserted local power beyond the gadfly role he'd been assigned, providing a model that the US did not want others to emulate. And by invading Kuwait, a country that is basically a British banking protectorate, he violated one of the cardinal rules of puppetdom: don't harass other puppets with good connections. For US policy makers, the choice between turning on Hussein and creating friction with another friendly imperial power was no choice.

The second reason for the US about-face with Hussein is that the US was shopping for a war in 1990, and Iraq presented itself as a likely candidate. With a tremendous effort of propaganda and international coercion, the US satisfied all its war "needs" at the time by selling, creating, and moving with great deliberation towards a war against Iraq....

A few days after the Iraqi invasion of Kuwait, US Senators could scarcely contain their joy in announcing that the B-2 "stealth" bomber could obviously not be scrapped now, as it had a "new mission." Of course, even if the US wanted to incinerate the Middle East with nuclear weapons ..., the "stealth" bomber would have been utterly superfluous. There was even talk that Hussein's missiles might have been the saving grace of the SDI/"Star Wars" program....

It was hardly a chance occurrence that the end of the Evil Empire pretext for US militarism in the Third World coincided with a rash of renewed militarism involving US troops, in addition to the extension of proxy forces, such as contras, Salvadoran death squads (in and out of uniform), UNITA in Angola, Cambodia's D.K. coalition (including the Khmer Rouge), the Afghani mujahedeen, etc. "Cold" wars, hot wars, drug wars, oil wars, star wars, any wars—the US was and is truly "in search of enemies." It took a few generations, but the Vietnam experience is now rewritten and sanitized history, and "we" are just spoiling for a good bash....

Another reason for US jingoism in 1990 was that, as one commentator noted at the time, "the Reaganomics bills are coming due." There were massive deficits, the S&L fraud, the Reagan years' colossal shift in wealth from the poor to the rich, etc. The US used the usual warmongering ruse to avoid dealing with severe domestic economic problems. The

A "gadfly" is literally one of a variety of flies that annoys lifestock. The word is also used to refer to someone who stimulates or annoys, especially through the use of criticism.

Clever turns of phrases can give your argument dramatic impact. But they can also make the debate appear flippant.

The Strategic Defense Initiative (SDI), popularly known as Star Wars, was a missile defense program launched by President Ronald Reagan in the 1980s.

"Jingoism" means extreme chauvinism or nationalism characterized by a belligerent foreign policy. A large proportion of the failure of savings and loan funds during the 1980s is thought to be linked to fraud.

Middle East action disrupted budget talks, and Bush promptly went on vacation.

Renewed militarism is an ideal form of denial.... Iraq was economically stressed out from its war with Iran, and Hussein no doubt used the invasion of Kuwait to unite, distract, and control Iraq's population, still reeling from some eight years of war. Indeed, Iraqi militarism parallels that of the US, not unsurprisingly, in that both were vying for control of oil, seeking a "new mission" for a bloated military machine, and attempting to avoid dealing with [big] domestic problems.

Moreover, deployment of US troops is extremely expensive—or lucrative, depending on your point of view. The early estimate was that deploying 50,000 US troops would cost $500 million per month. With the announcement that the US would send 250,000 troops or more, the cost may have risen as high as $2.5 billion per month. That's a lot of school lunches. Imagine spending that much on actual, pressing national emergencies, such as those in health care, education, homelessness ... the environment, etc....

> *Do you think the financial costs of war are worth paying if the reasons for going to war are sound? Was the Persian Gulf War worth its cost in money and in human lives lost?*

The plain facts of the Gulf War are these:
The United States encouraged (or, at the very least, did nothing to discourage) Iraq's invasion of Kuwait and then, turning diplomacy on its head, used that invasion to conjure a new war where there was no war, aggressively rejecting any peaceful solutions, including the last-minute virtual surrender of Iraq; the US then set its high-tech, meat grinder death machine on maximum kill, slaughtering 100,000 to 200,000 or more people in a 45-day orgy of blood, and wound up bulldozing mounds of corpses into mass graves in the desert, in scenes reminiscent of Nazi death camp footage.

> *Is a comparison to Nazi death camps justified in this context? What effect do statements like these have on an audience?*

Not unsurprisingly, though there were calls in the US media after the war to apply the Nuremberg principles to Saddam and try him for war crimes, no one here seemed to think of applying those principles a little closer to home.

The US war against Iraq was not a "just war"; it was not a moral war; it was not a war of collective self-defense against aggression. It was an imperialist war of aggression by US leaders who cynically spouted high principle as the rationale for continuing the arms race, dominating the "Third World," and diverting attention from the tremendous domestic problems which the war's billion dollar-a-day price tag only exacerbated.

It is important to see through the propaganda barrage and so to get a clearer picture of the state in which we live. The implications for action seem clear enough.

Summary

Both the World Socialist Movement and Benjamin Moss are highly critical of the Persian Gulf War, although for different reasons. According to the article issued by the World Socialist Movement, the Persian Gulf War was fundamentally about oil: In the case of the Iraqi invasion of Kuwait Saddam Hussein sought control of Kuwait's oil supply and easy access to the Persian Gulf. In the case of the United States and the allied military action against Iraq, the West sought to preserve the free flow of oil at market prices. The United States, along with its allies, went to war against Iraq, the World Socialist Movement argues, not primarily to free Kuwait or even to protect Saudi Arabia but to ensure its own continued economic and commercial prosperity.

Benjamin Moss demurs as to the real motives behind the war. According to him, the Persian Gulf War was driven not by economics but rather by politics. Moss suggests that the United States was "shopping" for a war at this time and moved deliberately toward war against Iraq. He argues that the war was motivated by several factors. First, the United States was worried that it would loose its influence in the Middle East if Saddam Hussein was allowed to retain Kuwait. Moss goes on to argue that the Persian Gulf War was also an opportunity to escalate the arms race—prior to the war there had been pressure to cut military spending as a result of deficits in the U.S. budget. Finally, he points out that the war was a distraction from domestic economic problems. Once the war started, the media would turn its attention away from domestic problems toward the fighting in the Persian Gulf.

FURTHER INFORMATION:

Books:

Mazarr, Michael J., Don M. Snider, and James A. Blackwell, *Desert Storm: The Gulf War and What We Learned*. Boulder, CO: Westview Press, 1993.

Useful websites:

www.pbs.org/wgbh/pages/frontline/gulf/
In-depth examination of the Persian Gulf crisis, including oral history interviews with political and military leaders and firsthand accounts of soldiers in the battlefield.
http://americanhistory.about.com/cs/persiangulfwar/
Guide to web resources providing background, facts, and chronologies of the Persian Gulf War.
www.washingtonpost.com/wp-srv/inatl/longterm/fogofwar/fogofwar.htm
Detailed analysis of war by the *Washington Post,* including photos and videos.

The following debates in the Pro/Con series may also be of interest:

In this volume:
Topic 16 Was September 11, 2001, the result of U.S. imperialism?

In *U.S. Foreign Policy*:
Topic 16 Should the United States take more responsibility for promoting peace in the Middle East?

September 11, 2001, pages 176–177

WAS THE PERSIAN GULF WAR
A WAR ABOUT OIL?

YES: Iraq's invasion of Kuwait
threatened Western economic
interests—the free flow of oil at
market prices

YES: It was a just war fought to
protect the freedom of the
Kuwaiti people as well as vital
economic interests

ECONOMIC INTERESTS
Was the Gulf War
fought to protect
economic interests?

VALUES
Was the war about
Western values such as
freedom and democracy?

NO: The Gulf War was
politically motivated. It was born
of a Western desire to dominate
the Middle East region.

NO: Many human lives were lost,
Kuwait continued to be ruled by
an unelected emir, and Saddam
Hussein remained in power

WAS THE PERSIAN GULF WAR A WAR ABOUT OIL?
KEY POINTS

YES: World freedom would have
suffered if Iraq had control of the
world's great oil reserves

YES: President George H.W.
Bush was facing severe domestic
economic problems at the time

WORLD STABILITY
Did the United States
and its allies go to war
against Iraq to protect
world stability?

DIVERSION
Did the United States go
to war to distract
attention from
domestic policies?

NO: Western powers did not
intervene for the sake of world
stability in other international
situations such as when Indonesia
invaded East Timor

NO: The war was an extremely
risky and expensive undertaking,
possibly costing as much as
$2.5 billion per month

Topic 16
WAS SEPTEMBER 11, 2001, THE RESULT OF U.S. IMPERIALISM?

YES
"SEPTEMBER 11: THE TERROR ATTACK IN THE U.S. AND ITS CONSEQUENCES"
STATEMENT BY THE ISG, SEPTEMBER 14, 2001
INTERNATIONAL SOCIALIST GROUP

NO
"STATEMENT BY THE PRESIDENT IN HIS ADDRESS TO THE NATION"
OFFICE OF THE PRESS SECRETARY, SEPTEMBER 11, 2001
GEORGE W. BUSH

INTRODUCTION

On September 11, 2001, groups of terrorists hijacked four commercial airliners in the United States and deliberately crashed three of them into major landmarks. The first hit the North Tower of the World Trade Center in New York City; the second hit the South Tower 17 minutes later. Half an hour later the third plane crashed into the Pentagon in Arlington, Virginia, which was damaged but not destroyed; both World Trade Center towers later collapsed. The total death toll in the three atrocities was estimated at 3,025. The fourth jet crashed in rural Pennsylvania when resistance by passengers forced the terrorists to abort their original plan.

Investigations soon revealed that the hijackings were carried out by Islamist militants. They were reportedly linked to Al Qaeda, a terrorist group headed by Saudi millionaire Osama Bin Laden, who had declared jihad (holy war) against the United States. In the wake of the September 11 attacks President George W. Bush proclaimed a War against Terrorism. Holding Bin Laden responsible for the attacks, Bush demanded his surrender by the Taliban government of Afghanistan, which had given him sanctuary. The Taliban rejected the demand, and the United States began air strikes against suspected terrorist hideouts in Afghanistan on October 7. By early December the Taliban hold over Afghanistan had been broken, but Bin Laden himself evaded capture, and no one knew if he was alive or dead.

Despite widespread revulsion at the attacks, and deep sympathy for the innocent victims, some political commentators in the Middle East, Europe, and the United States view the events of September 11 as the result of "U.S. imperialism." Miriam Webster's dictionary defines imperialism as "the policy, practice, or advocacy of extending the power and dominion of a nation especially by direct territorial acquisition or by gaining indirect control over the political or economic life of other areas; broadly, the extension or imposition of power, authority, or influence." Some analysts view the United States's interventionist foreign policy since World War II (1939-1945) and its global economic power and cultural influence as examples of the nation's imperialism.

"What I seek is what is right for any living being. We demand that our land be liberated from enemies. That our lands be liberated from the Americans."

—OSAMA BIN LADEN, FROM AN INTERVIEW BROADCAST ON AL-JAZEERA TELEVISION, 1998

In his writings and speeches Osama Bin Laden has directly attacked a number of areas of U.S. foreign policy. They include the presence of U.S. troops in Saudi Arabia following the 1990 Iraqi invasion of Kuwait, U.S. support for Arab regimes considered by Al Qaeda to be repressive—namely the absolutist monarchy of Saudi Arabia and the government of Egypt—UN sanctions on Iraq, and U.S. support for the republic of Israel. U.S. support of Israel is one of the main reasons for anti-American feeling in the Arab world. Most recently Al Qaeda has condemned the U.S. invasion of Iraq in 2003 and threatened a further

campaign of terror against the United States, Britain, and other countries that assisted in the action. Bin Laden and other Muslim extremists have characterized U.S. policy as selfish and determined by the acquisition and protection of economic resources, such as oil. They also view it as part of a U.S. campaign to repress the Muslim world. Al Qaeda exploits a wider perception in the Middle East that the United States is aggressive and materialistic, and aims to dominate Islamic culture and values.

Some U.S. commentators accept that there is resentment of their nation's global political and economic power, but they argue that U.S. foreign policy has been determined by a desire for stability, peace, and prosperity in the world. They see the United States as a peaceful nation that was attacked without provocation for reasons of religious fanaticism and jealousy.

Some Middle East observers also believe that the attack on the United States on September 11 was not a goal in itself but an instrument designed to help Al Qaeda's extreme brand of Islam flourish. They consider the attacks as part of an attempt to create a wider Islamist revolution to topple secular rulers in the Middle East—specifically in Saudi Arabia but also Egypt, which has been condemned by Al Qaeda for its dealings with Israel.

The first of the following articles contains a list of nations whose people might resent the United States and suggests that on September 11 the nation reaped what it sowed. In the second article President Bush states the view, which he has since maintained, that terrorism is an evil that must be obliterated from the face of the Earth. The possible motives of the terrorists are not matters for consideration.

SEPTEMBER 11: THE TERROR ATTACK IN THE U.S. AND ITS CONSEQUENCES
International Socialist Group

YES

The massive terror attack on the World Trade Centre, which has killed thousands of office and other workers, is indefensible in any terms. The political conditions which probably created it, however, are not so obscure. The perpetrators are not known at this time (despite all claims by the CIA), but the driving force behind them is most likely to be a deep hatred of U.S. imperialism generated by U.S. foreign policy—past and present.

We share the grief of the relatives of those who have lost their lives at their place of work. The civilian victims, like the great majority of the American people, cannot be held responsible for the barbarous policies of their government. But for the first time in recent times the U.S.A. is confronted with a huge attack on its own territory. Previously this has been the fate of the Vietnamese, the Cambodians, the Iraqis, the Yugoslavs, the Somalis, the Nicaraguans… you could quote a dozen more.

For years the U.S. government, and U.S. multi-national companies, have been imposing their will on the world by military force and financial power. They have been destroying local economies, imposing structural adjustment programmes, overthrowing popular governments, and putting the Suhartos, the Pinochets, the Marcoses, and the Mobutus in power—dictators subordinated to the U.S. who did not hesitate to slaughter their own people in the cause of U.S. policy.

Do you think the fact that the attack happened on U.S. home soil made a greater impact psychologically than if it had been on a U.S. embassy or other installation abroad?

Suharto was president of Indonesia (1967–1998); Augusto Pinochet was president of Chile (1973–1990); Ferdinand Marcos was president of the Philippines (1967–1986); and Mobutu Sese Seko was president of Zaire (1965–1997).

A response to misery

Under today's globalised economy, the rich are getting richer and the poor are getting poorer, and increased repression is used to keep the poor in their place. The mass misery which U.S. policy has imposed … on the majority of the world's population has created the conditions for the new feature in terrorism and resistance—the suicide bomber and now the suicide pilot.

In occupied Palestine there is no shortage of young men willing to sacrifice their lives in order to strike a blow against

COMMENTARY: The CIA

The National Security Act created the Central Intelligence Agency (CIA) in 1947. The CIA's mandate was to coordinate U.S. national security interests and correlate, disseminate, and evaluate any intelligence information of interest to the nation's security. From its beginnings the CIA was an independent body, responsible to the president through the director of Central Intelligence (DCI) and accountable to the people through the intelligence oversight committees of Congress. In 1949 the Central Intelligence Agency Act enabled the agency to use confidential fiscal and administrative procedures, and exempted the agency from many of the usual limitations on the expenditure of federal funds, thus protecting the secrecy of its budget. Some critics argue that this protection has allowed the CIA to conduct intelligence operations that are not necessarily in the best interests of the American people. The CIA has been accused of operating without consulting the president, planning to assassinate foreign heads of state or people who have allegedly threatened U.S. security, and running operations to try to force a president to act against official policy.

Some critics assert that the CIA's covert involvement in the affairs of other nations has fueled the hostility felt toward the United States in many parts of the world. However, CIA supporters argue that the agency has been essential in protecting U.S. interests and has prevented terrorist action and hostile enemy action against the country on many occasions.

The CIA and Osama Bin Laden

Afghanistan is among the many countries in which the CIA has had covert operations. Zbigniew Brzezinski, President Jimmy Carter's national security adviser, stated in an interview in 1998 that the CIA secretly supplied aid to the Mujahadeen to oppose the Soviet-backed government in Kabul from July 1979. Brzezinski claimed that the Taliban were seen as far less important than the destruction of the Soviet Union.

Between 1978 and 1992 the U.S. government allegedly contributed $6 billion in arms, training, and funds to the Mujahadeen factions. Ahmed Rashid, a correspondent for the *Far Eastern Economic Review*, claims that CIA chief William Casey supported Pakistan's CIA equivalent, the Inter Service Intelligence Directorate (ISI) in recruiting people from around the world to join the Afghan jihad. Between 1982 and 1992 at least 100,000 Islamic militants flocked to Pakistan, where recruits, money, and equipment were distributed to the Mujahadeen factions by an organization known as Maktab al Khidamar (MAK), a front for the ISI. Osama Bin Laden helped run MAK, taking complete charge of it in 1989. He set up terrorist training camps, and one of Al Qaeda's functions was to run these camps. Bin Laden became anti-American after the Gulf War. His terrorist campaign targeted U.S. interests. Some critics argue that the CIA is responsible for his activities.

Sanctions imposed after the first Gulf War in 1991 were designed to prevent Saddam Hussein using oil wealth to build up his military forces again. Oil could be sold to buy food and medicine, but the Iraqi government refused to do so.

These events took place in varying circumstances. Do you think they can all be equally described as "terrorist" acts? Can terrorism ever be justified? See Volume 1, Individual and Society, Topic 10 Is violent protest ever justified?

The Soviet Union invaded Afghanistan in 1979 and occupied the country until 1989. It was opposed by guerrilla forces that were well armed by the United States. Once the Soviets withdrew, these groups fought each other until the Taliban emerged as the dominant force in 1996.

George Robertson, defense secretary in Tony Blair's cabinet, was appointed secretary general of NATO in 1999.

the Israeli oppressor. Again, although such acts, particularly against civilians, cannot be supported it is easy to see how they come about. Palestinians are dying every day at the hands of an Israeli war machine supplied, backed, and bankrolled by the U.S.A. The war criminal [Ariel] Sharon is totally backed by George Bush—who is also no longer even interested in the so-called peace process.

In Iraq 1m civilians have perished through US sponsored sanctions and the destruction of the infrastructure of the country including the water supply and treatment plants. Today U.S. and British planes continue to bomb Iraq on a daily basis.

None of these crimes by U.S. imperialism justifies the killing of thousands of U.S. civilians, but they do help to explain the anger which is felt against the U.S.A. and its symbols of power.

It is said that this attack is the biggest act of terror of all time. But this would only be that case if it is non-state terror. Many acts of state terror surpass it, for example the nuclear annihilation of Japanese cities and the carpet-bombing of Dresden in WW2. Suharto killed 1m people in Indonesia. Millions were killed in Vietnam. The U.S.A. dropped more bombs on Laos and Cambodia during the Vietnam War than were dropped in the whole of WW2. If bin Laden is a terrorist he is not the biggest—even if he has done everything the U.S. accuses him of.

A monster of their own creation

The irony, in any case, is that bin Laden was a creation of the CIA during the Soviet occupation [of Afghanistan] and the Taliban—accused of harbouring him—was brought to power by the U.S. and its allies. In fact the proxy war between the U.S.A. and the U.S.S.R. in Afghanistan facilitated the development of well-trained, anti-socialist, Islamic militia network across the Middle East and further afield. Now we are told, in the most racists terms, that the civilised nations of the west are under threat from the uncivilised peoples of the East.

Bush has said that the U.S.A. is now in a state of war. Not only will those regarded by the U.S. as the perpetrators of the terror attack be punished (which may well be on flimsy or non-existent "evidence") but the countries accused of harbouring them will be attacked as well. [Tony] Blair has immediately said that he will back anything the U.S. decides to do (and no doubt provide bases and aircraft). But more than that his nominee at NATO, Lord Robertson, has declared that NATO will do the same. In fact NATO has declared that the attack is an attack on all NATO members and that the response will be in the name of all NATO members.... The UN has also backed Bush—and by a unanimous vote. Putin is backing Bush on the basis that it proves that what he is doing in Chechnya is right—since in his view the Chechens are terrorists as well. The Chinese bureaucracy is happy that it will give them a freer hand to repress human rights.

All this is carte-blanche for action against individuals and organisations accused of terrorism and against so-called rogue states accused of terrorism, and shows that the attack is not only indefensible, it is counterproductive.

The author is unhappy that there was almost unanimous backing for U.S. action in Afghanistan by the UN. However, there was very little backing in the UN for the action against Iraq in 2003. What do you think accounts for this difference?

Fighting the backlash

Whoever carried out the attacks in the U.S.A. the result of all this will be a new period of reaction. New political conditions more conducive to global capital are being created by this. Already anti-Muslim sentiment and anti-Arab racism is being stepped up—at [a] time when Muslim communities are already under attack from the far right. Asylum seekers will be targeted even more. New levels of repression are being prepared against those labelled by the authorities as potential terrorists. ...

Has anti-Arab and anti-Muslim feeling increased in the United States?

The effect that these events are going to have on a world economy is not yet clear. However, with the world economy moving towards recession before this happened it could push it over the brink. Certainly this has been one of the prime concerns of leading representatives of international capital as these events unfolded.

The job of the left will be to oppose this new reaction, defend civil rights, continue to support oppressed peoples, continue to defend asylum seekers and increase campaigning against the fascists. We have to oppose a new wave of xenophobia, defend those who are victims of the new reaction, and protest and organise against acts of war unleashed by Bush and his allies in the name of fighting terrorism. One thing is sure; the result of acts of war by U.S. imperialism in the present circumstances will be to create the condition for such acts of terror to be repeated.

Go to the CNN website—www.cnn. com—and the site of the British newspaper The Guardian— www.guardian unlimited.co.uk— and compare how the conflicts in Iraq and Afghanistan have been reported. Is there any evidence of an increase in anti-U.S. feeling since the wars began?

STATEMENT BY THE PRESIDENT IN HIS ADDRESS TO THE NATION, 2001
George W. Bush

NO

Go to www. whitehouse.gov/ news/releases/2001/ 09/20010911-16. html to see the full text of the speech and hear an audio version.

THE PRESIDENT:

Good evening. Today, our fellow citizens, our way of life, our very freedom came under attack in a series of deliberate and deadly terrorist acts. The victims were in airplanes, or in their offices; secretaries, business-men and -women, military and federal workers; moms and dads, friends and neighbors. Thousands of lives were suddenly ended by evil, despicable acts of terror.

The pictures of airplanes flying into buildings, fires burning, huge structures collapsing, have filled us with disbelief, terrible sadness, and a quiet, unyielding anger. These acts of mass murder were intended to frighten our nation into chaos and retreat. But they have failed; our country is strong.

A great people has been moved to defend a great nation. Terrorist attacks can shake the foundations of our biggest buildings, but they cannot touch the foundation of America. These acts shattered steel, but they cannot dent the steel of American resolve.

America was targeted for attack because we're the brightest beacon for freedom and opportunity in the world. And no one will keep that light from shining.

Today, our nation saw evil, the very worst of human nature. And we responded with the best of America— with the daring of our rescue workers, with the caring for strangers and neighbors who came to give blood and help in any way they could.

Immediately following the first attack, I implemented our government's emergency response plans. Our military is powerful, and it's prepared. Our emergency teams are working in New York City and Washington, D.C., to help with local rescue efforts.

Our first priority is to get help to those who have been injured, and to take every precaution to protect our citizens at home and around the world from further attacks.

The functions of our government continue without interruption. Federal agencies in Washington which had

Do you agree that the United States was attacked because the terrorists envied its freedom? Look at news coverage at the time by searching www.cnn.com and www.bbc.co.uk, for example, and see if there are other possible reasons.

A man holds the U.S. flag at a memorial service held at Ground Zero in 2002 in remembrance of the victims of the September 11, 2001, terrorist attacks in New York.

COMMENTARY: War against Terrorism

In his address to the American people reprinted here, President George W. Bush first used the phrase "War against Terrorism." In later statements he added that this would be a war on many fronts—intelligence, military, the battle for ideas—and that there was no particular point at which it could be said to have been "won." It would be a constant struggle against those who sought to use terror as a political tool.

The first phase of the war was the operation to remove the Al Qaeda organization from its bases in Afghanistan, along with the ruling Taliban government that had given it support. This was achieved between October and December 2001, with Afghan forces opposed to the Taliban joining a coalition of regular forces from the United States and many other countries. Although neither Osama Bin Laden nor the Taliban leader Mullah Omar were found, their organization was effectively crushed, and through international cooperation their financial support was largely cut off.

Alongside this military campaign homeland security was increased to an unprecedented extent in the United States. Airports and airlines became much more rigorous in searching both luggage and passengers, and once it became known that the September 11 hijackers had been armed with nothing more deadly than box cutters, the list of prohibited items for hand luggage grew enormously—from pens to metal cutlery. Where scanning of luggage had previously been haphazard—particularly on low-security domestic flights—procedures were put in place to ensure that every piece of luggage was now scanned for explosives or weapons. Flight attendants were trained in disarming would-be attackers, while plain-clothes armed marshals, posing as ordinary passengers, began riding on flights, trained to respond with armed force if terrorists attempted to hijack an airplane. Some airlines provided locks on cockpit doors and even armed their pilots as a final line of defense. Incidents such as the attempt by Richard Reid, a British-born Muslim convert, to explode a bomb hidden in his shoe during a transatlantic flight in December 2001 served to keep the issues of transportation security at the forefront of governments', airlines', and the public's attention.

Due to the apparent involvement of Al Qaeda in the September 11 attacks, the action in Afghanistan received perhaps the widest international support of any military response to aggression in the history of the United Nations. Dozens of countries either voiced support, sent troops, or provided technical backup and cooperation. However, some voices warned that military operations were insufficient, and might even be counterproductive, against a terrorist enemy. Countries with experience of long-running terrorist campaigns—from Spain and Great Britain to India and Sri Lanka—have found that progress in ending the campaign only comes about when those waging it feel that their grievances are being taken seriously.

to be evacuated today are reopening for essential personnel tonight, and will be open for business tomorrow. Our financial institutions remain strong, and the American economy will be open for business, as well.

The search is underway for those who are behind these evil acts. I've directed the full resources of our intelligence and law enforcement communities to find those responsible and to bring them to justice. We will make no distinction between the terrorists who committed these acts and those who harbor them.

We stand together

I appreciate so very much the members of Congress who have joined me in strongly condemning these attacks. And on behalf of the American people, I thank the many world leaders who have called to offer their condolences and assistance.

America and our friends and allies join with all those who want peace and security in the world, and we stand together to win the war against terrorism. Tonight, I ask for your prayers for all those who grieve, for the children whose worlds have been shattered, for all whose sense of safety and security has been threatened. And I pray they will be comforted by a power greater than any of us, spoken through the ages in Psalm 23: "Even though I walk through the valley of the shadow of death, I fear no evil, for You are with me."

This is a day when all Americans from every walk of life unite in our resolve for justice and peace. America has stood down enemies before, and we will do so this time. None of us will ever forget this day. Yet, we go forward to defend freedom and all that is good and just in our world.

Thank you. Good night, and God bless America.

Very few alleged terrorists or their backers have been "brought to justice"—that is, brought to trial in a court. Do you think it would have been better to try to capture the individuals most responsible and bring them to court rather than fighting a more general war?

This is the first time the president used the phrase "War against Terrorism." Do you think this is a war that can be fought with conventional military means, or will it require a different response?

Summary

The first article was published under the auspices of the British-based International Socialist Group, a Trotskyist (left-wing) political organization. It condemns the destruction of the World Trade Center and the deaths of innocent people, but suggests that the attack may have been a reprisal against U.S. imperialism, which it blames for injustices in many parts of the world. The article cites Cambodia, Chile, Iraq, Indonesia, Nicaragua, the Philippines, Somalia, Vietnam, Yugoslavia, and Zaire as some of the nations that have suffered either from direct U.S. military action on their territory or from Washington's support for an unpopular regime. U.S. foreign policy is seen as the principal cause of these injustices, but U.S. multinationals are also criticized: Together they are accused of having "created the conditions" for the events of September 11, 2001. The article points out that suicide attacks were developed as a method of warfare by Palestinians, who have suffered at the hands of Israel, which is described as having a "war machine supplied, backed, and bankrolled" by the United States. The article also questions the guilt of Osama Bin Laden and observes that the Taliban, who were harboring him, were originally U.S.-backed.

The second article is a transcript of the address to the nation broadcast by President George W. Bush on the evening of September 11, 2001, immediately after the terrorist attacks. Although U.S. intelligence had not yet identified the perpetrators, the president gave a significant indication of future policy when he said, "We will make no distinction between the terrorists who committed these acts and those who harbor them."

FURTHER INFORMATION:

Books:

Bacevich, Andrew J., *American Empire: The Realities and Consequences of U.S. Diplomacy.* Cambridge, MA: Harvard University Press, 2002.

Cooley, John K., and Edward W. Said, *Unholy Wars: Afghanistan, America, and International Terrorism.* Sterling, VA: Pluto Press, 2002.

Crockatt, Richard, *America Embattled: 9/11, Anti-Americanism and the Global Order.* New York: Routledge, 2003.

Useful websites:

www.geocities.com/weisskirche/terror.html
Progressive Praxis site with links to resources giving many different viewpoints on the war on terrorism.
http://libwww.syr.edu/news/forum/terrorismforum3.html
Syracuse University Forum page on "The Global Response to Terrorism," with links to articles and other resource pages with further links.

The following debates in the Pro/Con series may also be of interest:

In this volume:

Topic 15 Was the Persian Gulf War a war about oil?

In *U.S. Foreign Policy*:

September 11, 2001, pages 176–177

WAS SEPTEMBER 11, 2001, THE RESULT OF U.S. IMPERIALISM?

YES: The United States has consistently interfered in the affairs of other nations

YES: The United States only wants to end repressive regimes and give everyone equal rights

INTERVENTION
Is U.S. foreign policy too interventionist?

CULTURE/POLITICS
Is it fair for the United States to impose its own politics and culture on other countries?

NO: The end of the Cold War has made a world policeman more urgently needed than ever before; the United States is uniquely qualified to perform this role

NO: There is such a thing as national sovereignty. It is important for individual countries to be able to conduct their affairs and to behave in ways native to their culture without criticism.

WAS SEPTEMBER 11, 2001, THE RESULT OF U.S. IMPERIALISM?
KEY POINTS

YES: Many countries have suffered greatly as a result of U.S. interventionist foreign policy. Sanctions, for example, cost millions of lives in Iraq. It is justified if it brings about change.

YES: The United States once bankrolled Bin Laden; he is therefore a U.S. creation

JUSTIFICATION
Can U.S. interference in other countries' affairs in any way justify September, 11, 2001?

NO: An "eye-for-an-eye" is not right. We live in a civilized world, and talking is better than terrorism.

NO: Thousands of innocent people died on September 11, 2001. There is no way such a loss of life can ever be justified.

GLOSSARY

Age of Discovery period of the late 15th and early 16th centuries in which European explorers first encountered many parts of the world in America, Africa, and Asia.

Al Qaeda international Islamic terrorist network founded in the late 1980s by Osama Bin Laden and associates. It is thought to be behind several acts of terrorism, including the events of September 11, 2001.

Arawaks Native Americans originally from the Venezuelan mainland. Using Trinidad as a stepping stone, they spread up the Caribbean and beyond.

Bill of Rights the first 10 amendments to the Constitution, which were ratified on December 15, 1791.

Civil Rights Movement a popular mass movement that emerged in the United States during the late 1950s and gained a measure of equal rights for black Americans through nonviolent protest.

Civil War conflict fought in the United States from 1861 to 1865 between the Northern states (the Union) and the Southern states (the Confederacy).

COINTELPRO acronym for counterintelligence programs, carried out by the FBI from 1956–1971 against U.S. political dissidents.

Columbus Day a national holiday commemorating the anniversary of the landing of Christopher Columbus in the Americas (in the Caribbean) on October 12, 1492.

communism a political ideology based on the writings of Karl Marx (1818–1883). It advocates common ownership achieved through the overthrow of capitalism by revolutionary means.

Constitution the written codification of the basic principles and laws by which the United States is governed. It was ratified by the necessary nine states by June 1788.

Constitutional Convention the 1787 meeting of state delegates in Philadelphia that drew up the Constitution.

Democratic Party one of the two major political parties. Historically referred to as the "party of the common man," its origins go back to 1792 and its name to 1828.

Enola Gay the U.S. B-29 aircraft that dropped an atomic bomb on the Japanese city of Hiroshima on August 6, 1945.

Equal Rights Amendment an amendment to the constitution to counter sex discrimination. First put before Congress in 1923, it was finally passed by the Senate in 1972, but has still not been ratified by the required number of states.

fascism an extreme right-wing political ideology that glorifies the nation or the race. The term originated in Italy in the early 20th century.

First Amendment part of the Bill of Rights that protects freedom of speech, freedom of the press and of assembly, and the freedom to practice one's own religion.

McCarthyism the right-wing patriotism that underlay Senator Joseph R. McCarthy's early 1950s campaign of accusations against and investigations of suspected communists in U.S. society.

Manhattan Project code name for the government program, set up in 1942, that developed the world's first atomic bomb. The name derived from the Manhattan Engineer District, the project's early home.

National Socialism the doctrines and policies of Adolf Hitler's National Socialist German Workers' party, which ruled Germany from 1933 to 1945. Also called Nazism.

New Deal a program of social and economic reforms passed by President Franklin D. Roosevelt from 1933 to 1939 to counter the effects of the Great Depression.

Nineteenth Amendment addition to the Constitution preventing denial of the vote on the grounds of sex. Also known as the Susan B. Anthony Amendment, it came into effect on August 26, 1920.

Pearl Harbor attack by Japanese carrier-borne aircraft on the U.S. naval base at Pearl Harbor, Oahu, Hawaiian Islands, on December 7, 1941. It brought the United States into World War II.

Persian Gulf War also called simply the Gulf War, the conflict between a United States-led coalition and Saddam Hussein's Iraq that took place in January and February 1991 in response to the Iraqi invasion of Kuwait in August 1990.

prohibition U.S. state and federal legislation that outlawed the manufacture, distribution, and sale of alcohol, 1920-1933. See also temperance movements.

racism a belief that some races are inherently superior to others, which often gives rise to discrimination.

Reconstruction the period from the end of the Civil War in 1865 to 1877, during which defeated Southern states were readmitted to the Union with governments based on racial equality.

Republican Party one of the two major U.S. political parties. Founded in 1854, it is also known as the Grand Old Party and stands for limited government and low taxes.

Seneca Falls Convention the first women's rights convention in the United States. It was organized by women's rights activists Elizabeth Cady Stanton and Lucretia Mott and took place in July 1848.

slavery the ownership of one person by another, in which the owned person must work for and obey the other.

Suffragists a group of women who campaigned in the early 20th century for women's right to vote.

Taliban an Islamic fundamentalist group who were effectively rulers of Afghanistan from their capture of the capital Kabul in 1996 until being ousted by a U.S.-led military campaign in late 2001.

temperance movements organizations that urged people to moderate or cease their consumption of alcohol. With close links to church groups, they were key in the introduction of federal prohibition. See also prohibition.

Three-Fifths Clause a clause of Article I, Section II, of the Constitution that enabled states to count three-fifths of their slave numbers when quoting their population for representation purposes. It benefited the Southern states, since higher populations meant more representatives in the lower house of Congress.

Tripartite Pact an agreement of September 1940 between Japan, Germany, and Italy, stipulating that if hostilities broke out between one of the signatories and a country not already involved in World War II—between Japan and the United States, for example—the other signatories would support their ally.

Vietcong a communist guerrilla force that operated in South Vietnam during the Vietnam War. See also Vietnam War.

Vietminh (the League for Vietnamese Independence) organization that sought to free Vietnam from French colonial rule and also resisted the occupying Japanese forces during World War II.

Vietnam War Southeast Asian conflict in which the United States intervened on the side of South Vietnam against the Vietcong and communist North Vietnam. Direct American combat involvement lasted from the mid-1960s to 1973, making the war the longest armed conflict in U.S. military history. See also Vietcong.

Watergate a political scandal of the 1970s, in which people connected with Republican President Richard M. Nixon's reelection committee were caught attempting to break into the Democratic Party national headquarters in the Watergate building in Washington D.C. The scandal led to Nixon's resignation in 1974.

Acknowledgments

Topic 1 Should Americans Celebrate Columbus Day?

Yes: From "Remarks by the President on Signing of Columbus Day Proclamation" by George W. Bush. Courtesy of the U.S. Department of State.

No: "Nation Should Not Celebrate Columbus Day, Terrorism of Native People" by Darren Kroenke. Copyright © 2001 by Darren Kroenke. Used by permission.

Topic 2 Were the Framers Racist?

Yes: "The Bicentennial Speech" by Thurgood Marshall, Annual Seminar, San Francisco Patent and Trademark Law Association, May 1987. Public domain.

No: "Spike Lee and *The Patriot*" by Stuart Buck (www.enterstageright.com). Copyright © 2000 by Stuart Buck. Used by permission.

Topic 3 Was Slavery the Cause of the Civil War?

Yes: From "Cornerstone Speech" by Alexander H. Stephens, Georgia, March 1861. Public domain.

No: "Causes of the Civil War" by Randy Golden (www.georgian.com/history/why.html). Copyright © by Randy Golden. Used by permission.

Topic 4 Was Reconstruction a Success?

Yes: "The Freedmen's Bureau" by *Harper's Weekly*, Editorial, July 25, 1868. Courtesy of HarpWeek.com.

No: From "Reconstruction and Its Failure" from *The Black Experience in America*, published on the web 1996. First published by Twayne Press in 1972 as part of the *The Immigrant Heritage of America*. Copyright © Norman Coombs. Used by permission.

Topic 5 Did the Nineteenth Amendment Improve the Position of Women in Society?

Yes: "Bush Proclaims August 25 as Women's Equality Day," White House press release, August 16, 2002. Courtesy of the Office of International Information Programs.

No: "21st-Century Equal Rights Amendment Effort Begins" by Twiss Butler and Paula McKenzie. From *National NOW Times*, January 1994. Used by permission of the National Organization for Women.

Topic 6 Was Prohibition a Disaster?

Yes: From "Alcohol Prohibition Was a Failure" by Mark Thornton, Cato Policy Analysis No. 157, July 17, 1991. Copyright © 1991 by The Cato Institute. Used by permission.

No: "Dry Law Is Worker's Friend" by *The New York Times*, July 31, 1923. Copyright © 1923 by The New York Times Co. Used by permission.

Topic 7 Should the United States Have Supported the League of Nations?

Yes: "How the League of Nations Ended Up as Debris" by Robert Fisk. Copyright © 2002 by *The Independent*. Used by permission.

No: "Speech in Opposition to the League of Nations" by Henry Cabot Lodge, Washington D.C., August 12, 1919. Public domain. Used by permission.

Topic 8 Was the New Deal "New"?

Yes: From "New Deal" by James T. Patterson, Grolier Online article on The American Presidency (http://gi.grolier.com/presidents/ea/side/newdeal.html). Used by permission.

No: "Franklin D. Roosevelt's New Deal" on www.studyworld.com.

Topic 9 Did Franklin D. Roosevelt Provoke Pearl Harbor?

Yes: From "FDR's Infamy: Pearl Harbor, 60 Years Later" by Srdja Trifkovic, December 7, 2001. Reprinted with permission from the website of *Chronicles: A Magazine of American Culture*, a publication of The Rockford Institute in Rockford, Illinois.

No: From "Part V. Conclusions and Recommendations," Report of the Joint Committee on the Investigation of the Pearl Harbor Attack, July 20, 1946. Public domain.

Topic 10 Was It Necessary to Drop the Atomic Bomb?

Yes: From "If the Atomic Bomb Had Not Been Used" by Karl T. Compton, *The Atlantic Monthly*, December 1946. Used by permission.

No: "Was Hiroshima Necessary to End the War?" by Gar Alperovitz in "50 years Since the Bomb: A Packet for Local Organizers" (www.warresisters.org). Used by permission.

Topic 11 Did the United States Overestimate the Threat of Communism in the 1950s?

Yes: From "Introduction: Confrontation by McCarthyism" by Dennis Merrill in The *Documentary History of the Truman Presidency*, Vol. 25, *President Truman's Confrontation with McCarthyism*, 2000. Copyright © Dennis Merrill. Used by permission.

No: From "Speech at Wheeling, West Virginia" by Senator Joseph McCarthy, February 9, 1950. Public domain.

Topic 12 Did the Civil Rights Movement Improve the Position of Blacks in Society?

Yes: From "Interview with Rosa Parks" on Scholastic website, January-February 1997 (http://teacher.scholastic.com/rosa/interview.htm). Used by permission.

No: From "Which Way for Blacks in the USA—Black Nationalism or Socialist Revolution?" by Rob Sewell, marxist.com, February 1999. Copyright © 1999 by Rob Sewell. Used by permission.

Topic 13 Did the FBI Persecute Dr. Martin Luther King, Jr.?

Yes: From "The FBI's Vendetta against Martin Luther King, Jr." by Morton Halperin, Jerry Berman, Robert Borosage, and Christine Marwick in *The Lawless State: The Crimes of the U.S. Intelligence Agencies*, Penguin Books, 1976. Used by permission of the Center for National Security Studies.

No: From "The Beast as Saint: The Truth about Martin Luther King, Jr." by Kevin Alfred Strom in "Speech, American Dissident Voices" radio program, January 15, 1994.

Topic 14 Was the Vietnam War Avoidable?

Yes: From "Vietnam Veterans against the War Statement" by John Kerry, Senate Committee on Foreign Relations, April 23, 1971. Public domain.

No: From "Peace without Conquest" by Lyndon B. Johnson, Address at Johns Hopkins University, April 7, 1965

(www.lbjlib.utexas.edu/johnson/archives.hom/speeches.hom/650407.asp). Public domain.

Topic 15 Was the Persian Gulf War a War about Oil?

Yes: From "Economic Causes of the Gulf War" by World Socialist Movement, Socialist Standard, November 1990 (www.worldsocialism.org). Used by permission.

No: From "The Gulf War: Origins and Motivations" by Benjamin Moss (www.users.qwest.net/~mbenjamin4/mypages/thoughts/gulfwar2.html).

Topic 16 Was September 11, 2001, the Result of U.S. Imperialism?

Yes: "September 11: The Terror Attack in the U.S. and Its Consequences" by International Socialist Group, Statement, September 14, 2001. Used by permission.

No: "Statement by the President in His Address to the Nation" by President George W. Bush, Office of the Press Secretary, September 11, 2001. Public domain .

The Brown Reference Group plc has made every effort to contact and acknowledge the creators and copyright holders of all extracts reproduced in this volume. We apologize for any omissions. Any person who wishes to be credited in further volumes should contact The Brown Reference Group plc in writing: The Brown Reference Group plc, 8 Chapel Place, Rivington Street, London EC2A 3DQ, U.K.

Picture credits

Cover: Library of Congress; **Corbis:** Bettmann, 65; **Getty Images:** 95; **Library of Congress:** 13, 37, 51, 69, 107; **National Archives:** 124/125, 133, Jon Reekie, 6/7, 46/47; **Photos12.com:** Collection Cinèma, 29, 30; **Rex Features:** Ron Sachs, 209; **Richard Jenkins:** 86/87; **Robert Hunt Library:** 171, 183; 188/189; **Topham Picturepoint:** The Image Works 18

SET INDEX